D0938243

Good Looking

The MIT Press   Cambridge, Massachusetts   London, England

Barbara Maria Stafford

Good Looking

Essays on the Virtue of Images

This book was set in Garamond 3 by Graphic Composition, Inc., and was printed and bound in the United States of America

Library of Congress Cataloging-in-Publication Data

Stafford, Barbara Maria, 1941–
    Good looking : essays on the virtue of images / Barbara Maria
  Stafford.
       p.   cm.
    Includes bibliographical references and index.
    ISBN 0-262-19369-8 (alk. paper)
    1. Visual communication.   2. Postmodernism.   I. Title.
  P93.5.S73   1996
  302.23—dc20   96-7079
                                                        CIP

For Fred

Contents

List of Illustrations

The example of some wonderful, path-breaking people in all areas of visual communication convinced me the time was right for the emancipation of images. John Callaway, who will probably be surprised to find himself mentioned in these pages, demonstrates nightly the intelligent conversation possible on television. As director of the William Benton Program in Broadcast Journalism at the University of Chicago, he warmly welcomed me into discussions about the actualities of contemporary media. The demise of Benton House and his subsequent departure leaves me inexpressibly bereft. The thing of it is, John, your fears about "the age of blinding light" forced me to address the specter of thousands of images ceaselessly and contradictorally clamoring for attention.

Marilyn Miglin, founder of the Destiny Institute and leader of the Roundtable for the Year 2000, embodies the grace and foresight needed in the practical life. Under her enthusiastic guidance, an engagement with all aspects of visualization moves forward in concrete projects. Our small band continues to grow, but I want to single out Robert Beck, James Kahn, Kathy Kapp-Simon, Marc Karlan, Kaarina Koskenalusta, Jerre Levy, Gwil Newman, and Carol Sexton for their sustaining interest in imaging. Suzanne Ghez, Director of the Renaissance Society at the University of Chicago, quietly mounts intensely thought-provoking exhibitions of contemporary art year after year. I am grateful she allowed time for friendship. Thanks also to Mary Mahowald, a philosopher and fellow member in the MacLean Center for Clinical Medical Ethics, who encouraged my explorations of pragmatism.

Salvatore Settis, Director of the Getty Center for the History of Art and the Humanities, kindly invited me in the spring of 1994 to be a Visiting Scholar at that extraordinary institution. During those precious weeks, and, now, in 1995–1996 as a Getty Scholar, he, Alex Weintraub, Herbert Hymans, Marsha Reed, Fran Terpak, Don Williamson, and too many others to enumerate enabled me to pull my distracted thoughts together. A monthlong stint in the always energizing Herzog August Bibliothek in Wolfenbüttel, Germany, let me rethink the historical end of things. Drs. Sabine Solf and Gillian Beppler incorporated me into the wider circles of that erudition-laden village. Dave Hickey's courageous voice, speaking a different kind of art criticism, inspires me to keep going against the current. Peter Schjeldahl opened my eyes to another kind of writing for a wider audience.

Back in the Art Department at Chicago, I remember the intellectual excitement of Michael Camille, the down-to-earth rectitude of

Charles Cohen, the early morning eye-opening conversations with Tom Cummins, the irreverent wit of Ingrid Rowland. Gratitude, as ever, to graduate students old and new, but especially to the courageous group in the experimental seminar on "Pragmatism and Art History" that I taught in the fall of 1994. I affectionately cite Seth Almansi, Fiona Cho, Rebecca De Roo, Anthony Elms, Jr., Katherine Haskins, Lisa Hernandez, Mark Hinchman, Elizabeth Liebman, Christina Nielsen, Elizabeth Siegel, Freida Tesfagiorgis, and Namita Wiggers. Thank you to our accomplished, generous, and encouraging experts in the art of practical life for their *pro bono* contributions. Anselmo Carini, Robert A. Clifford (of the law firm Corboy, Demetrio, Clifford), Chad Kainz, Mary Mahowald, Marilyn Miglin, and David Teplica, M.D., opened our eyes and minds to tasks leading beyond the university. Meanwhile, at home, and as always, none of this would have been conceivable or executable without my husband, Fred. His refining suggestions infuse the whole enterprise.

I am long overdue in publicly thanking Larry Cohen, my supportive editor at the MIT Press who, perhaps unwisely (!), never cried no. Something must also be said about the MIT Press in general. Designers, like Ori Kometani, and copy editors, like Matthew Abbate, have made it possible for me to incarnate my arguments visually. Defying predictions of the imminent death of serious publishing, the Press has resiliently fashioned hybrid books alive to the complexity of the new media. Whatever persuasive ability I possess to create imaginative uses for historical knowledge was surely enhanced through excellence in production and flexibility in format.

Versions of some of these essays were published in the following journals and books. They are arranged in order of their appearance here: *Consumption and the World of Goods,* edited by John Brewer and Roy Porter (Routledge, 1993); *Studies in Eighteenth-Century Culture,* 25 (1995); *Getty Trust Newsletter* (Summer 1994); *Ecumene,* 2 (Spring 1995); *Humbert de Superville Retrospective Exhibition,* edited by Jaap Bolton (Leiden, 1996); *Design Issues,* 11 (Winter 1995); *Heterotopia: Postmodern Utopia and the Body Politic,* edited by Tobin Siebers (University of Michigan Press, 1994); *Visions of Empire: Voyages, Botany and Representations of Nature,* edited by David Miller and Peter Reill (University of California Press, 1996); *Configurations,* 1 (Fall 1992). I gratefully acknowledge permission to reproduce this material.

Good Looking

1

Jan Breughel de Velours, *Vision,*
1634. Oil. (Photo: Courtesy The
Prado, Madrid.)

"Velvet" Breughel's allegory of *Vision* projects unbounded longing.
Sight is seated pensively in a high-
ceilinged gallery encrusted with
paintings, tapestries, busts, prints,
coins, medals, jewels, decorative objects, and scientific instruments.
Searching for intellectual patterns
in a maze of images, she embodies
visual pragmatism at labyrinthine
work, alert to the imaginative demonstration and constructive potential of human ingenuity, past or
present.

Introduction: Visual Pragmatism for a
Virtual World

A Constructivist Manifesto

Recent academic rhetoric is saturated with terms of rejection, revision, revolution; but manifestos, even of renunciation, remain in short supply. Writing about what is wrong in old optical formats and new imaging technologies is relatively easy. Harder is proposing mind-opening analogies between historical displays of visual intelligence and computer-age information viewed through the eyes. Being digital requires designing a post-Gutenbergian *constructive* model of education through vision. But I am not convinced, with Nicholas Negroponte, that a hypermedia future entails obliterating the past.[1] The crux of the matter, I think, seems more Darwinian than cataclysmic. Today's instructional landscape must inevitably evolve or die, like biological species, since its environment is being radically altered by volatile visualization technologies. This ongoing displacement of fixed, monochromatic type by interactive, multidimensional graphics is a tumultuous process. In the realm of the artificial, as in nature, extinction occurs when there is no accommodation. Imaginative adaptation to the information superhighway, even the survival of reflective communication, means casting off vestigial biases automatically coupling printed words to introspective depth and pictures to dumbing down.[2]

The bound book has led a charmed existence since typesetting was invented in mid-fifteenth-century Mainz. This longevity, no doubt partially owing to a Darwinian flexibility, makes me optimistic about its mutated persistence. Become more virtual informational space than stable artifact, the traditional volume can find another life as an interconnective environment. Lines of copy interface with users very differently when presented in hybrid Web pages, and acquire unsettling mobility when reformatted, amended, and emended electronically. The digital imaging revolution is crucially reconfiguring how we explore and comprehend ideas from urban planning to photography.[3] Yet in spite of the arrival of what I have termed the "age of computerism"[4]— rapidly replacing modernism and even postmodernism—a distorted hierarchy ranking the importance of reading above that of seeing remains anachronistically in place. All the while, computers are forcing the recognition that texts are not "higher," durable monuments to civilization compared to "lower," fleeting images. These marvelous machines may eventually rid us of the uninformed assumption that sensory messages are incompatible with reflection.

I have serious trouble with the deprecating rhetoric that stakes out bookish literacy as a moral high ground from which to denounce a tainted "society of spectacle." Contemporary iconoclasm, like early modern versions, rests on the puritanical myth of an authentic or innocent epistemological origin. Clinging to the Rousseauean fantasy of a supposedly blotless, and largely imageless, print ecology ignores not only contrary evidence from the past but the real virtues of colorful, heterogeneous, and mutable icons, whether on or off screen.

These essays, then, are unfashionably positive and frankly polemical. Their perspective is simultaneously pragmatic and theoretical. As practical acts of affirmation, they challenge an implacable system of negative dialectics arcing from the moral denunciations of Plato to the coercive aesthetics of Adorno to the war metaphors of Foucault.[5] In short, they offer case studies, stretching from the lens to the computer era, presenting an alternative view of the pleasures, beauties, consolations, and, above all, *intelligence* of sight. They argue that imaging, ranging from high art to popular illusions, remains the richest, most fascinating modality for configuring and conveying ideas. More broadly, they prismatically interconnect seers and seeing within a sensory web productive of cultural signification.

Yet it is not enough to show the intellectual, spiritual, and physical demands of making, observing, and exhibiting spatialized media, whether pre- or postmodern. I want to combat the sophism that images do only destructive work within our institutions. By engaging the epistemological uncertainties and educational upheavals of an electronic future, I seek to demonstrate their capacity for good interventions. Further, I ask how the practice of image study can regain pertinency at a moment when the traditional visual disciplines, like all the rest, are coming unmoored from their original purposes. From this dual perception of revolutionary opportunity and impending Armageddon, the following essays call on established and aspiring imagists across disciplinary boundaries to confront the fundamental task of remaking the image of images. Freeing graphic expression from an unnuanced dominant discourse of consumerism, corruption, deception, and ethical failure is a challenge that cuts across the arts, humanities, and sciences.

As manifestos on the knowingness of visual communication, from scientific illustration to on-line interactivity, these studies have another immediate context. They specifically counter the hierarchical "linguistic turn" in contemporary thought. The totemization of language as a godlike agency in western culture has guaranteed the identification of writing with intellectual potency. Ferdinand de Saussure, the early twentieth-century founder of structuralism, strengthened the biblical coupling of meaning with naming by formulating the opposition of signifier/signified.[6] These verbalizing binaries turned noumenal and phenomenal experience into the product of language. Not only temporal but spatial effects supposedly obeyed an invisible system, the controlling structure of an inborn ruling *écriture*.

Forcing human cognition to become synonymous both with computational codes or abstruse texts and with the ability to decipher them resulted in downgrading sensory awareness to superficial stimuli and false perceptions. Most damagingly, Saussure's schema emptied the mind of its body, obliterating the interdependence of physiological functions and thinking. It is not surprising that, up to now, an educational economy materially based on language has either marginalized the study of images, reduced it to a subaltern position, or appropriated it through colonization.[7] In most American university curricula, graphicacy remains subordinate to literacy. Even so-called interdisciplinary "visual culture" programs are governed by the ruling metaphor of reading. Consequently, iconicity is treated as an inferior part of a more general semantics.

Establishing a universal linguistic unconscious was central to Noam Chomsky's much publicized debates in the mid-1950s with B. F. Skinner.[8] The often-maligned father of behaviorism had tried to erase consciousness from psychology's subject matter. Skinner spent most of his beleaguered career measuring how rats pressed down levers and pigeons pecked at disks, seeking in these reinforced operations the explanation for why organisms do what they do.[9] Chomsky, on the contrary, tied mental concepts to innate "computationalist" discourse in which an automaton neurology manufactured strings of propositional symbols. The equally controversial linguist's theory inspired the invidious comparison of algorithms used to write computer programs with human conceptualization.[10] What was left out of this, and the subsequent rationalist cognitive science quest for a parsing grammar of the mind, was the developmental link between perception and thought. This vital omission, now being rectified in the metaphor and mental imagery research of Lakoff and Johnson among others,[11] contributed significantly, I believe, to poststructuralism's "linguistic turn" and its splintering strategies of differentiation. While the intellectual work of criticism assumed the status of a superior generative language, its base physical object was fragmented into a multiplicity of scattered and uprooted propositions.[12]

Modeling comprehension as a kind of ascetic, even anaesthetic, information processing allowed influential academic areas such as semiotic and deconstructive literary theory or interpretive anthropology to reconceive the material subjects of their inquiry as decorporealized signs and encrypted messages requiring decipherment. So Clifford Geertz's narrational view of ethnography as "thick description"—influential on new historicist tendencies in recent scholarship—treated artifacts, behavior, and culture as if they were layered pages in a book demanding sustained decoding.[13] Although himself a persistant critic of the single-minded quantifying pretensions of the social sciences, Geertz paradoxically reduced communication to inscription. Not unlike Chomsky, his cultural textology assumed that language provided the most basic grid for getting at the meaning of what, after all, were intricately patterned ceremonies, rituals, and gestures.

While the problem of consciousness has returned to cognitive science after its Skinnerian banishment,[14] the conjunction of *psyche* with *logos*—especially in artificial intelligence systems—has not helped the status of images. An unfortunate consequence of the metaphor that treats brain function as modular, but ruled by a common syntax, is the intellectual imperialism of collapsing diverse phenomenological performances, whether drawings, gestures, sounds, or scents, into interpretable texts without sensory diversity. Cartesian reductive tendencies, intensified by advances in high-tech instrumentation, have leaked out of robotics into the humanities. The example of cybernetic disembodiment lurks behind unbiological abstractions such as "spectacle," "spectatorship," "gaze." Derived from observational apparatus, these static concepts ignore the variability of optical sensations in different times, places, and individual beholders.

I am arguing that we need to disestablish the view of cognition as dominantly and aggressively linguistic. It is narcissistic tribal compulsion to overemphasize the agency of *logos* and annihilate rival imaginaries. Martha Nussbaum's subtle remark about dogmatic Stoicism's guarding itself against the lure of poetry applies to the obsession with language in contemporary methodologies.[15] Semiotic, poststructuralist, and deconstructivist translations of the pictorial can be equally self-protective and unidirectional. Typically, these interpretive systems do not allow the "reader" of the depiction to be changed or gain insight through an avenue of expression different from the literariness of the criticism. Derrida's perverse praise of blindness provides a case in point. Claiming that drawing is inadequate to render the "sufferings of sight," he extols the superiority of writing "without seeing."[16]

Culture studies are no less problematic when they disseminate a bifurcated and essentializing world picture of observed annexed subjects and narrating free agents. Thus, in a reprise of Derrida, one hears that the invisible depths of postcolonial identity emerge only through discourse since the true self eludes surveillance. Homi Bhabha, echoing Frantz Fanon, reduces visuality to an evil, doubling colonial eye that either strips the individual of her proper representation or negatively mirrors the alien appearance projected by an oppressor.[17] In the face of such sweeping schematizations, knowledgeable artists and art, architectural, or design historians should ask what ever happened to the notion of *complex* imagery and revealing portraits. The facile complaint that images are merely and always trumping reproductions drowns any memory of their originality and plenitude. Since when does working with surfaces qualify as shallowness? It's a bizarre logic, indeed, that tautologically identifies mimesis with copying whatever sits on a plane (as if that were a simple process!), and, from this restricted definition of resemblance, leaps to conclude the inherent superficiality of imitation.

Anne Hollander's intuition that western fashion offers a visual escape from the trap of unquestioning custom suggests a compelling optical counterpoint to the inscription of racial or ethnic stereotypes.[18] A world rather than a national literature, according to Goethe, had the obligation to make available works from different times, places, cultures.[19] But this desirable effort of translation is not the sole, or even the most effective, means for facilitating exchange. I consider an unforeseen benefit of media "disembedding"[20] to be precisely the global traffic in fugitive visions. Large populations, from both "traditional" and "modern" societies, are being exposed and educated to the hybrid ways in which people everywhere wish to, and do in fact, look. Recognizing alternative styles of being and manifold appearances undermines false assumptions about constant meanings and inherited roles. As a confessed enthusiast for images, then, I deplore the one-sided estimation of language that has installed it as the paradigm for depth, seriousness, thought, even our very identity.

It is not hard to see that the multifaceted campaign to establish the primacy and innateness of our linguistic faculty is challenged by the materialist approach to the mind. Intense debates over Darwin's theory that organisms were born of blind chance and evolved according to the quirks of matter have refocused attention on the origin and configuration of all species. Both adaptationist and ultra-Darwinian investigations into human and animal reasoning[21] open up the question of the sensorium's role. The philosopher Daniel Dennett is a spokesman for the latter camp, stating that to have evolved a capacity for awareness, living creatures must have a sophisticated, unified informational organization endowing them with cognitive capabilities. Empirical processes like learning, in this account, are a tool by which natural selection has created complex biological systems. This new turn in the study of consciousness proposes that life is more than selfish genes by bringing the formative powers of perception into productive engagement with a no longer discrete and hierarchical organ of thought. Urging humanity to "grow up," he comments that Darwin's great legacy consists in his distribution of design throughout nature.[22] The lesson in this for imagists is that, if there is no hope of discovering an absolute trace or essential mark in life's processes that counts more than the rest, then, similarly, we must select, conserve, invent, and compose our artificial environment so that it becomes humane for all.

Yet, in spite of his Darwinian conviction about the importance of design, Dennett remains strangely language-centered. For him, the unfolding stream of human consciousness occurs in a massively parallel-processing brain, a virtual James Joycean linguistic machine. Only now, with the integrative neuroscientific philosophy of Paul and Patricia Churchland, "the body-minded brain" of Antonio Damasio, or Owen Flanagan's insistence on "the missing shade that is you," is the iron grip of a univocal language-like prototype for cognitive activity starting to erode.[23] Understanding, imagined as a combinatorial and synthetic physical function, has the potential for taking into account a broad range of multisensory endeavors. This suggests that truly enlarging the horizon of the emergent sciences of the mind (cognitive science, neurobiology, linguistics, AI, philosophy) should entail learning from the transactional visual arts about the experiential structures of thought. Ironically, the aesthetic, historical, and humanistic dimensions of perception remain virtually absent from the new interdisciplinary matrix in which cognitive being is about to become embedded.[24]

The controversy over who or what is designing nature, then, has been at the heart not only of genetic and reproductive research but of neurobiology. The much-publicized "decade of the brain," bridging the 1980s and 1990s, spectacularly opened a window onto the living mind. Multidimensional medical imaging (CT, PET, MRI) transparently displayed both the permanent neural anatomy and the acrobatics of evanescent emotion. Seeing neurons firing and witnessing localized functions in simultaneous performance suggest that it is more accurate to speak, not of separate art, artists, or art historians, but of interconnective images, imaging, imagists. Bennett Reimer's insistence that the application of arts education must be extended by showing its pertinency to every symbol sphere is even more true in light of this lately revealed cross-cortical power.[25] An array of devices, discoveries, and practices, then, are encouraging us to relocate narrowly categorized "art objects" elsewhere, into what I have termed "imaging." In this borderless community without physical territory, spatialized phenomena belong to larger constellations of events. Creating a map of ongoing debates, organized around central issues or substantial questions arising from this evolving geography, will be a major task confronting the new imagist. Such a "hypermediated" person will have become a reality when we are hard-pressed to say what his or her discipline is.

Optical technology itself is spurring an integrative revolution. Yet it is staggering how loath we visualists have been to transform ourselves. Where are our blueprints, blue-sky or realistic, for guiding media convergence on screen?[26] The conservatism of the supposedly new and old art history, its secondhand reliance on "discourse," on recirculating other fields' methodologies, tropes, rhetoric, has meant the loss of any intellectual and moral leadership that we might have exerted. If we have nothing particular to contribute to formerly linguistic fields and professions now undergoing radical *visual* metamorphosis, we confirm our irrelevance both within institutions of higher learning and in a decentralized electronic society.

These essay-manifestos, then, are constructivist in another sense as well. They call for some real risk-taking. It is one thing to embrace the agendas, definitions, and theories provided by other disciplines—

themselves, ironically, in the throes of blurring or dissolving—and quite another to reconceptualize visuality historically, and in the light of that past lens culture to devise cross-cutting projects for the emergent cyberspace era. We no longer face the nagging question of whether and how we might establish boundaries for art history, as Victor Margolin remarks about design studies.[27] Rather, we confront mutable fragmenting and coalescing forms of humanistic, scientific, and technological knowledge that temporarily converge because of imaging—an activity itself constantly changing. It seems infeasible, either intellectually or financially, to sustain multiple, linear specializations in art, craft, graphic, industrial, film, video, or media production and their separate histories. Instead, we need to forge an imaging field focused on transdisciplinary *problems* to which we bring a distinctive, irreducible, and highly visible expertise.

If Gianni Vattimo is correct that the effect of networked mass media is a "weakening" of immutable or Heideggerian Being,[28] then giving shape to metamorphic Becoming is the challenge. Suddenly, possibilities for configuring a shifting artificial environment open up. Bodynet, part of the innovative Things that Think project of the MIT Media Lab, implicitly challenges Baudrillard's claim that the simulacrum killed reality.[29] In an uncanny permutation of the premodern notion that there is no inanimate matter, explored in my *Voyage into Substance,*[30] this research center envisages designing intelligence into everyday products. A new sensing, networking, and automating technology is to vivify "dead" objects, making them responsive to human needs or emotions. Doorknobs, chairs, toasters, even jewelry will contain implanted silicon chips to perform smart operations by perceiving the desires of their owners. Clothing could recover a patient's vital signs and transmit them to a doctor's database, or adjust to the thermal conditions of different climates, obviating the need for a large wardrobe.[31]

All told, when freed from nihilism and liberated from asymmetrical relationships, material artifacts and graphic presentations can regain their rightful cognitive share. In the magical era of ubiquitous computing, art history's mission to retell the story of conventional media without a consideration of their future is over. Even its disciplinary name sounds archaic. But the efficacy of appearances—whether old or new—and the imaginative possibilities of thinking in, through, and with them is not anachronistic. Imaging may even begin to formulate its own questions and confidently say something about its own ends. It might think about itself instead of just being thought about by others.

In spite of incessant talk concerning interdisciplinarity, something is wildly out of kilter when, at the end of the twentieth century, no alternative metaphor of intelligence counters the nineteenth-century standard of the printed book.

THE THROWAWAY MEDIUM

The passionate visualist, roaming the labyrinth of the postdisciplinary age, is haunted by the paradoxical ubiquity and degradation of images: everywhere transmitted, universally viewed, but as a category generally despised. Spectatorship itself has become synonymous with empty gaping, not thought-provoking attention. Some might object to this inclusiveness, replying that disdain is reserved for machine-generated simulations, or that most people value medical scans, or that, surely, canonical works of art in museums are exempt. Yet none of these caveats gets at the heart of a deeper problem. We have lost faith in the creation of good images; we have no confidence that good looking can be agreed upon or fostered. Already in *Body Criticism* and *Artful Science,* I uncovered an entrenched antivisualism pervading western neoplatonizing discourse from the Enlightenment forward.[32] Will enthusiasm for etherealized environments, data glasses or gloves, and Internet epiphanies automatically change the reflex that associates graphics with illiteracy, delusion, shape-shifting, and coloring emotion? I fear not.

This Orwellian disenchantment with the iconic affects not only a broad spectrum of the educated public but, more disturbingly, those of us in colleges or universities professing to know something about how imagery functions. No matter where one looks, a balanced, let alone a constructive, demonstration of the power of sophisticated images to communicate something other than misinformation, violence, pornography, and callous consumerism to tuned-in viewers is absent. Their visionary role in speculating about the conduct of life is obliterated by a relentless discourse of voyeurism and trickery. John Dewey's perceptive remark, in *Experience and Nature,* that the fine arts as well as the industrial technologies are affairs of practice molders forgotten.[33]

But why should it concern those of us working in the visual arts, film, video, computers, and design, or anyone else for that matter, that spatializing media are declared to be *intrinsically* prone to ethical violations? Even as the din grows louder over plagiarism, misappropriation of written evidence, incomplete research, and errors of fact, images are perceived as more treacherous, requiring greater control, tougher proscriptions, than verbal modes. Why, in short, is the view of optically presented material as more corruptible and less mindful than typeset texts the most intractable bias? Equally the most ancient and the most modern of discriminations, aniconicity is also the most fundamental, underlying harassments against women, people of color, other races, different classes. The unfair assessment of representations as always unfair is itself the first bias for many. Consciously or unconsciously grounded in a faulty sight, this initial misperception is reified into an absolute judgment about the taintedness of the instrument and not the fallibility of the errant perceiver.

Beyond exposing the dubious assumption that pictures, their creators, and their beholders *essentially* lack integrity, or basically are not as cognizant as language purveyors,[34] there are other pressing reasons for making public the affirmative actions of images throughout time and across civilizations. The exhilaration of living in the on-line era is dampened for me by the worry that manipulable graphics will again, and more resolutely than ever, be identified with the unethical modifications possible in *any* replicating medium. Will we ever dig ourselves out of Plato's irrational shadow realm? Escaping from the cave involves, not outlawing the ghosts, but recognizing that such infringements are as old and as new as human nature.

The venerable plight of appearances turned me into an essayist. Their dissolution in the all-purpose solvent of wired fraud changed me into a public advocate. In the age of the throwaway image, when digital "banks" stockpile, license, and sell volatile conglomerated media to customers through CD-ROM catalogs, or subscribers download, use, and reuse hybrid graphics through the agency of commercial servers, it becomes impossible to divorce thinking about past illusion-producing art from contemporary imaging modalities. Digital plagiarism and the illegal redistribution of printed works, pictures, and photographs evoke historical problems concerning the ownership, transmission, and display of material objects. To date, the legal discussion over who owns the rights to immaterial cyberproperty transferred over the national information infrastructure ignores this potentially illuminating avenue of inquiry.[35]

But how to wed the study of the early modern period with reflections on the science-fictionalized realm of distance learning, telecomputing, animation, video, home shopping, and court TV? Why not abandon the chronological enterprise entirely and embrace the here and now? Ultimately, I was reluctant to forsake a stretch of time that had inspired and sustained my work over the last twenty years. Without its anchoring example, the electronic web of America OnLine, Prodigy, and CompuServe fragmented into instantaneous Post-It notes and intangible connections. So I just made the long eighteenth century longer.

Reckoning with shattered categories and crumbling institutions suggests an even greater reason for integrating historical knowledge with current events. As graduate education everywhere grows imperiled and traditional employment opportunities dwindle for highly trained and focused students, what kinds of embodied knowledge will survive the corporate tendency to convert individual aptitudes into remote expert systems? On one hand, we are faced with the specter of narrow "consultants" (without permanent jobs), and, on the other, with "generalists" (a euphemism for people with minimal skills). Donna Haraway's myth of a new species, a synthetic blend of human and machine, does not exhaust the implications of such pay-for-use utilitarianism.[36]

The trend toward automation has moved from the factory into the office, blueing the white collar. In a deregulated society, citizens find themselves as deregulated as industries. Jobs are being taken away not just from auto assembly line laborers but from the service and management force, from secretaries, sales personnel, telephone operators, bank tellers, lawyers, journalists, publishers, editors. Can professors and their students lag far behind? Mind you, the work all these people perform has not disappeared. On the contrary, it is being done directly between customers and robotic systems. In light of increasing layoffs across all sectors and the steady squeezing of survivors to produce even more, home shopping aptly epitomizes the destabilizing directness accompanying the spread of the Net. Such computerized immediacy will certainly cause other types of employment—from stockbrokering to in-class instruction—to vanish if it is not thoroughly reconceptualized and the value of *mediated* encounters stressed.

Add to this ubiquitous telemarketing impulse the threat of abolishing the NEA and the NEH, or even the proposal that the NSF be privatized, and we have the permanence of impermanence reified. The vulnerability of higher education, where even college degrees offer no guarantee of entry to secure jobs, further underscores a general sense of the decrepitude of the humanities and the sciences, their perceived lack of compelling aim or clear intellectual purpose within an ironically named "information society." I do not see that we are preparing our students for the reality that the Information Superhighway is a brand-new toll road and not the same old freeway.

Startlingly, the emergence and convergence of media is simultaneously a wholly ancient and an utterly modern phenomenon. As a deliberate shock tactic, then, these essays brusquely juxtapose distant periods and earlier types of graphic communication with those of the present. I do this believing the eighteenth century uncannily recuperates what we have repressed about our own times. Hal Foster's nuanced analysis of the Surrealist fascination for the outmoded[37] pertains to my invocation of the Enlightenment. The auratic-explosive eruption of an old-fashioned epoch into the contemporary scene disrupts both a Luddite nostalgia for the pretechnological era and the empty ecstasy of netsurfing. Like André Breton's melancholic flea markets or Walter Benjamin's ruined arcades, obsolete optical apparatus and discarded mechanisms are the ghostly remains of lost practices we need to redeem. Relics from an artisanal age haunt current ephemera. To spark a connection between the supplanted and the alien, I have mounted remote scenes in a futuristic frame and edged our virtual world with forgotten representational strategies.

THE "IN-VIEWNESS OF ENDS"

But even this transdisciplinary and transtemporal initiative does not go far enough. I believe we must finally renounce the institutionalized notion that only the "pure" study of anything, including images (whether defined as formal, theoretical, critical, historical, cultural, neurological, psychological, biographical, museological), is admirable. If not for its intellectual merits alone, then because of the recent spate of books damning the beleaguered university,[38] serious consideration should be given to the proposition that a great part of our most meaningful inquiry goes on precisely because it gives thought to practical ends. The Princeton sociologist Donald Stokes convincingly argues for developing a national agenda of understanding-driven and use-inspired science.[39] His central thesis urges joining "pure" inquiry to applied ends following a nonlinear model of research.

Independently, but likemindedly, I have resisted oppositional dualisms. The more we can demonstrate real functions for images, and the greater the comprehension they foster across disparate dimensions—running the gamut from virtual museums, to hypothetical surgery, to a revolutionary visual model of the law[40]—the more integral they, and we, will become to our digital age. The longing for renewal and reinvention, shimmering in every corner of the academy, stems partially from the sense of living at a precarious juncture where supplanting people, businesses, and traditional skills has become the norm. Engaging new equipment at the design and content level means we will less likely be split across irreconcilable generational divides or be outpaced by an inhuman nanosecond immediacy.

Dewey's evocative phrase, "the in-viewness of ends," captures this projection in real time of the possible consequences of any mental or physical operation.[41] At present, an arbitrary theory, offered as a candidate for aesthetic contemplation in competition with its own subject matter,[42] and an avant-garde opticality, conceived as self-enclosed visual plenitude,[43] have played themselves out. Pursuing these romantic roads terminated in frustration at the limits stopping freewheeling subjectivity. But they also led to a boundless cynicism condemning all forms of persuasion as specious and manipulative.[44] Pulled both by the ideological power struggles accompanying the disintegration of the "canonical" disciplines and by dangerous administrative drives to tailor the curriculum solely to the marketplace, teachers need to demonstrate more effectively how images contribute to the informed conduct of life.

Neither an unimaginative utilitarianism nor a constricting instrumentalism, classical American pragmatism struggled to overcome the unproductive conflict between ideas and experience. Peirce, James, Royce, and Dewey insisted that human endeavors were not diminished when steered by a purpose. In differing ways, their philosophies exemplified transactional process and Emersonian presence.[45] By overturning the wholesale skepticism of the British empiricists, Dewey, in particular, developed a more generous, juster apprehension of sensory phenomena beyond aesthetic trumpery. His educational philosophy stands in stark contrast to a neo-Kantian, postwar model of art history that removed the discipline from democratic social goals and the amelioration of existing circumstances.[46] Following his lead, I suggest that images should be freed from the idealist identification with *trompe l'oeil,* the contemptuous judgment that they always pretend to fool the viewer into thinking that unreal things are real. Such a nonabstract, anti-Platonic stance would have as its touchstone the cumulative somatic and spiritual experiences felt by interconnected organisms coexisting in a material world. Developing an integrated, nonpolarized view of the varieties of visual experience means that the good, bad, and mixed properties of imaging would never be a foregone conclusion. As is true for any other human production, decisions about value would depend upon individual and community use during the course of a lifetime.

In retrospect, I now see that the essays in this book are gropings along a pragmatic path. Some steps are sure, others tentative. Yet all footfalls lead in the direction of visual scholarship that is always driven by the need for understanding and alert to potential use. I hope they prove helpful to other imagists similarly searching. Pragmatism's stress on human choice, organic growth, contingency, continuity, transition, novelty, permeates the three groupings into which these studies have been clustered. In the first part, I ask what possible consequences a knowledge of the eighteenth century could have for the era of artificial intelligence, microprocessing technologies, desktop publishing, and virtual light. Although the early modern period serves as a guiding thread throughout, in this opening section it becomes woven into a future-is-now tapestry. The epoch of heteroclite mixtures offers exceptional insights into the heterologies of the twenty-first century. The Enlightenment, too, was forced to rethink and restructure all forms of scientific and cultural display at a revolutionary moment of converging and overturning informational formats. This strong bond, tying past to present, should dispel any aura of quaintness or irrelevance still clinging to the notion of the eighteenth century for a contemporary audience. In turn, our *fin-de-siècle* machine dream of direct electronic exchange, when set in cameo relief, emerges as part of a venerable utopian desire for unmediated human connections. Ironically, such spectral confrontations were enabled, then and now, by optical media that appeared not to exist.

What does an expanding expertise in the myriad facets of art production, reception, exhibition, and interpretation offer the telepresent age? More generally, in the second part I explore what an overarching and innovative imaging discipline could look like. How might it assist scripturalist professions such as law, journalism, business, and text-based fields such as history, sociology, comparative and national literatures, all being funneled on line and on screen? In the Faustian conversion from linear thinking to mosaic presentation, typical of the new media, can we suggest models for how to cope?

The areas of bioethics and moral theory have quickly become topics of intense public interest and scrutiny. In the third part, I try to put a familiar face on the neurosciences and medical technology. I show how aesthetics, originally signifying sensory knowing, has much to contribute to the wrenching dilemmas of diagnosis, prognosis, and treatment springing from the Human Genome Project, genetic research, and reproductive engineering. Indeed, American medical education, accustomed to heeding "hard" sociological concerns, could benefit from the "softer" reflexive examination of ambiguous, and frequently contradictory, realities. Images not only possess a cognitive quotient but they can refine our imaginative, emotional, and spiritual lives, make us intelligent in the body and sympathetic in the mind. Conversely, the cerebralizing drive to "theorize" art history might be compassionately tempered by looking at painted, sculpted, and built forms as complex experiential achievements, as the best of conscious human activity at work. Case-based decisions, emerging from a contextualized clinical model, emphasize precisely such situational intersections of visuality, learning, and the world.[47] Seeing the patient, documenting the examination, and assessing congeries of symptoms paint the suffering person in primary colors.

2

Pompeo Batoni, *Time Revealing Truth,* c. 1745. Oil. (Photo: Courtesy Museum of Art, Rhode Island School of Design.)

Radiant truth, vanquishing dark unreason, was the emblem of the Enlightenment. Time, education, and progress, it was anticipated, would eventually defeat blinding errors and clouding illusions. The binary structure of Batoni's painting illuminates the two poles of this struggle. Practical reason was to turn this abstract ideal of perfectibility into a pragmatic weapon aimed at false belief, superstition, zealotry. The *philosophes* argued that all people must cultivate a truth-seeking capacity within themselves. At the end of the twentieth century, the memory of both the utopian aspiration and the dismal failure of that reforming project continues to torment us.

I   Enlightenment/Re-Enlightenment

The Visualization of Knowledge from the Enlightenment to Postmodernism

1

3

Kenneth Snelson, *Chain Bridge Bodies,* 1991. Cray-computer-generated atom landscape. (Photo: Courtesy the artist.)

We are preoccupied with time. If we could learn to love space as deeply as we are now obsessed with time, we might discover a new meaning in the phrase to live like men.

—Edward Abbey, *Desert Solitaire*

The shift in imaging, from reconstructing an alternative three-dimensional world to simulating events that the artist has not witnessed, can be traced in the work of the American sculptor Kenneth Snelson. Fluidly moving from the creation of elegantly balanced tensile towers to equally idealizing self-contained atomic environments, his installation becomes an arena for meditating on the wonders of a selective reality. The computer-generated *Chain Bridge Bodies* projects an eerie sense of completeness, incorporating the viewer into a realm as magical as the moon landing vista we saw flickering on our television sets on July 20, 1969.

The production, management, and consumption of the flood of bytes spilling out of worldwide databases and computer networks has become a universal obsession.[1] It is not accidental that this overwhelming volume of information coincides with a mounting concern for bolstering and maintaining language literacy. Yet the simplistic identification of verbal skills alone with a properly "humanistic" education is profoundly disturbing. It does not take into account the conceptual and perceptual revolution that has been occurring in the presentation of knowledge since the eighteenth century. Equally limited, to my mind, is the notion that visual materials should be used in education merely to convey information—that the illustrated data derived from graphics is important, but not the image itself.[2] Inscribed into this equally linguistic bias is the false severance of *how* things are presented from *what* they express. Anyone dismayed by the concealed manipulations often operating in broadcast journalism or political advertisement must see the danger inherent in such a division.

However briefly, I wish to show that present-day written forms of communication were already being challenged, and even swept aside, in an earlier era. My view is that this turn of events does not necessarily represent cultural decline or a great social evil. In fact, it provides a splendid opportunity for exiting, at last, from Plato's cave. The new-found power and ubiquity of images calls for innovations in teaching and for altering venerable but unexamined epistemological models and textual metaphors ("codes," "alphabets," "letters," "spelling," "grammar"). I believe that only a serious training in visual proficiency will allow us to assimilate, integrate, and understand a holographic and multidisciplinary reality increasingly filtered, transformed, and synthesized through three-dimensional imaging. Furthermore, as the battle over government funding of the arts and humanities is proving, those of us involved with the visual arts cannot be content simply to champion freedom of speech and to produce or consume innovative artistic works. We are also responsible for articulating to a wider public that an understanding of the communicative modes and tactics of images is essential to a thorough, humanistic education. We must strive to develop future directions and strategies to prepare broad and informed constituencies for technology's ever-advancing power to make the invisible visible.

If our postmodern times are indeed preeminently visual times, they can be set in valuable relief against an earlier chapter in the history of visual communication. For it was precisely in the eighteenth century that the persisting rationalist philosophical attitude toward images hardened into systems. Such theories claimed that pictures and perceptual apprehension, in the words of Baumgarten, were an inferior gnosis.[3] This consumption of presuming and popular images by an official hermeneutic of higher interpretive words was evinced in the academic demotion of pictures to an ornamental, or merely craft, status when bereft of a superior nonvisual method.[4] Paradoxically, but not surprisingly, this attempt at textual control occurred in a century unprecedented for sophisticated visual practices, technological inventions, and sheer pictorial production. The prejudicial implications of continuing to see images linguistically, that is, as a lesser, transitory, and illusory form of written communication, are still playing themselves out.

Early twentieth-century modernism was characterized by printed manifestos, by a conceptual abstraction,[5] by painted word games,[6] by alphabetic and numbered collages and calligrams,[7] by what one contemporary architectural critic has termed "the writing of the walls."[8] Conversely, the late twentieth century is the media age of vocal, aural, and, above all, optical rhetoric:[9] of television cinematics and video spectacles, of interactive computer displays,[10] of performance art, procedural art,[11] fractal and math art,[12] holography,[13] and of that hyper-advertisement, the blockbuster exhibition. We are awash in entertainment and information presented sensorially. On the domestic front, it is now possible for the average person to assemble a small-scale television station within his or her four walls. New wraparound audio systems coupled to gigantic screens seem to be fostering a society of romantic solitaries communicating with other electronically generated specters. On the biological and cosmic front, the Human Genome Project and the Hubble Space Telescope are already spewing forth data by the gigabyte. Imaging lies at the heart of both this private creation of evanescent ghosts and the public decipherment and cataloging of reams of elusive facts and figures that would otherwise remain uninterpretable. Instead of sequencing three billion pieces of DNA, scientists, relying on a visual metaphor, now favor sketching out a "road atlas" of the genome indicating genetic markers or distinct biochemical features. Yet the overarching human need to find meaningful visual patterns, whether in the living of a life or the conduct of research, has not been seen as a *positive* aspect of the broader drive toward the visualization of knowledge initiated during the Enlightenment. Giving shape to, or mapping, experiential confusion requires learning and special skills. The history of the general move toward visualization thus has broad intellectual and practical implications for the conduct and the theory of the humanities, the physical and biological sciences, and the social sciences—indeed, for all forms of education, top to bottom.[14]

The multiple ramifications of this far-ranging aesthetic process rest submerged in a culture that, despite its clear reliance on a spate of images, remains ironically mired in a deep logocentrism.[15] By logocentrism I mean that cultural bias, convinced of the superiority of written or propositional language, that devalues sensory, affective, and kinetic forms of communication precisely because they often baffle verbal resolution.[16] To produce a new world of perspicuous and informed observers (not just literate readers) will, I believe, require a paradigm shift of Copernican proportions. As more and more people are producing and consuming their own productions, and as cable television, video cassettes, and Internet communities further particularize and decentralize messages, the need to suture together a shared culture becomes greater. These marvelous and sophisticated contemporary machines to think by belong among the technological apparatus characterizing a long evolution in perception. Knowing something about the common myths surrounding images, their past uses and structures, would help to forge models for future interactive communication as the old linguistic hierarchies fracture. In the era of personal broadcasting and the demassification of visual consumption, perceiving should be given at least as much attention as reading, if not more. These activities

4

Transverse section of the brain. Upper left: PET alone. Upper right: MRI of the same slice. Lower left: PET and MRI. Lower right: metabolic activity. (Photo: Courtesy Dr. Malcolm Cooper, Center for Imaging Science, University of Chicago.)

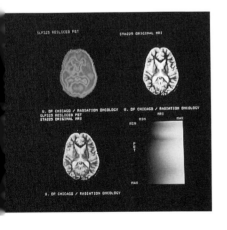

(as we are increasingly learning from the neurosciences)[17] are not merely interchangeable functions or skills. Interconnected (or possibly orchestrated in a network), yes; the image subsumed or generalized to extinction in a number- or text-based logic, no.

Like the twentieth-century electronics revolution, eighteenth-century technology encouraged the privatization of pleasurable beholding. While not yet making it feasible for people to spend more time at home and less time going to their places of work, shops, or theaters, it nonetheless initiated a consumer-driven flexibility in visual communication. New graphic techniques widened the possibilities of articulation within a given medium and provided greater subjective choice in what one was able to see. Eighteenth-century aesthetic and technological innovations, and the visual skills to analyze them, thus have much to teach the twentieth century about the presentation, construction, and interpretation of graphical messages of all sorts.

If one were to raise a periscope to survey the contemporary sea of visual information inundating all disciplines, what might one behold? I call attention to a few upwellings. Understanding their significance within the current structure of knowledge is enhanced by knowing that they still reverberate with allusions developed in the early modern period. The burgeoning field of neuroscience has led to the spatialization and visibilization of the brain's concealed terrain in a kind of neural photography.[18] A few examples must serve. Computer simulations of the brain's interconnected nerve cells provide neuroscientists and cognitive psychologists with literal insights into the dynamic processes by which the mind thinks, senses, feels. Medical imaging devices transparently and noninvasively open opaque surfaces, permitting physicians to gaze into formerly hidden depths. X-ray tomography (CT) exposes bone structures. Magnetic resonance imaging (MRI) gives a cross-sectional picture of the architecture of the brain at different levels or "cuts." Computers are then used to reconstruct in visual form a three-dimensional translucent display in rotation, or a hovering transparent brain. Its inner parts can be dissected at a touch of the keyboard by stripping away the skull's layers electronically. Difficult craniotomies can thus be rehearsed visually. Positron emission tomographic (PET) scanners provide portraits of the brain as a whole caught in the act of thought. This instrument is a kind of neo-Albertian window on mental operations, and by its means we can view clairvoyantly spatiotemporal patterns of activity arising from neural performances. Mobile chromatic shapes map various cellular and electrochemical properties of the brain involved in diverse sensory and affective processes. Most spectacularly, the superimposition of PET and MRI (figure 4) is leading to the establishment of detailed three-dimensional correlations between specific functions and their location in the brain.[19] As with widespread genetic screening, these imaging breakthroughs are fraught with ethical concerns. Lured by the physiognomic fallacy, what if insurers, employers, and other institutions try to exclude, through prognostic tests, individuals who carry the "wrong" genes or mental "defects"?

Spectacle has also entered the domain of physics. The American sculptor Kenneth Snelson, in his essay-portrait of the atom, longed for the day when computer graphics might allow us to sit "in a theater and observe the true wonders of the microphysical world."[20] In a three-decade-long project, which came to fruition only because of computer simulation, Snelson went beyond any currently realizable atomic model. He conjectured about the "atomic condition" as he saw it, from within, from the electron's perspective, not from the physicist's external and bombarding point of view. He thus challenged the thesis of the founding fathers of quantum theory that no pictorial representation could be devised to permit an unmediated description of the quantum world of untrackable quarks, interactions among electrons, and mysterious quantum exchanges among particles. The mathematical theory of de Broglie, Bohr, Schrödinger, and Heisenberg aimed only to describe systematically the response of apparatus.[21] Yet Snelson's gossamer computer panoramas poignantly hark back to the Enlightenment's desire for diaphaneity. Like Piranesi and a host of early modern antiquarians, he desired to render perceptible an ephemeral realm not directly perceivable.

Supercomputers thus permit us to see internal and external worlds anew. Again, it is dynamic visualization that can transform an incomprehensible data file into more than a meaningless string of bits and pieces or an infinite series of unrelated fragments. Consequently, many astrophysicists, radiologists, meteorologists, and engineers have begun to decry the widening gap between the accumulation of raw numbers and their transformation into a visual format enabling practical analysis.[22] Thunderstorm modeling and the animation of planetary magnetospheres represent only two small instances of how visualization of complex data—otherwise literally unimaginable—is now critical to the advancement of many fields of science.[23] In addition, there is a renaissance of widespread serious interest in the use of graphics in the mathematical field of statistics,[24] made evident in well-designed charts and histograms. Moreover, and more importantly, pictorial tools for the discriminant analysis of multivariate data are being created. Chernoff's heads, or schematic faces—operating on the principle of much-in-little advanced by eighteenth- and nineteenth-century caricaturists—prove that statisticians, like the rest of us, need succinct images to help them think about multiple and heterogeneous variables.[25]

Legal practice, too, has become increasingly cinematic. Trials are now routinely shaped by reliance on so-called demonstrative evidence in the form of videos. The filming of everything from dramatized mugshots, to "a day in the life" of a victim, to the reenactment of crime, gives the old problem of the nature of accurate witnessing and judging a new urgency. The ambiguities surrounding eyewitness testimony, specifically, are set in sharp relief.[26] How does the law establish objective visual criteria for simulating a performance meant to capture "what really happened" during a transitory event viewed by many subjects, seen from different perspectives, under a variety of emotional conditions, and remembered differently? In short, what constitutes reliable visual evidence? How does the jury member, or the trial lawyer for that matter, recognize distortion or bias, not only in the verbal account given by witnesses but in the film or virtual version of that account? Given the lavish increase in sophisticated court exhibits, in scale models, multicolored charts, computer simulations, and multimedia shows, how does a visually unsophisticated jury distinguish responsibly between a message corresponding to the complexities of the actual experience and a contrived but purportedly objective point of view? As G. C. Lichtenberg, the superb eighteenth-century German commentator on Hogarth's graphic works, remarked, the great hermeneutic problem in life lies not in ferreting out truth or lies but in exposing "very clever false interpretations."[27]

But the paradigmatic postmodern visual condition—the dissociation of hand from eye, cause from effect, stimulus from response, skill from signal—is to be witnessed in the business world.[28] Here, at the site of desktop workstations and far-flung databases, the Enlightenment's fundamental contribution to the epistemological structure of the late twentieth century is most evident. In the corporate Platonic cave—a windowless, mirrored, or darkly glazed high rise—smooth and shiny surfaces reflect simulacra. The new workplace is an information-rich organization in which physical labor and tangible objects related to administrative, productive, and personnel activities have become etherealized into prismatic apparitions weightlessly flitting across a computer screen. This new immaterialism was set in motion by Bishop Berkeley.[29] The production of intangible "liteness" by the media, and the consumption of the phantasmatic by a broad public, is part of a greater and daily dematerialization. Solid or manufactured objects evaporate into unreal or evanescent appearances through the intervention of circuitry. In a world where information is just *there,* users increasingly neither know nor care where the free-floating and autonomous debris originated.

This present-day sense of the societal ambiguity of technology, accompanied by mixed feelings of excitement and unease, returns us squarely to the Enlightenment. The eighteenth-century preoccupation with visionary territories was linked to an awareness that history had many potential realizations. Eluding certainty, the look of a bygone civilization could only be imagined or visualized through chance finds, partial discoveries. Contingency, variability, and fluctuation—the signs of cultural unmooring—were endemic to a period experiencing an explosion of discontinuous and odd finds demanding representation. Optical classification of the strange, the scattered, and the singular, in turn, was inseparable from the technological reproductive innovations needed to simulate them. Among the consequences of this dual development were sustained reflections on the possibilities, subtleties, power, and beauty of visible history and on the importance of visual instruction of all sorts. The age's chief aesthetic theorists—Dubos, Caylus, Diderot, Falconet, Addison, Shaftesbury, Hogarth, Reynolds, Winckelmann, Lichtenberg—drew an important distinction that is largely forgotten by twentieth-century verbally shaped disciplines. With great sophistication, these thinkers differentiated between imagery used as equivalents to discourse (or as illustration) and as an untranslatable constructive form of cognition (or as expression). In viewing broadcast journalism, for example, we have to come to grips with this distinction, realizing that we need to coordinate and interpret not only what people say but *how* they say it, judging their veracity by the style of what they observably *do.* The art of visual conversation is aided by a format that encourages speakers seated face-to-face to perform their arguments at length. Such interactive communication calls upon the discernment of an audience that, although absent, is urged to participate as if it were present.

It is on this major, and profoundly educational, role of imagery that I wish to linger. Images are not only architectonic, they are iconoclastic in destroying specious certitudes and in revealing ignorance or the limitations of human comprehension. The unique perspective of the eighteenth century on the affective and pleasurable training value of pictures, coupled with the rise of a special technology for visualization, has much to teach the modern viewer about the analysis of contempo-

rary visual material. Unlike the intervening age of photography—
which unwittingly fostered the illusion of neutral supports for information, the reception of reality without toil and the self-explanatory
nature of sight[30]—the eighteenth century, I believe, initiated the pedagogical struggle to comprehend the full power of visual arrays now realized in our twentieth-century culture of pictorial information. Three
examples, drawn from the varieties of visual history created during the
Enlightenment, epitomize how understanding an outmoded visual acu-
ity might shape more astute observers of the contemporary scene. They
are: the preservation of fragmented cultures; the exhibition of biodiver-
sity; and the externalization of somatic experience.

The desire to present a visual stratigraphy of artifacts from an
era long since vanished elicited from the tireless Venetian etcher Giambattista Piranesi (1720–1778) one of the greatest graphic innovations
of the age.[31] His radical experimentation with etching, a corrosive
chemical procedure for "biting" a copper plate, was matched only by
William Blake's later revision of reproductive engraving. The English
poet-illuminator punningly termed his own acid stereotype process the
"infernal" method because it required printing, or exposing to light,
what was literally buried beneath an impervious ground, or covered
over by drawing.[32] Relying on the same surface and depth analogy implicit in the intaglio procedure, Piranesi performed perceptual rescue
work. He systematically unearthed the mutilated remains of Italian antiquity and placed them, miniaturized, between the covers of heroically
scaled albums. Unlike modern archaeological restorations, Piranesi's
paper excavations in black and white did not despoil eroding monuments of their pathos (fig. 5). Thus the "suffering" surfaces, stuccos,
ornament, and even aging dirt of the tombs and cinerary urns lining
the Appian Way were left intact.[33] From the countless walls, temples,
baths, and amphitheaters of the *Antichità Romane* (1756), to the republi-
can and baroque monuments of the *Delle Magnificenza ed Archittetura de'
Romani* (1760), to the subterranean chambers, cisterns, and corridors
of the *Descrizione e disegno dell'emissario del Lago Albano* (1762), Piranesi
uncovered and retrieved the decaying corpse of Rome. Wielding the
etcher's needle like a scalpel, he applied surgical procedures (learned,
I suggest, from medical illustration) to turn the still-living fabric of
architecture inside out (fig. 6). In fact, he appeared to be following Vesalius's lead. The great sixteenth-century anatomist's emotion-laden
attitudes had recently received engraved reinterpretation by Jean Wan-
delaer for Albinus's 1725 Leiden edition of the *De humani corporis fab-*

5

Giambattista Piranesi, *Appian Way,*
from *Le antichità romane,* 1784, II,
frontispiece. Etching. (Photo: Courtesy Getty Center, Resource
Collections.)

6

Giambattista Piranesi, *Section of the
Tomb of Alessandro Severo,* from *Le
antichità romane,* 1784, II, pl. 32.
Etching. (Photo: Courtesy Getty
Center, Resource Collections.)

7

Giambattista Piranesi, *Pantheon: Interior of the Portico,* from *Vedute di Roma,* 1769, pl. 82. (Photo: Courtesy Department of Special Collections, University of Chicago Library.)

8

Felice Fontana (?), anatomical figure, eighteenth century. Wax. (Photo: Courtesy Wellcome Institute Library, London.)

rica.[34] The anatomist's muscled dead were mobilized by the architect into lithic *écorchés.*[35] Blasted nudes became analogues for hollowed-out ruins, for an eviscerated, but still potent, antiquity. As an intuitive explorer of monuments, he closely resembled the great analyst and extrapolator of the human body. Vesalius was the first to unite the separate functions of lecturer, dissector, and practical demonstrator. Similarly, the artist-technologist was the foremost delineator and antiquarian, interpreter and defender of the changing urban landscape of Rome. As patient *ostensor,* the Venetian etcher invited participation from his audience. His searching fingers of light and dark obliged the viewer's eyes to follow (fig. 7). In this visual and manual process of fleshed-out, not reductive, showing, Piranesi, like the Renaissance anatomist and his important eighteenth-century successors,[36] put his own hand to the business of demonstration, to grip the attention of the beholder.

The intaglio process lent itself to taking physiological soundings. In the *Section of the Tomb of Alessandro Severo,* the superficial or deep registration of various architectural "tissues" to longer or shorter exposure to acid, to more or less delicate or rough stimulation by the etching needle, clarified the complex vertical structure. Piranesi's experimental method for visibilizing the "irritability" of the ancient fibers on copper plates belonged to the inductive mentality determining the practices of such Hallerian contemporaries as Felice Gaspar Ferdinand Fontana (1730–1805) (fig. 8) and Leopoldo Marcantonio Caldani (1725–1813).[37] Like them, he captured the elusive passage of time by palpably probing and poking beneath the veneer. Marring and smoking the shiny surface literally mimicked the pitting of smooth exposed stone and mortar. The arduous and lengthy process of physical exploration and visionary recreation was compressed into large and magnificent prints. What had been a piecemeal act of retrieval became comprehensible to the viewer through corporeal reenactment. The beholder, too, spent time looking, searching, and visually wandering among the *membra disjecta* of ruins.

The power of Piranesi's expressive hieroglyphics arose from collaging complex spatiotemporal events without blurring differences (fig. 9). Significantly, this late baroque interactive approach to visual knowledge avoided classificatory schemes based on linear sequence, similarity, and homogeneity. The grotesque, disruptive, and heterogeneous appearance of these architectural prints suggested that supposedly canonical monuments were simply the accidental results of what had been left over or dug up. Piranesi carefully demonstrated, and asked us to evalu-

9

Giambattista Piranesi, *Plan and Elevation of the Tomb of Alessandro Severo,* from *Le antichità romane,* 1784, II, pl. 31. Etching. (Photo: Courtesy Getty Center, Resource Collections.)

ate, how his subjective taxonomy might serve as a guide for ordering a lost material world. Yet this vision of totality was always provisional, alterable through the discovery of new remnants.

What Lessing and his followers never understood was that the expressive spatial arts are not exclusively spatial. In fact, they prod viewers to experience time by inviting us to engage in the construction or deconstruction of the image.[38] Piranesi's "surgical" methods of demonstration are revealing from this temporal perspective. He cleverly made use of accidental sections that gaped like wounds in deteriorating masonry. The decaying pilasters in the interior of the *Portico of the Pantheon* only gradually exhibited the details of their internal structure to sight. Like Fontana's anatomical waxes containing nesting parts, the areas for intensive study were systematically controlled and progressively highlighted.[39] In addition, multiple images were displayed limblike on the same plate to avoid confusion and to draw attention to conflicting information (fig. 10). This anti-illusionistic strategy offered the viewer multiple options. Seams or scars indicated speculative solutions, especially appropriate when a monument was partially buried under accumulated debris. Piranesi thus responsibly sutured the certain to the conjectural. He trained the observer, as he trained himself, in the fine art of probability, that skill in estimating the unknown by knowl-

10

Giambattista Piranesi, *View and Profile of the Tomb of L. Arunzio,* from *Le antichità romane,* 1784, II, pl. 11. Etching. (Photo: Courtesy Getty Center, Resource Collections.)

11

Ferrante Imperato, *View of Museum,* from *Historia naturale,* 2d ed., 1672, frontispiece. Engraving. (Photo: Courtesy Getty Center, Resource Collections.)

edgeably judging a maze of seemingly isolated and dispersed objects. The architect-etcher began by anatomizing, or visually separating, parts, and ended by organically synthesizing what he dismembered into a heroic span of views. This series endures because it continues to help the modern beholder reintegrate and recontextualize historical fragments into a living urban totality.

Piranesi's innovative expansion of the orthodox boundaries of building types was the consequence of showing the dramatic effects of contingency operating within material culture. He made manifest the alien look of a complex antiquity known only through stray traces. Displaying the fragments of a broken lineage, of course, had been central to Renaissance collections housed in a study or self-contained room (fig. 11).[40] The eighteenth-century scientific quest for origins, ancestry, and genealogy, however, was permeated by the conviction that such a trove of visual objects possessed a unique capacity to teach, to uncover the relation of known parts to an unknown whole. The creation of galleries, museums, libraries, and natural history cabinets was grounded in a visual encyclopedism persuasively encouraging cross referencing in a disparate public that strolled and paused before minute details and eye-arresting features (fig. 12).[41] Such visual searching and bodily travel, roaming from the insignificant to the significant and back again,

12

Claude du Molinet, *View of the Library of Sainte-Geneviève*, from *Cabinet de la bibliothèque de Sainte-Geneviève*, 1689, frontispiece. Engraving by F. Ertinger. (Photo: Courtesy Getty Center, Resource Collections.)

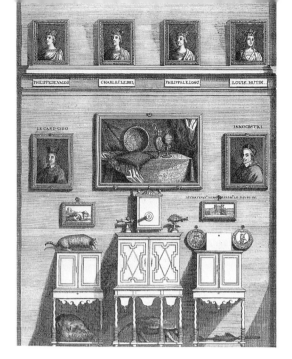

prompted mental locomotion. The fluid particulars of a rising phenomenal tide were exhibited as trophies of the ebb and flow of a metamorphic world (fig. 13).[42]

Mimicking the startling juxtapositions typical of the baroque *Wunderkammer,* or magical case of memories with its special boxes and rarity-filled niches, this pragmatic form of historical reconstruction exposed uncertainty, the interruptions existing in contemporary systems of categorization.[43] Like Piranesi's etching style, the exhibiting method was abrupt, even jarring. Unlike the false coherence implied by the linear sequences found in annals or narratives, the assemblage and montage of curiosities resembled a mosaic whose tesserae were simultaneously accessible to sight. Artificial and natural, pagan and Christian, ordinary and exotic artifacts provoked an immediate awareness of the miscellaneous and chance act of finding itself. These elaborate three-dimensional collages demonstrated how we learn painstakingly by gathering and arranging bits and pieces in the dark. There is always more evidence, always another, and better, mode of organization. Stray specimens of cultural and natural remains—portraits of historical figures, *trompe l'oeil* still lifes, exotic animal species, scientific instruments, sports of nature, and marvels of metal casting—jostled one another on charged tables and cluttered walls. Instead of concealing the absence of connections, the dynamic layout summoned the observer to fill in the gaps.

13
—
Claude du Molinet, *A Wall of the Room Housing the Collection,* from *Cabinet de la bibliothèque de Sainte-Geneviève,* 1689, pl. 5. Engraving by F. Ertinger. (Photo: Courtesy Getty Center, Resource Collections.)

This inextricable combination of recreation and research was intimately tied to the dialogic aspect of visualization. The mix of popular fun and serious scholarship, characterizing the display of early modern collections, was especially evident in the spectacle provided by fossils. Their wonder-inspiring power derived, at least partially, from being natural historical "monuments" left behind by the Flood (fig. 14).[44] Significantly, our contemporary bio-ecological aesthetic[45] originated in the eighteenth century when intrinsic value, and even vitality, was first widely ascribed to natural antiquities or petrified "singularities." According to Diderot, Robinet, and Delisle de Sales, nature imaged forth the record of its ongoing transformation in stony pictograms.[46] Graphic granite carried traces of decipherable development marks. Dendritic and map agate bore the imprints of mountainous and forested terrain. These delightful gifts from the past were taken to be hieroglyphics exhibiting the geological record of their internal growth and organization.

Through the broad dissemination of stunningly engraved folios, such as the Swiss Jean-Jacques Scheuchzer's natural-theological Bible, fragile casts were consumed as instructive visual records of otherwise invisible earth events. Geological and geographical concepts such as great age and distance were spatialized as subtly graduated depth. Intangible and imperceptible occurrences, such as the slow passage of time, received tangible and perceptible representation in terms of nearness or remoteness from the viewer. The team of Augsburg engravers responsible for Scheuchzer's eight-volume work created poignantly veiled prints of fossil fish that obliged the eye to struggle. To discover long-since vanished species, the observer had to excavate them visually from the occluding sediment—a nuanced physical, emotional, and intellectual experience that escaped words. The beholder's role was essential to the performance in that she supplemented the *nonfinito.* Small plaques broken from an immense ancient ocean floor were vignettes excerpted from a global spectacle now graspable only in scattered segments. These lithic picture-sculptures offered access to an otherwise unknowable past. As the user's eye "handled" unfamiliar objects, he or she also learned them.[47] The intricately organized and labeled plates encouraged diverting interaction. They depended upon the viewer's playful, hide-and-seek engagement with extant and extinct organisms (fig. 15).

14

Jean-Jacques Scheuchzer, *Monuments of the Flood,* from *Physique sacrée,* 1732, I, pl. 57. Engraving by I. A. Corvinus. (Photo: Courtesy Getty Center, Resource Collections.)

15

Jean-Jacques Scheuchzer, *Fossil Remains* (*Work of the Fifth Day of Creation*), from *Physique sacrée,* 1732, I, pl. 19. Engraving by I. A. Corvinus. (Photo: Courtesy Getty Center, Resource Collections.)

But the union of laboratory science with aesthetic experimentation was perhaps best exemplified by the technological innovation of color printing. This major development in simulation originated in the mid-1740s with Jacques Gautier Dagoty's jealously guarded system for creating chromatic anatomical reproductions that were "true to life." In the opinion of their inventor, these two-dimensional automata surpassed those of his mentor and eventual rival, J. C. Le Blon. The latter's multiple-plate mezzotint, or improved three-color process, led to the manufacture of "printed paintings." By midcentury, L. M. Bonnet's production of facsimiles of full-color pastels[48] finally achieved the difficult coordination of Newton's spectrum on eight plates. French science was thus given the technology for visual cognition. By the 1780s, the refined toolwork of J.-F. Janinet's imitation of *manière de lavis,* and C. M. Descourtis's method of superimposing a limited range of colors, provided mineralogy with the means for representing the elusive tints needed to render a convincing transparency revealing inclusions. More importantly, I suggest that it was specifically through these graphic technologies that the fledgling science of crystallography was able to conceptualize, by laying bare, the hidden processes of crystal and mineral formation. Analogously, it is doubtful whether either meteorology or romantic landscape painting would have flourished at the close of the eighteenth century without the invention of aquatint. This Anglo-French resin-based chemical process (roughening metal plates directly with acid) not only made possible the convincing representation of wetness but allowed the viewer to contemplate in detail the vagaries of cloudy weather.

For the Enlightenment, powers of discernment, visual acumen, and the development of probing habits of sight were requisite skills, and not just in the domain of natural history. Perspicuity was the primary literal and critical tool for delving into the architecture of the body. Art and medicine shared (and, indeed, still share) somatic metaphors of sign, symptom, and hand or touch. Their tactile procedures interanimated one another on many fronts. None, however, was more central than the need to perceive and make public that most private, elusive space of all: the human interior. To return to my opening premise, I want briefly, and by way of moving toward a conclusion, to develop a contrast in this biological sphere between a verbal and a visual way of knowing.

The strategy for "reading" hidden terrain was derived from rational philosophy. Dissection interrogated the inert body by violently laying it bare—much like the deductive dismembering of a coherent thought by a syllogism. The aim of the anatomical method, and I use the term now with its broader epistemological connotation of measured vertical penetration, was to get at a fundamental truth that lurked beneath a merely visible, unimportant appearance or surface.[49] Such an invisible gem of transcendent value, it was believed, could be made manifest only through calculation, the division of the organism into computable parts. The analytical and separating knife of reason successively descended from the epidermal (appearance), to a subcutaneous myology, to attain, finally, the bedrock of bone itself (character). This slicing resembled the parsing of a sentence to arrive at clear meaning or the cutting of a corpse to reach the seat of life. One example, taken from particle physics, will have to stand for the ubiquity of this epistemological method for forcible entry in our contemporary culture. I quote Roy Schwitters, the Harvard physicist, on the importance of the proposed, but now abandoned, supercollider designed to search for the delicate traces of ghostly particles: "We're going in [to the fundamental particles] with wrecking bars and sledge hammers to try to find the treasure."[50]

What a contrast this rational-linguistic system of attack makes with visual cognition embodied in noninvasive and nondestructive medical probes (see fig. 4). Recall that these instruments for the remote "laying on of hands" transmit ghostly streams of light and dark messages requiring a new science of sensory detection. To make biological knowledge from copious symbolic information, the medical connoisseur of the future, like his artistic counterpart, will have to know how to decode at a distance. She must learn to interpret the infinitely nuanced and ambiguous phantasms emitted by the living human organism as they painlessly float in space. Conversely, the anatomical, lexical, and logical mode of knowing tends to render insensate the objects of its scrutiny. By splitting, fragmenting, and isolating biota in frozen moments, the procedure is antithetical to the mutable and metamorphic life processes it purports to reveal.[51]

Both methods entailed psychological ramifications. The outer features of the body, especially those located on the face, had been used since antiquity to infer an individual's unique, but masked, history. Yet plumbing the character, essence, temperament, spirit, aura, or inner life of a person from a marked exterior has proved as difficult as pinning down elusive prions, zoo particles, or the Higgs particle. Physiognomy and phrenology involved *reading* the hidden properties of the soul and the intellect. The analysis was anatomical, depending upon the supposed legibility of fixed features and the bony topography of the head. Significantly, mental augury was raised to scientific status in the late eighteenth century through the publications of Johann Caspar Lavater and Petrus Camper.[52] Interpreted as systems of forecasting, such logocentric methods extracted semantic meaning from isolatable looks. As such, they continue to have profound implications, evident not only in the screening for genetic predispositions but in cosmetic surgery.[53] Plastic surgeons use computer modeling in which noses, lips, or eyes are so many recombinant spare parts. These biological fragments stock a seemingly infinite database of corporeal "readymades." This physiognomic application of electronic imagery thus confirms Marcel Duchamp's prediction that the category of readymades would eventually embrace the entire universe of objects.[54] Now that the body has become a constructed artifact, the client may select his ideal and ageless persona, frozen in youth, from a repository of reproducible items. Removal is also an option. Wrinkles, creases, and folds can be erased, thus further expunging any tell-tale signs of mortality or a personal past. Parenthetically, this cosmetic development appears to follow logically from the Leibnizian premise that all discrete data are combinable.[55] When extended to the genetic level, the application of a biological *ars combinatoria* conjures up visions of sperm banks and of decontextualized, faceless couplings occurring in petrie dishes, or otherwise at a remove from particular human bodies.

Similarly, in eighteenth-century physiognomic analysis, the body became any body. This ahistorical abstraction was compounded from excisable qualities. Separable properties or characteristics were thus endowed with a meaning and value irrespective of the individual context in which they inhered. By contrast, the pathognomic theory developed by Georg Lichtenberg[56] disputed the establishment of a presumed correspondence between timeless, buried essence and stilled portions of the anatomy. The German natural philosopher and art critic called, instead, for the visualization of mutable appearances. The full range of human activity was to be captured in expressive gesture, fleeting pantomime, and ephemeral emotions. This performative method—enacted with paint and brush on springy and responsive canvas, or fingers pressed in clay, or burin and needle exposing metal—aimed to sort out feelingly the transitory and colored diversity of internal life as lived. This optical auscultation or palpation of a particular body's surface should be seen as analogous to the artist's personal style in expressively handling materials. Thus the perspicuous painter, sculptor, architect, and printmaker, like the sensitive physician, could train himself and the willing viewer to perceive and make visible the invisible motions of the heart.

In sum, my point has been that we have been moving, from the Enlightenment forward, toward a visual and, now, an electronically generated culture. Since the time of Plato, however, this visual culture and its magician-creators have suffered from a low status.[57] The Platonic analogy is especially apt in view of the contemporary proliferation of technological wizardry and the resulting bodilessness of virtualized things. The shadowy video screen and the ghostly computer semblance remind us of the philosopher's consignment of fantastic or sophistic appearances—associated with nonexistent or false objects—to the bottom of his divided universe. He deemed such bewitching phantasms, or dim visibles, to be as indeterminate as the chromatic blur hovering in water and as confusingly deceptive as dreams. His Neoplatonic followers, in particular, located these insubstantial and overwhelming "illusions," along with fluid fictions in general, in a subterranean cavern. That distant sensory darkness was situated at the antipodes from the true and sunlit intellectual verities (*archai*) accessible to rational philosophy.[58] But it is precisely these unseizable images—unlike delusory "clear and distinct" words or "reliable" numbers identified with reason—that, paradoxically, do not lie. As kinetic, probable, and interactive forms of expression, they openly attest to the conjectural and fluid nature of life lived in the middle zone. They help us to organize and make sense of that floating world, or *milieu,* stretching considerably below certitude and somewhat above ignorance.

I believe, then, that it is time that we, as imagists, looked to another quarter—the structure and activity of visual cognition itself—for both our praxis and our methods. We must frame a unified theory of imaging from the intersections of the old historical arts with the new optical technologies. True interdisciplinarity would be grounded in the acknowledgment that perception (*aisthesis*) is a significant form of knowledge (*episteme*), perhaps even *the* constitutive form.[59] It is also time to assert that innovative collaboration can occur only in a community of intellectual equals. Moreover, creating such a hybrid art-science of visualization would help to avert a greater social and cultural danger. It offers the model for a concept of learning that challenges us not to remain unskilled and naive ingesters of misinformation we did not help to produce.

As we have seen, we possess artistic models and visual methods of analysis—many deriving from the eighteenth century—for not receiving pictures passively but entering and reassembling them actively. Yet the poverty of our current observational skills is such that the specter looms of an engulfing, abstract and invisible technology more sophisticated than its uncomprehending users. The time has also come, then, to cease being disembodied receivers and transmitters of a cynical linguistic propaganda packaged graphically. Educated seeing is precisely about recognizing that information cannot be separated from the manner or style of its display. As Piranesi, Scheuchzer, and Lichtenberg demonstrated, the enlightened observer—with the guidance of the artist—patterns and constructs reality through dynamic interactions.

Let us prepare for this alternative future. In that illuminating image-world, the spatiovisual disciplines would model themselves upon the special characteristics of their "graphicacy."[60] I foresee that glad day when feared and despised images, and underrated affective sensory experience in general, are released from their penumbrous prison. It cannot be mere utopianism to hope that the historical process, begun in the eighteenth century, coupling advances in imaging techniques with advances in technology must ultimately lead out of Plato's ill-lit and second-class hotel for ghostly transients. No longer defined as subjugated illustrations, or just more efficient conveyors of extant verbal information, images would be recognized as free agents indispensable in discovering that which could not otherwise be known. In that coming Enlightenment, our public policy and our pedagogical practice would finally coincide. Visual lessons and visual means learned from the past could be applied imaginatively to tackle current problems in imaging.

Display and the Rhetoric of Corruption

2

Can art history disappear as a field? Does anything prevent its becoming absorbed, eventually, by a discipline of social history or ethnography? Since we use their methods increasingly, and they more and more use material objects as "texts" through which to pursue reconstructions of a now immaterial past, what will differentiate art history?

—Martha Kingsbury, Program Announcement, College Art Association, Annual Meeting, Seattle, 1993.

No species of reasoning is more common, useful and necessary to human life than that derived from the testimony of men and the reports of eye witnesses and spectators. . . . The problem with this kind of testimony is that it hinges on the truth of a general maxim: no objects have any discoverable connection together, and that all the inferences, which we can draw from one to another are founded merely on our experience of their constant and regular conjunction.

—David Hume, *Of Miracles* (1748)

This essay is a meditation on one protracted question. Why do images seem to pose a special epistemological problem, in ways that written words do not, for researchers in the humanities, social, biological, and physical sciences? Not much has changed since eighteenth-century *philosophes,* echoing Plato's fear of *mimesis,* condemned the "Oriental despo-

16

Benedetto Ceruti and Andrea Chiocco, *View of the Museum,* from *Musaeum Franc. Calceolari jun. Veronensis,* 1622, frontispiece. Engraving by Hieronymus Viscardus. (Photo: Courtesy Getty Center, Resource Collections.)

This crowded treasury bears witness to the fascination and even devotion once accorded to the universe of objects. But the miscellaneousness and materiality of its contents could also be used to indict a corrupting, parallel world in which viewers all too easily got ensnared. As contemporary media critics remark about simulating technology, sensuous animations lure viewers to play in category-defying cyberspace. Analogously, polymathic collections were seen by later systematizers as a Land of the Lotus Eaters, beckoning beholders into a hypnotic realm of conspicuous surplus and uncontrollable substitutes.

tism" of the eye and the superstitious gaze of pagan idolaters.[1] In the continuing contest over how to wrest the full-strength sense datum from its diluting representation, only the intervening technology—largely derived from the entertainment industry—has altered.

The 1993 International Summer Consumer Electronics Show presented a dizzying display of futuristic multimedia products.[2] Info-tech fantasy and techno-hyperbole characterized exhibits centered on the trail-blazing convergence of personal computers with interactive gadgets. According to the sponsors, our planet is about to be inundated by wall-sized high-definition television and wrap-around high fidelity sound. The promise of ever more lifelike experiences through virtual reality, and ever more realistic illusions through digital simulation, prompts me to ask what role remains today for the visual expert. When the basements of America vibrate to VCRs and laser disk players or are awash in stereo video games requiring special helmets, earphones, goggles, and gloves allowing hordes of people to caper in a Nintendo landscape, is there anyone left who does not understand this form of communication? Indeed, who is still capable of saying what information "uncontaminated" by instruments and graphics might look like?

I want to argue that, traditionally, when animation capabilities advanced and a corresponding premium was placed on creating more "naturalistic" effects, the Platonic rhetoric of visual corruption became invoked by techno-skeptics. In the domain of the artificial,[3] where scenery is endlessly painted through the agency of hidden numbers emitted by a CD-ROM player, the memory of silent texts continues to evoke nostalgia. Late twentieth-century Luddites yearn for some supposed pristine existence before the advent of on-screen displays and home cinema. Especially among postmodern critics,[4] the desire to flee the promiscuity of audiovisual surround theater has led to the romanticized slide into the chaste realm of aniconic linguistics.[5]

Mustering persuasive arguments on behalf of perceptual expertise, then, seems all the more pressing today. As interdisciplinarity becomes a booming academic industry,[6] what case can be made for specialization in the changing techniques, material processes, and rhetorical strategies of image construction and reception? This question is unavoidable because of two major and, I believe, connected aspects of the information revolution. Both involve the intertwisting of aesthetic with ethical issues. First, cases of nonprofessional desktop criminals who "borrow" illustrations and then alter them are distressingly common.[7] Violations of copyright through the flagrant theft of scanned imagery, the production of unauthorized duplicates, and the electronic manipulation of digitally encoded intellectual property threaten the notion of a unique or authentic work. More troublingly, technological craftiness implies that there is something inherently corrupt about pictorially conveyed information since it permits, and even appears to facilitate, such tampering.

The growing sophistication of electronic mimicry and the explosion of unlicensed private publishers who fiddle with software add a new dimension of uncontrollability to the venerable notion that images are dangerously transgressive and ungovernable. To the destabilizing reality of a generalized lifting, scavenging, and morphing of found bits and pieces of optical data can be added a second, disquieting social phenomenon. On one hand, electronic infringement by everyman debases visualization by calling attention to the problematic practice of borrowing. Even legitimate and openly acknowledged imitation necessarily undermines the long-standing, if mythic, ideal of an unmixed original.[8] On the other hand, the proliferation of software has, paradoxically, created two classes of citizens separated according to whether they *need* images or not.

DOS for Dummies, dubbed an "irreverent primer for the perplexed,"[9] is directed precisely at that expanding home market that has been purchasing cheaper and faster computers but is unable to understand the manual. The division between a technologically literate elite, capable of deciphering arcane symbols and hermetic instructions, and the great unwashed ignorant consumer is growing. What has not been remarked, however, is that the Macintosh's display of icons or Microsoft Corporation's development of Windows contains the biased assumption that pictures are for digital illiterates. While it is admirable that abstract commands are being made graphically concrete, I am as troubled by the association of images with a "technology for dummies" as with their reflexive link to corrupting substances.

These dual issues of electronic copying by the unscrupulous and the assumption that knowledge does not come full-strength through figures require historical situating. My purpose here is to examine a single, but crucial, aspect of the linguistic bias as it hardened into its modern binary opposition during the eighteenth century. Inhabitants of the contemporary era of telepresence and subscribers to computerized long-distance learning may find it eye-opening to ponder how graphics became entwined with dubious, if appealing, packaging and fairground huckstering.[10] The radical sensory skepticism, ushered in by Cartesians,

17

François-Saneré Chérubim d'Or-léans, *A Newly Invented Instrument for Drawing All Sorts of Objects in Proportion,* from *La dioptrique oculaire,* 1671, pl. 28. Engraving. (Photo: Courtesy Herzog August Biblio-thek, Wolfenbüttel.)

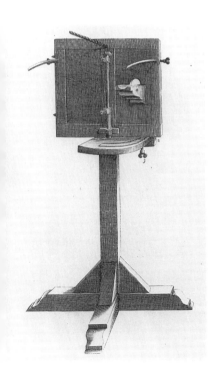

British empiricists, and French sensationalists, identified visualization with the lures of sophistry. For iconoclastic philosophers and enlight-ened reformers, image manipulation was the hallmark of the charlatan equipped with the latest technology projecting deluding special effects. In the increasingly arduous early modern quest for reliable means of dissecting true visual proof from false appearance, the crucial point was how to free images from a welter of contaminants. Who would reduce these light and color composites to homogeneity? Who, or what, would purge adulterating ambiguity, expunge error, exaggeration, and other carnal abuses so that ocular evidence might be rational, a pure and perfect surrogate for the real thing?[11] The French Oratorian Chérubim d'Orléans's monumental and seemingly automatic apparatus for cap-turing and recording transitory optical epiphenomena embodied this post-Cartesian purificatory wielding of disciplining devices (fig 17).[12] Heroically scaled measuring and calibrating setups were intended to subjugate the visual concupiscence of a luxury-loving baroque society.[13]

To understand this accumulating and instrument-driven power of script within modern visual culture, Bruno Latour's model of "black-boxing" is helpful. A black box contains those assumptions broadly held not to need reconsideration. Its sealed contents have become a mat-ter of obedient quotation or undissenting and indifferent passing on.[14] I wish to weaken the grip of the linguistic on the present intellectual scene[15] by exposing past iconoclastic impulses still concealed within this leaky black box. The suppressed premise maintaining the inferior-ity of images (and, conversely, the superiority of texts) is predicated on the privileging of language as standing for all higher handless and sightless cognitive activity.[16] Hermeneutics, defined as the interpretive, exegetical, and theoretical procedure performed on a resisting text, fos-tered such a hierarchy by ranking close reading above the ostentatious shallowness of sight. The historical emergence of difficult discourse was contingent on the moral censure of fast and loose gazes. Thoughtless visible experience has as its foil the internalized, invisible patrimony of literate civilization.

The decoding hermeneuticist derived his status from the al-leged capacity to probe beneath deluding surfaces. Criticism, as rational purification, proceeded initially from the microscopic examination of sacred scriptures, to the detailed scrutiny of profane literature, to the relentless interrogation of images as translatable symbols. Specifically, it was the misunderstanding of Kant's *Critique of Judgment* that allowed the fleeting percept to be dominated by the durable concept.[17] The conflation of the imagination with the understanding made it seem as if permanent form and volatile content were identical and so totally explainable. Once sensory data were transformed into enigmatic characters, an elite cadre of decipherers emerged to unlock their secret codes and veiled messages unavailable to the ordinary beholder.[18]

It is not accidental that the critical condemnation of visual quackery—judged to be a sort of empty conjuring or voyeuristic display[19]—coincided with the rise of a neoclassical "methodism" and a romantic "algebraicism." These late eighteenth-century artistic movements, usually conceived as divergent, actually converged in their attack on a Lockean optical epistemology.[20] Their most notable theorists—from Winckelmann to Baudelaire, from Novalis to Coleridge—posited an abstract systematics, that is, an aesthetical logic directed at the demolition of rococo legerdemain. For reformers, conspicuous signs of manufacture signified circus juggling and mountebank trickery. Flamboyant hypervisibility not only deviated from good taste, it served as a counterexample of nondiscriminating gullibility.

In order for text-based theories, systems, and methods to become autonomous referents, divorced from the sensory sphere above which they floated, the matter and manner of vision had to be demoted to intellectual nullity, to the realm of the merely showy or the fantastic. This further subsumption of the visible to the invisible occurred as texts were allowed to exert power far beyond the legitimate networks in which they originated.[21] The illicit extension of literary operations, and with it of criticism, can be witnessed in the eclipse of eighteenth-century popular science demonstrations by the authoritative scholarly publication. These magical shows were a pan-European form of instructive entertainment.[22] Here I can only sketch the social and epistemological processes that led to the accretion of metaphors of pollution and idleness around machine-generated images. Corrupt, feminine, facile simulations were entangled simultaneously in the craft domain of luxury commodities and the dirty regions of technology. In either case, they were regarded with suspicion, seemingly evading virile and honest labor. Analogies to the spoiling empiric and the sophisticating conjuror persistently eddied around the manually produced and commercially reproduced phantasm.

We need to consider, in addition and however briefly, key factors contributing to the new status of language in Enlightenment pedagogics. Recent literacy studies have revealed the growing split in early modern Europe between a popular, but lowly, oral culture and a polite,

18

Louise-Elisabeth Vigée-Le Brun, *Comtesse de Cérès,* 1784. Oil. (Photo: Courtesy the Toledo Museum of Art, Gift of Edward Drummond Libbey.)

upwardly mobile middle-class company of readers and writers (fig. 18).[23] What has been insufficiently emphasized to date is the fact that this past oral culture was also fundamentally visual. Beginning already with the great seventeenth-century religious polemics, literacy was seen as a weapon in the Protestant arsenal fending off Catholic idolatry.[24] To their detractors, "Romish traditions" and the monstrous impurities of Jesuitical baroque art relied on superstitious speech, wanton gestures, and abominable fetishes to reach the common unlettered man and woman through multisensory spectacle.[25]

Crushing mindless credulity (verbal and visual) with knowledge or reason (writing) was not just at the core of mass education drives from the eighteenth century forward; it was also the chief goal of the Enlightenment. Pictorially conveyed religious doctrines continued to be disseminated in catechistic iconographies throughout the Catholic territories of the old regime. One typical exemplar, issued by the Barefoot Carmelites ministering to the Bavarian provinces, taught visualization strategies through the creation of hybrid figures (fig. 19). The theologians devising the manual noted that five areas lent themselves to imaging: the growth of self-knowledge, the suppression of human vanity, the heightening of virtue, the fostering of inner prayer, and the contemplation of divine things.[26]

Counter-Reformation Catholicism's struggle to embody difficult mental processes and convey them to illiterate viewers is being reiterated by the contemporary computer archivist seeking to conceptualize elusive topics.[27] Like present-day pictorial research, the *Ichnographia* sought visual analogues for abstract psychological conditions, metaphors for the warring passions alternately activated by divine light or by empirical data entering through the doors of the senses.

Significantly, the positive aspects of such compound modes of representation were forgotten in the *philosophes'* campaign to eradicate institutionalized religious tyranny. Using similar but satirically subversive pictorial strategies reformers such as Goya worked at defacing the grotesque empire of brutish and greedy monks (fig. 20).[28] A true son of the Enlightenment, the Spanish painter detested the demonic spells cast by modern thaumaturges and hoped they might give way before reasoned public discourse. Ridiculing corruption, then, was part of a more generalized anti-imagistic intellectual agenda. The politics of a cleansing iconoclasm called for the overthrow of the despised priestly mirage of counterfeit miracles, fraudulent marvels, and emotion-tugging portents. Under the banner of reason and morality, the super-

19

Visualization of the Passions of the Soul, from *Ichnographia,* 1779, pl. 64. Engraving. (Photo: Courtesy Getty Center, Resource Collections.)

20

Francisco de Goya, *They Are Hot,* from *Los Caprichos,* 1799, pl. 13. Etching and aquatint. (Photo: Courtesy the National Gallery of Art, Washington, D.C.)

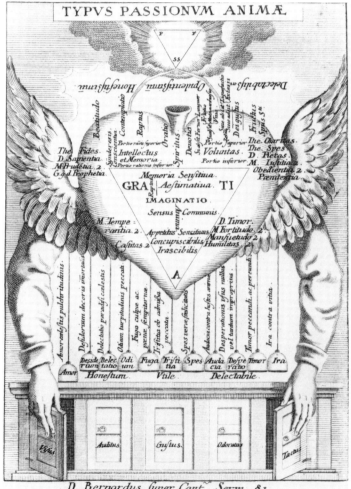

natural became a legacy of authoritarianism needing to be brought down to earth.[29]

David Hume's widely disseminated tract, *Of Miracles* (1748), must stand for this immense class of literature intended to stamp out fanaticism. One of the greatest skeptics in the history of philosophy, the British empiricist inveighed against the propensity of humanity to be drawn to the singular and the extraordinary. The acme of fictionality was the fabricated eyewitness account. Appositely, he argued that optical errors flourished "chiefly among ignorant and barbarous nations, or if civilized people admit them, they received them from ignorant and barbarous ancestors." This specious oral and visual testimony "captivates" its audience and subdues them as "every Capuchin, every itinerant or stationary teacher" knows.[30]

Hume's disproof of visual proof raises a second historical condition contributing to the ethical and intellectual destruction of images and the identification of their makers with con artists. From 1750 onward, a newly quantified probability theory joined forces with a legal insistence on measuring the degrees of certainty on which people could ground rational belief. This calculating mentality, weighing the credibility of texts versus images, confirmed the high enlighteners' conviction that written testimony was more reliable than speech and, certainly, than visual evidence.[31] But such an assumption contained a profound paradox.

To return to hermeneutics, its emergence in the form of the "higher criticism" in the second half of the eighteenth century, and its full-blown formulation during the romantic era, were predicated on just such intense religious and scholarly polemics. The biblical *critica sacra* and the mythical *critica profana,* developed by Enlightenment philologists and comparatists, made a major impact on nineteenth-century art explication and literary exegesis.[32] Moreover, this elaborate *ars critica* continues to undergird our twentieth-century overestimation of text-modeled interpretation. Resembling those technological wizards priding themselves on the complexities of computing's written programs, eighteenth-century students of variora rejoiced in manipulating esoteric ciphers. Yet, ironically, ever more sophisticated means of textual analysis resulted in the impasse of circularity. Interpretation collided with the equally intense Humean perception of the impossibility of proving definitively that a recorded event had actually occurred since the modern interpreter had not been present at the time to *witness* it.

Here, then, is the nub of a fundamental incongruity lurking at the heart of romanticism. The present-day seer was a sham, resembling an inauthentic fairground charlatan, not an authentic prophet. Through sheer skill, craft, or technical trickery, poet and painter were able to imaginatively simulate mythical, historical, or religious scenes they had never, in fact, beheld. Conjuring and artistry were thus one. Alexandre Decamps's moody *fantasmagoria* of the *Villa Doria Pamphili* allows us to reflect on the hermeneutic problem of persuading an audience that such fictionalized persons and recreated settings had once existed (fig. 21). The French romantic painter's ghostly *fête galante* suffers from a triple spatial and temporal dislocation. Past and present are strangely at odds. He creates simultaneity where, historically, there can be none by collaging the fabled Renaissance garden, allusions to Watteau, with the crisp umbrella pines rising above nineteenth-century Rome.

Like today's postmodernists, the first generation of romantics felt crushed by the infinite task of comprehending, interpreting, and, above all, reading every single thing in greater and greater detail.[33] Significantly, this project of futile retrieval was essentially negative, that is, ironical and *critical*. Since the maker knew that convincing visions had to be artificially induced or fabricated, they belonged to the domain of the illusory. As the magical products of cunning manufacture, artistic imitations were the immoral antithesis of pure nature. Free from doctoring, the organic world offered apparent escape from human contamination and tinkering. The aesthetic and ethical problems surrounding the insincerity of romantic creations relate directly to current talk about electronic chicanery through computer sleight-of-hand.

21
—
A. G. Decamps, *The Villa Doria Pamphili, Rome,* nineteenth century. Oil. (Photo: Courtesy The Wallace Collection.)

We have come full circle, returning to my initial question. At a time when an anonymous information superhighway increasingly leads to every home, how one regards images and their proper use is no small matter. Today, Leibniz's melancholic assessment that there are no absolutely new phenomena under the sun, only recycled copies and excerpted reiterations, appears both true and inescapable. The sad baroque awareness of the *vanitas* of the arts and sciences remains apt.[34] Their proud claim to originality comes undone when we realize that technology enables anyone, at the push of a button, to appropriate drawings, film stills, song clips (fig. 22). Yet the realities of multimedia manipulation and plunder do not free us from the obligation of choosing which permutations are acceptable—regardless of technological feasibility.[35]

Worry about digital hybrids has resuscitated the old Platonic and Judaeo-Christian rhetoric of corruption, judging all human creation to be heteronomous and tainted. But a concomitant backward-looking drive, seeking to reestablish bookish literacy to its late nineteenth-century position of preeminence, offers no help in dealing with the dilemmas of global on-line services. Experts in the many historical facets of imaging can, I believe, contribute something positive to the postmodern quandary. They can educate the public concerning earlier technological shifts and upheavals caused by drastic changes in the processes of duplication. It should not be left to the text-bound legal profession alone to decide what constitutes optical larceny or information as property.[36]

In the widespread postmodern denigration of the aesthetic,[37] what is forgotten is that from Leibniz to Schiller, the term connoted the integration of mental activity with feeling.[38] *Aisthesis,* as perception or sensation, has in post-Cartesian and especially post-Kantian thought become separated from cognition. Rediscovering its pragmatic capacity to bridge experience and rationality, emotion and logic, seems all the more important in the era of virtual reality and seemingly nonmediated media. The awareness that images can sustain the continuity of thinking, not merely serve as fictionalizing counterfeits or pseudo-intellectual goods, brings both an ethical and an aesthetic dimension to the computer age.

22
—
Michael Rentz, *The Vanity of All Human Things,* from Franz Anton, Graf von Sporck, *Der sogennante Sinn-Lehr und geistvolle . . . Todtentanz,* 1767, frontispiece. Engraving. (Photo: Courtesy Getty Center, Resource Collections.)

The Eighteenth Century at the End of Modernity

3

In this essay, I want to draw attention to three areas in which the Enlightenment produced public and private discourses that corresponded to, and were simultaneously very different from, its intentions.[1] We are heirs to those mirrorings and anamorphoses. The intersecting rhetorics of corruption, progress, and transformation not only continue to shape how we currently organize the data of our disparate experiences, but they affect the structuring of as yet nonexistent realms of knowledge.

Viewed from without and within, today's academic landscape looks fractured and fractious. On the street or behind the walls, the dominant metaphor of hypermodernity remains Walter Benjamin's *shock*.[2] Psyches and systems everywhere are in the throes of "breaking down," "going to pieces," and "fragmenting." Universities and colleges are not exempt from the effects of worldwide shattering. Beset by fiscal pressures from the outside and methodological critiques from the inside, they, too, suffer the physical trauma of polemical wear and tear. The eighteenth century knew all about making and rupturing rigid categories. The business of metamorphosis is always unsettling.[3] But undoing apparently clear classifications of identity, gender, and social or racial stereotypes can also signal protean flexibility, not chaotic destruction.

No one denies that civilizations and cultures are falling apart in a technologically altered and accelerated environment. As mass society becomes unglued, what structures will suture the life of the mind? What patterns will be assumed by established, but no longer unified, fields in their revolutionary transit from discrete and vertically organized modes of inquiry into the nonhierarchical computer era of "inter," "trans," "multi," "sub," and "hyper"?[4] Beyond the destruction, erosion,

23

Giambattista Piranesi, *Decorative Capriccio,* from *Opere varie,* 1750, pl. 1. Etching. (Photo: Courtesy Getty Center, Resource Collections.)

Piranesi's grotesques are images of incredible freedom and lightness. Postmodern in their lack of fixity and hybridity, these inventive etchings display a democratic attitude toward the heterogeneous elements making up a composition, showing the creative process to be about both self-fashioning and the fabrication of a dynamic and shifting universe of forms. The great Italian architect, interior designer, antiquarian, draftsman, and polemicist pictures practical knowledge in action. His prints conjure nonexistent things and unsayable significations into being. Communication is sensory, performative, and always in formation before the eyes.

appropriation, or absorption of the disciplinary "other," what hope is there for a common revitalization? Can we avoid both the narrow-bore view of single departments as well as the careless collapse of the many into the indeterminate one? Borrowing a metaphor from architectural history, it seems that neither the preservationist's advocacy for protecting all aspects of the curricular environment nor the developer's passion to level its isolated monuments takes into account a broader concern for community values.[5] I am not arguing for essential and permanent features of reality that can be reduced misleadingly to normative types of behavior or raised to transcendent standards. This popular misformulation of Aristotelian universals precludes the possibility of searching for common or recurring characteristics of experience among very different actants.[6]

George Rousseau recently lamented the absence from the American scene of the engaged intellectual capable of addressing a non-academic audience.[7] James Winn similarly argued that we pay a heavy price for overspecialization. Indicative of the larger rift between practice and theory in today's "service economy," the damaging separation of those who create and perform works of art from those who analyze them in our universities and humanities institutes further cuts scholars off from an educated general public.[8] Yet that same public must vote to support the funding of cultural and research activities.

Extending these scholars' thoughtful perceptions, I suggest that the central issue is not whether to salvage this or that crumbling specialty. Nor is it simply a matter of razing blasted subject matter, bulldozing the outmoded and rapidly disintegrating ruins of an unilluminated pre-feminist, before new historicist, and *avant*-poststructuralist era. Rather, the great problem is the steady degradation of higher learning in *everyone's* eyes.

REENCHANTING

To enhance our collective endeavors not only in the sight of the public but in our own apprehension, it might prove useful to identify three ways in which the contemporary disenhancement of scholarship derives from taking Enlightenment battles to their violent, and even repellant, conclusion. I think it is striking, and not only to an art historian, how the high enlighteners' emphasis on rational systematics and sensory duplicity destroyed the cognitive importance of somatic experience. The long afterlife of corporeal alienation leads me to take up, first, the humanities' and social sciences' loss of visual appeal. Digging up the dirt in academe's groves, debunking myths, and hooting at hoaxes was, of course, a favorite eighteenth-century sport. What was not foreseen by even the most prescient of *philosophes* or mordant of satirists, however, was the turn to the ugly that accompanies the current passion for denunciation. The Algerian feminist Hélène Cixous has remarked that the two fundamental lessons of living are slowness and ugliness.[9] She intended by this *appercu* to encourage us to allow ourselves to be drawn within the physical object. In that fleshly and certainly not conventionally attractive space, compounded of material thing and feeling perceiver, we might relearn to see in ways prior to the disembodied and distanced gaze. Appositely, Cixous's Ovidian vision of female and male psyches deformed by the altering presence of other bodies is fluidly mutable. Initial repugnance for experiences we thought distasteful becomes transformed into respect through intimate association.

I wish to argue that such transvaluation of the negative into the positive is rare in the current normalizing of the pessimistic intellectual, bent on extirpating secular mortal sins. No one surveying institutions of higher learning can fail to be struck by the fallenness of the arts and sciences. As if fulfilling the prophecy of human corruption preached by Descartes, Hobbes, Hume, Boulanger, and Voltaire, broken disciplines are seen as monstrous memorials to global rot.[10] From the perspective of the literate public, the apparent erasure of disciplinarity indicates a scholarly failure to manage empirical chaos, to control our phenomenal and unruly objects of study within an autonomous system. For reform-minded academics making the case for oppressed groups, the early modern physiognomics of fraud still obtains. Detecting deceit imprinted on the political and religious face of society, however, has now shifted to exposing the ubiquitous error of our cultural ways, the falseness of western "-ologies" and "-isms."[11] In the past as well as the present, to be enlightened was synonymous with being critical, especially self-critical. The mind must be purged of animal instincts, sensual emotions, and coloring feelings that might entangle the perceiver with the heteronomous world. No less than in Rousseau's time, the illusory arts are seen as dishonest, contaminated by the matter of the world and the substance of the body.

Powerful new media have exacerbated the nostalgia for primitive environments not yet besmirched by the duplicities of the video screen or the computer monitor.[12] Baudrillard's shallow hyper-specter, that *simulacrum* without origin or reality, represents the apogee of eighteenth-century yearning for deep and authentic models stripped of their sensory veil or disguising dress.[13] The end of modernity is marked precisely by this uneasy sense that literacy has come to an end. For many, meaningful sounds and coherent texts have been drowned out in the fire-hose flow of data. Pedagogy's venerable scribal skills seem defiled by hidden systems of connected, but variously formatted, electronic apparatus that manipulate, modulate, synchronize, and digitize information by numbers through endless entertainment channels.[14]

Our late twentieth-century objects and methods of study, then, stand accused of decline, adulteration, or counterfeit, no matter the camp. My purpose is not to take sides, or to stake yet another theoretical claim, but to draw attention to how the Enlightenment rhetoric of corruption has become the postmodern discourse of ugliness. The Frankfurt School did much to spread a radically negative method, that is, the "negative commitment" to subvert the instrumental world.[15] Neoplatonizing critiques that destroy oppressive dichotomies would not have shocked Diderot or Lichtenberg. Today, the taxonomy of antipathies has changed: anti-castration, anti-ego, anti-homo, anti-media.[16] Condemnation and essentialism go hand in hand. A longing for mythic purity underlies Fredric Jameson's desire to annihilate capitalist production, shot through by the irrationality of the commodity system generating worthless and superfluous goods.[17] Similarly, the failure of Kant's moral will, cleansed of Humean passions, fuels Michel Foucault's trope of power relations as punitive and militaristic.[18]

"Oppositional" criticism, or the radical critique of contemporary culture guided by practices operating within the academy, the arts, and international politics, also inflects the work of "new" Marxists and new historicists.[19] Relying in different ways on the Lacanian model of cognition as fissured with gaps and lapses, Louis Althusser and Stephen Greenblatt transferred the barbaric caesuras of the fractured unconscious onto a collapsing and divided society.[20] Metaphors of the riven and the polluted underlie descriptions of competing "advocacies," "saturating hegemonic systems,"[21] despotic "imperialisms," delusory "fetishes," and money, land, class, or gender "biases." Significantly, these political and intellectual tyrannies are conceptualized visually, thus extending the eighteenth century's iconoclastic attacks on conspicuous affluence and ostentatious luxury.

If any importance remains attached to the aesthetic, beyond that of being just another dirty word,[22] it might well consist in the practical ability to render things magical through subtle modes of perception and thinking.[23] I am suggesting that unless we reenchant our

damaged art, literature, history, science, and even epistemology by rescuing it from an implacable logic of venality, it is difficult to see why a
larger public should be drawn to support the study of what we ourselves
loathe. The demystifying and deconstructive strategies of postmodernist debates are extensions of Enlightenment polemics against superstition, priestcraft, and repressive political domination. Ernest Gellner
identified this demolishing demon lurking in post-Cartesian philosophy with the reification of reason, objectivity, language, and logic.[24]
The epistemological "devil" symbolized the tricking and lying appearances preventing humankind from knowing anything with certainty
about the phenomenal world. Accordingly, whether in Cartesianism or
empiricism, the mind was vaporized into a dream. Identity was subjected to corrosive doubt. The senses were equated with delusion, and
the imagination turned into a factory for the production of spellbind-
ing apparitions.

Gellner's mapping of the trajectory of modern philosophy raises
the question of whether the new interdisciplinarity conceives of itself,
too, as a confrontational comparative diabolics.[25] Will universities become the arena where hostile methodologies and their road warriors
slug it out over the merits and demerits of a world capitalist system
and shrinking local diversity? That, I think, would signal a spent modernism without Enlightenment. Aptly, Werner Schneiders has written
of later eighteenth-century philosophy's unprecedented construction of
a mission for itself.[26] One could argue that, even much earlier, Shaftesbury, Addison, and Steele borrowed the Gnostic notion of scattering
sparks of divine light to combat atheism.[27] Transforming the concept
from its religious connotation to that of a secular embassy, the *philosophes* as new missionaries of intellectual virtue militantly battled on
behalf of right reason, moral truth, and human perfectability. Like the
Cathars of old, a more perfect elite set out to convert the credulous,
promiscuous, and backward-looking dupes of feudalism. Error was to
be eradicated through compulsory education and redemptive literacy.
The understanding had to submit before the clarity of analytical argument. Resistance proved futile. When persuasion failed, then psychological or physical force was enlisted. Schneiders, in the spirit of Isaiah
Berlin, coupled sacred teaching with holy war, the failure to effect lasting political reforms with the despair of idealists turned ideologues.[28]
Ironically, a frustrated purism gave rise to the most corrupt totalitarian-
ism and the cannibalism of the modern police state.

Contemporary Catharism,[29] with its emphasis on rigorous mental ascetic rituals and linguistic or social purification, follows in Descartes's and Kant's footsteps. Good moral character and worthwhile intellectual projects are conceived as necessarily negative and skeptical, qualities that have historical roots in the perceived need to dislodge vice-ridden human beings from their evil and dissimulating tendencies. Ideological discourse, in the words of Judith Shklar, put hypocrisy at the forefront of the vices.[30] Kant's *philosophia militans,* or the aggressive offensive mounted by the three *Critiques* against nonmentalized experience, embodied this major relocalization from outer to inner goals, from revolutionizing the masses to radical self-improvement. The long eighteenth century, then, is not only contiguous with, but central to, romanticism. The problem of shattered illusions and the aggrandizement of thwarted desire led to the destructive claims of absolute egotism.[31] It also elevated the superstition denounced by Voltaire into an alternative and autonomous fantastic, fraught with the violence implicit in any binary construction.[32]

If, on one hand, the failure of the Gospel of Reason yielded the despotic subjugation of those who thought otherwise and the Satanic glorification of the autonomous individual will, it resulted, on the other hand, in the loss of mission. This terrible sense of impotence and inauthenticity, however, goes far beyond Gellner's or Schneiders's analysis of the plight of modern philosophy. For what is the mission of the humanities and social sciences today? What remains for them to *do* after having had their corrupt motives, westernizing progressivist rhetoric, and factitious recuperation of cultural differences exposed? What shall we do, at the ash end of modernism, after everything has been debunked, but escape into formal systems or internecine war? This reflexive flight into the interior or exterior is acted out as fields preoccupy themselves with their theories, logical structures, and, above all, their flawed development laid bare to public misanthropy.

The hazard in implacably extirpating corruption, no matter how laudable the aim, is the zealotry of the anti-corrupt. Inherited from the *philosophe*'s drive to eradicate religious credulity, the compelling need for rigorous truth and intellectual purity *above all other virtues* can lead paradoxically to personal, social, and scholarly vandalism.[33] Subjecting wayward fields to cleansing ascetic practices betrays the eighteenth-century nostalgia for an authentic, prelapsarian moment when cultural production supposedly had not yet been penetrated by the distortions of the western imagination or the capitalist commodity system. I am suggesting that the single-minded hunting down of counterfeit scholarly activities disturbingly dead-ends in an iconoclastic antiaesthetics of ugliness or unvisualizability. Can we really afford unquestioningly to embrace postmodernism's negative dialectics, its antiocular suspicion that all forms of representation are voracious, dominating, and duplicitous simulacra?

REDOING

The Enlightenment is inseparable from a rhetoric of progress extolling the importance of tireless doing. If the attack on corruption forms the unstated background to the postmodern interdiction of essentialism, totalizing systems, and the technology of spectacle, then the reification of ceaseless production inversely stands behind the current drive to redeem the discarded. The environmental slogan "recycle, reduce, reuse" brings me to a second, fundamental link between early and late modern views. Picking up the pieces, finding the materials, and gathering the concepts together in the flea market of global modernity positively challenges both the high modernist vision of constantly making something new and the tribalist impulse to cling to the old by separating into self-contained and homogeneous units.

While the grand unitary plans of eighteenth- and nineteenth-century states are crumbling, European and non-European customs are being reelaborated, reconceived, and reconstructed. Like the patchwork of rough-hewn *objets trouvés* and factory surplus clothing being torn, dismembered, and then sutured by antiestablishment fashion deconstructionists such as the Malinese Lamine Kouyaté,[34] bits and pieces of the postcolonial world are being jaggedly sewn together. This global undoing of decaying systems goes beyond simply unraveling the seamless garment of orderly historical progression. Importantly, rather than a smoothing over or radical annihilation of bodies of difference, a Piranesian scarred beauty consonant with diaspora and hybridity is emerging.

This affirmative Leibnizian *ars combinatoria,* redevising fragmenting heritages and coarsely weaving formerly alien cultures together, is also accompanied, however, by a sense of estrangement and loss.[35] Who can deny the disquieting aspect of late modern unlivability, or ignore the collapse of the rhetoric of hard work leading to economic improvement, when faced by the human castoffs inhabiting the contemporary jungle of urban life?

The distinguished American painter James Rosen's plangent effacements of famous portraits after Gainsborough and Reynolds are

24
James Rosen, *Nelly O'Brien,* from
Homages to Reynolds, 1987. Water-
color. (Photo: Courtesy the artist.)

25
James Rosen, *The Age of Innocence,*
from *Homages to Reynolds,* 1989. Oil.
(Photo: Courtesy the artist.)

ethereal elegies to the spent vision of progress.[36] Their physical indeterminacy and optical minimalism simultaneously promise a glimpse into the eighteenth century while withholding the possibility of ever recuperating that era in its rich coloration and volumetric palpability (fig. 24). Significantly, the *Homages to Reynolds*—like his other "erasures" of extant work from Giotto to Ingres—involve a knowing "redoing" of spectral originals. Thus rethought, *Nelly O'Brien* (1987) exists both as a ghostly survivor into the present and as a disembodied and unseizable apparition from the past. At the end of modernity, viewers are obliged to admit that they witness clearly neither the British academician's sitter nor her society. The observer's effort to pierce the historical blur or rend the veiling camouflage manages to excavate only the most tenuous marks leading from that vanished age to ours. Less transparent stain than clouded blot, *The Age of Innocence* (fig. 25) is no less uncannily and ironically imported into our world. This phantom of lost youth has the unsettling effect of a damaged photographic negative imperfectly capturing a shadow. The voids and vacancies shattering the paradise of myth prompt the beholder to look more intently. To move deep into the elusive image is to retrace the path from Schillerian naiveté to postmodern sophistication, from distant fall and caesura to recent chiasmus and absence.

Neither incomplete copies nor faded originals, Rosen's muted repaintings are exemplars of modesty for living within the littered posthistorical landscape. In his anti-waste economy of artistic thrift, Reynolds's figures are recycled from their secure position as static museum objects to circulate again as destabilizing symbols of an alien incursion. Reconfiguration demonstrates how familiar identity can become unfamiliar and the unnerving stranger a comforting presence. Just as the day seems over for the romantic estimation of the entirely new,[37] so the will appears gone to sustain the Enlightenment metaphor on which it rests, that of modernity as dynamic progress.[38] Rosen's self-effacing afterimages are helpful in indicating how lifeless narratives might be resuscitated when inserted into other, vivifying situations. Conspicuously lacking the sentimental pessimism and bourgeois nostalgia frequently accompanying preservationist arguments, these bleached pictures on the margin of visibility manage, paradoxically, to reinvest the back and forth movements of history with meaning. Precisely because they do not pretend to be autonomous, godlike "creations," such magical works reenchant human production. Rehabilitated, cultural goods function neither as shallow commodities nor as illusory simulacra. The go neither relentlessly forward nor revivalistically backward. Consequently, the process of making is not invested with impossible linear and mechanical expectations.

RE-ENLIGHTENING

Pondering the relations of the past rhetoric of corruption to the present discourse of fallen signification leads us to looking again at the tacit assumptions of progress. At first glance, there seems nothing marvelous about the charges and countercharges surrounding politicized education and its discontents. One group argues that the maintenance of strict standards and the pursuit of disinterested inquiry has been tainted. Another group, inspired by developments in feminism and multiculturalism, claims that recent academic work has only brought into the open far-from-pure conflicts that have existed all along. I am suggesting that, in this often acrimonious national debate about what constitutes authentic teaching as opposed to sophistic advocacy, the sheer delight and pleasure of wonderment in what we do has gotten lost. The suppressed violence of Enlightenment progressivist dualisms has erupted in academic antagonisms: "self-serving" agendas versus "impartial" scholarship, regulation versus free speech, the contestation of received ideas versus the promulgation of timeless verities.[39]

What has been forgotten, in the present takeover of the past project of modernity, is that eighteenth-century philosophers wanted to enrich ordinary life. Jürgen Habermas has remarked that, instead of giving up on the idea that the arts and sciences could promote understanding of the self, the world, and its institutions, the twentieth century could fruitfully look to the Enlightenment's hermeneutics of everyday communication.[40] Enchantment is no less fundamental to learning than it is to aesthetic experience. The enlighteners believed that humanity could be amazingly transformed, but not through the counterfeit spells of devils or the tricking incantations of imposters. The re-Enlightenment of contemporary disillusioned instruction might draw a lesson from this love for curious, prodigious, and astonishing things. Early modern usage is rich in the perceptual language of marvels.[41] Cunningly wrought artifacts and natural oddities provoked *stupore* in viewers suddenly confronted by the *strano, straordinario,* or *raro.*[42] The anomalous leads onlookers beyond the normal, but is capable likewise of revealing the unusual lodged in the prosaic and the quotidian. Brute facts and intractable objects can be made to address the imagination and thus awaken a genuine enthusiasm to know.

Antiocular invectives concerning the "pornography of information" and the "obscene ecstasy of communication"[43] have served to obscure the opportunities, challenges, and indeed wonders beckoning from another quadrant of the scholarly galaxy. Admittedly, like the supernatural prodigy, transcendence through miraculous technology remains an equivocal phenomenon. Nonetheless, the far-flung computer universe of a new, decentered spatiality is being greeted with a guarded *jouissance* by many cyber-professors.[44] Reminiscent of the eighteenth-century infatuation with ghostly *fantasmagoria,* the changing spectacle of the universe, and outlandish monsters, virtual culture is inspiring the reawakening of a deadened appreciation for *meraviglia.* Designs for computer-mediated experience, behavior, but above all for *collaborative interaction* via hypermedia are springing up everywhere.[45] Dreams of integrative studies, the construction and visualization of new domains, modeling alternative worlds, and fostering global connectivity are dancing in the heads of researchers interested in reshaping their fields.

I say this with the full realization that electronic information is also causing much epistemological angst over the blurring of distinctions between the organic and the artificial, and the inequalities separating the haves from the have-nots. Nevertheless, by way of conclusion, I want to focus on the positive consequences of redesigning the language paradigm, traditionally operating in scholarship, into a space for the production of multiple and integrated *patterns* for human use.[46] I believe that identifying and coordinating emergent areas is not infotech fantasy but a way to have collective conversations, from diverse perspectives, around common problems in visuality and visual culture.

One of the inescapable ramifications of the computer revolution has been the revelation that the image is not merely a quasi-idea, a "material" bit of sense datum requiring reification into a higher and "abstract" mental concept, but that it *is* that concept. David Summers has convincingly shown how the widespread misinterpretation of Saussurian signification has led not only to the prevailing authority of linguistics as a disciplinary and epistemological model, but to the specious analogy of images to the arbitrary signifier of language.[47] I am extending his perspicuous argument here to suggest that we have to get beyond the false hierarchy of lowly somatic, and elevated mental, activity. Privileging abstract, disembodied meaning by placing it above physical perceptions and tangible technologies results in continuing to think in terms of warring oppositions and clashing polarities. How can the technological objects and information we have created interface with human beings if they are believed destitute of cognitive worth?

Beyond the obvious discrepancy inherent in trying to separate pre- from postintellectual structures, there lurks the implicit devaluing of practical vis-à-vis theoretical activity. Yet, ironically, it is precisely in the area of situated praxis that we *dixhuitièmeistes* are most needed. As the paper culture world of the old regime becomes transformed into the computer graphics universe, historians can help in locating and adjudicating the meanings forming along this permeable boundary. Moreover, we should give some thought to devising pragmatic research agendas that go beyond merely using the computer as a word processor. This powerful and revolutionary medium has the potential to be reshaped into a flexible, diversified, and ethically responsible learning machine.[48]

The reconfiguration of current disciplines into an appealing enterprise is, I believe, a visual design problem. Presently divided into discrete forms of practice (engineering, architectural, industrial, graphic, stage, and fashion), a reconceptualized notion of designing would involve generating a persuasive argument for its centrality to social life.[49] Why not also to intellectual life? Distinct specializations, individual research projects, and a dizzying diversity of disciplines might be challengingly reimagined. Much as in the rococo *Gesamtkunstwerk* or in a delightful cabinet of curiosities, meaning would reside less in the unique creator and more in the constructive interaction with individual percipients. Feminism has been especially powerful in showing the importance of craft modes of production and polysemic forms of reception.[50] As the previously separated media of television, radio, telephone, and mail are merging into patterned image-word-sound composites, crafting significant interaction in all knowledge domains becomes crucial.

We are traveling along a new road devoid of the customary signposts and without a map. It is simply a fact that optical fiber networks are actually redesigning cultures in ways that factional strife and mutual recrimination are not. While we splinter in the name of interdisciplinarity, a vast, single communications channel simultaneously disintegrates and unifies multiple identities into a telepresent identity. Paradoxically, just as collectively we are becoming more aware that information has been packaged, that is, presented to us by design, we are less conscious that it is anything but design.[51] At a historical moment singularly allergic to the affirmative gesture, our academic culture of experts stands apart from rethinking one of the major practical issues of *everyone's* life world.

Learning from Enlightenment aspirations and impasses, we can demonstrate why our intellectual problems and concerns matter today. If design involves the planning and patterning of any act toward a desired end, then artifacts and images, texts and technology, mass-produced products and discrete art objects, even area studies and curricula, are changing cultural forms requiring constant good shaping. Instead of focusing on the Manichean battles that erode and divide us, we might try fashioning common problems for study. Through the smoke of late modernity glimmers the re-Enlightenment. Journeying flexibly into the twenty-first century entails an open-minded encounter with the realm of the artificial. Extricating ourselves from the debilitating pessimism accompanying the failure of modernist straight-line trajectories seems to involve some creative wandering. Not deterministically going forward or panglossianly staying behind means reenchanting, re-doing, and reenlightening the fields of inquiry we have inherited from the past.

The New Imagist

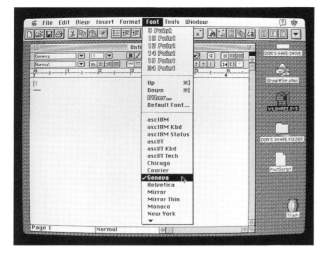

EXPERT WITHOUT QUALITIES

As we shift irrevocably from a lens to a digital culture, I am struck by the dissolution of familiar things, categories, structures. What first attracted me to art history was the alluring materialization of thought occurring in teeming museums, riveting objects, beautiful paintings, multifocal collages, shadowy films. At the threshold of another millennium, our heightened perception of instrumentalized artifice, of ubiquitous technological mediation—extending into the inner reaches of the body and encouraging travels into alternate sensory realms—has left viewers both excited and uneasy. Our awareness of ever more sophisticated interventions, without knowing precisely who is producing them and how the effects are produced, has resulted in wishful expectation for, and boundless cynicism concerning, the media reengineering of actions, feelings, events. Cyberspace in particular, with its convergence of formerly distinct media into a single multimedium and its erasure of marked boundaries between transmission modes, raises worries about potential invasions of privacy, theft of intellectual property, credit card fraud, "cracker" terrorism, and remailed child pornography.[1]

Both a liberating form of international communication and a freewheeling outlaw culture, the telepresent environment is, not surprisingly, reconfiguring learning. Yet utopian visions of the virtual classroom as drawing worldwide modem owners together has not diminished nagging fears about a vast, homogenizing conduit of information. If predictions prove accurate, fiber optic cables will have the capacity to channel different data sources such as newspapers, e-mail, video, and television into a single stream of messages controlled by a few powerful invisible agents. Further, there is a fear that financially

26

Apple Macintosh color display M1212 with Word 6.0. (Photo: Courtesy Donald Williamson.)

Philippe-Jacques de Loutherbourg's late eighteenth-century invention of the *Eiduphusikon*—a backlit, continuously unfurling painted panorama accompanied by *sons et lumières*—quickly descended the stage of Drury Lane to invade the domestic parlor (fig. 27). As in today's personal computer revolution, sensory technology increasingly abandoned the public sphere to colonize the private interior. Both old and new machines capture the mass appeal of devices that are at once optical toy, miniature theater, and illusionistic spectacle in motion meant to be seen in the dark.

strapped institutions might use electronic technology simply to cut faculty costs by forcing instructors to teach huge numbers of students online or on-screen. How do we turn disembodied information into a quality education, that is, into a high-level interaction connecting the difficult process of thinking to individual faces and responsible voices? In the currently polarized atmosphere of elation about the coming non-physical frontier, and suspicion about the smart, anonymous equipment creating it, all forms of visual manifestation, including those skillfully wrought and beguiling substances called works of art, are susceptible to being identified merely with passive entertainment, deceptive advertisement, or, in the case of aggressive television, with incitements[2] to real-life violence.

This essay argues that if you take any media problem old or new—posed by the Eidophusikon or the laptop—and push it far enough, it becomes an image problem (fig. 27). In light of current debates over how digital information can be organized, interpreted, and taught, we need to go beyond conventional art, architectural, or design history. Such sweeping reappraisals of mission and perspective can be summed up by a paradox: we have to shape a disciplined transdisciplinary imaging field. As both preparatory specialization and overarching area, this transcategorical kind of inquiry would refocus and reshape the contents of the humanities, biological, physical, and social sciences. With an eye to my conclusion, I suggest we must define the new imagist—an expert who does not yet exist—in order to help anticipate, illuminate, and interconnect unsuspected visualization issues arising across the spectrum and accompanying the global pictorialization of knowledge.

This future imagist faces a daunting task, not just because these are difficult intellectual challenges but because the sensory modalities conveying the messages are frequently considered contaminating or, worse, mindless. The current enthusiasm for immersive environments, that is, placing a person inside a scene by restoring peripheral vision and filling out the periphery, is a case in point. The craze for hypersimulation—accomplished by wearing a special headset, with earphones and small screens in front of each eye, wired to computers—tends to exaggerate the instability of all forms of exhibition. The user feels surrounded by an animated spectacle that shifts with each turn of the head. The unreflective tendency to collapse the varieties of illusion into an all-inclusive virtuality, and sapient beholders into potentially unethical "users," does not take into account important differences among media.

While the new, speeded-up processes favor anonymous automatism and clandestine manipulation, display does not necessarily entail deception nor, *contra* Guy Debord, must it be a subjugating instrument of unification forcing diverse phenomena into an unreal fusion.[3]

Machine euphoria, spurred by on-line pedagogy, network collaboration, and the promise of wider access to emergent global infrastructures, however, has obscured the intellectual and emotional complexities of human choice. As several states (Maine, Utah, Virginia) hurry to establish an electronic college to replace brick and mortar campuses, the focus, troublingly, remains on EDNET equipment, not on preparing discriminating viewers. While recognizing the crucial value of a convergent web of video, voice, and text for reaching otherwise inaccessible students, I am concerned about depersonalized distance learning. The art of seeing and conceiving is more than just "a guy's arm on a TV screen," to quote Robert A. Bryan, former provost at the University of Florida.[4] Ironically, at the moment when very different kinds of images have become morphed into generic simulations or digital recombinants, the very institutions that used to assume responsibility for demonstrating their intelligent design are being volatilized. University walls, enclosing outmoded compartmentalized programs, no longer appear solid. They, too, have become porous, thinned by cyberspace.

To return to my core issue: how are past and present technologies of representation to be reconciled? Or will the obsession with virtuality drive out the important study of earlier types of apparatus-mediated vision? In the postmodern era of degravitation, disconnectedness, and disembodiment, how might visualization as an innovative, integrating and bridging field spanning the arts, humanities, and sciences be imagined from and within a historical perspective? It's a point worth making again that the explosion of multimedia—that unstable collage of video, audio, text, and graphics collected within an electronic interface[5]—raises serious questions concerning the kinds of training needed to navigate meaningfully through a blurred and fluid informatic realm. Should we speak of a multimedia designer, a digital culture-creator, a cyber-aestheticist, an applied visualist, an experimental connectivist, a synthesthesiologist, a pragmagist (combining pragmatism with imagist)? As yet there is no adequate term or concept for what humanists and scientists must become, or for the transmedial medium in which we must develop proficiency.[6] Nietzsche's confident call for the New Man has become, at the close of the twentieth century, a nag-

27

Eiduphusikon, *Panorama of an Excursion to London,* front and back views, 1880. (Photo: Courtesy Getty Center, Resource Collections.)

ging anxiety about the unspeakable artifices of animation. Gropings toward appropriate nomenclature demonstrate the intellectual difficulty of seizing the almost magical ways in which telecommunication technologies have transformed our very consciousness.

This remarkable proliferation of nameless phenomena and category-evading characteristics indicates larger educational, epistemological, and societal uncertainties. Think, for example, of how talk about only one modality of expression seems old-fashioned in the face of enchanted worlds conjured by video games. CD-ROM effortlessly weaves together picture, music, and narrative into an alternate universe where everything is simultaneously serious and amusing. Similarly, expertise, with its connotation of directed or unilateral focus, requires rejustification at a time when advanced computing artfully mixes animations and stills to produce ever more "realistic" effects. By extension, solitary scholarship is open to charges of anachronism in an era extolling collaboration—an interaction itself hard to define. Even data, with its evocation of chunklike content, dissolves as it becomes relayed through the EtherNet. Monolithic-sounding information fragments in the process of being subsumed or hooked up into microchip-driven systems.

Ambiguous apparatus, paradoxical presentations, tattered taxonomies, unspecialized specialists—like Robert Musil's man without qualities—all point to inevitable personal and professional upheavals. The inability to classify equivocal artificial phenomena sets in relief a pressing question. What sorts of practical skills should every citizen possess to ethically and intelligently use, analyze, and disseminate digital apparitions? In the transdisciplinary epoch, what committee or program will assume the obligation to the public good to teach the different ways a wide range of visual materials are produced so that consumers can discern their reliability? Not surprisingly, journalists are wrestling with similar issues of accountability[7] because news today is routinely gathered, selected, and distributed electronically. Imagists must also struggle to codify principles and practices that would reintroduce an awareness of craft, tangibility, and physicality into a society growing accustomed to seamless spectacle. Getting beyond feeling adrift in phantasmagoria entails demonstrating how graphics have been put together.

CONNECTING AS COLLECTING

But we need to redesign the image of images not just because of the spread of ghostly media or the precipitous undoing of geographically located institutions. The concepts on which time-honored disciplines and many professions have been based are in crisis, I believe, because of a deeper stereotype. In spite of their prevalence, images in western culture continue to retain the low cognitive and moral status initially accorded them by Plato. The advent of the University of Illinois at Chicago's virtual reality "Cave," where computer-fired projectors located behind walls and ceiling throw images on the surfaces of an empty room,[8] can only entrench the perception of all appearances as purveyors of sensory delusion. It remains an unexamined irony of the current drive to visualize everything that images continue to be discussed, both in the academic and the life world, primarily as by-products of a simulating and stimulating technology. It is to the intelligence of imagery, largely ignored in the public debates over mass media and the decline of alpha-numerical literacy, then, that I now wish to turn. Images do conceptual work in a wide range of processes, from medical teaching tools, like the National Library of Medicine's "electronic cadaver," to the multitude of icons enhancing computer-based dictionaries and encyclopedias. More basically, pictures constitute the stuff of memory, the way in which the brain internally displays thoughts to itself.

The graphic capacity to give vivid shape to abstractions illuminates some major implications of how we currently envision information. While it is common to remark on the generation of quantities of data as a result of the computer revolution, the fact that there are actually two sorts of information has not received serious attention. One type lends itself to integration, the other to linkage. This is an important distinction. The difference between systematically merging (i.e., collapsing) individual characteristics, processes, or media, and connecting separate entities into inventive arrangements, has far-reaching repercussions. These range from how we conceptualize the interdisciplinary convergences occurring in our colleges and universities, to so-called one-stop shopping for health care services, to the seamless editing of video tapes offered as evidence in personal injury and criminal trials, to the inlaid look typical of Mosaic, an Internet browser, and of commercial servers. The two, very different, kinds of impact become clear when we visualize discrete bits, pieces, or categories of things whose operations have become amalgamated and thus covert. Contrast this blend to an assemblage whose man-made gatherings remain overt, and so available for public scrutiny.

28

Frederick Ruysch, *View of Cabinet of Curiosities,* from *Opera omnia,* 1720, frontispiece. Drawn and engraved by C. Hüyberts. (Photo: Courtesy Herzog August Bibliothek, Wolfenbüttel.)

These dual attitudes toward the meaning-making powers of visual presentation can best be understood through an art historical contrast. It is helpful, I think, to imagine these antithetical views of data as opposite approaches to collecting and collections. The history of images, then, is indispensable for recognizing the cognitive potential of contemporary multimedia displays. Turning, first, to the disjunctive jumble stored in an eighteenth-century cabinet or chamber of curiosities, the modern viewer is struck by the intensely interactive demands it places on the visitor (fig. 28). Not unlike when one faces the sophisticated icons on a Macintosh monitor, significant relationships must be discovered among incongruous objects. Both the computer and the *Kunstschrank* compel the viewer to select from a parade of responsive miniaturized pictures. Cryptically juxtaposed paintings, statuary, medals, coins, minerals, fossils, extraordinary materials housed alongside the most ordinary, are crowded into a variety of three-dimensional containers. Boxes, shelves, drawers correspond to the desktop and toolbar festooning the caselike electronic screen. When unlocked, either chest exhibits a heap of singularities. Artful eccentricities beckon the viewer to search for some greater bond that might join such improbabilities together. The metaphor of traveling among beautiful strangers is apt, because the compartmentalized organization makes even the familiar appear unfamiliar. And, in spite of insistent borders, the beholder senses that such extravagantly disparate objects must somehow also be connected. Reminiscent of confronting a vast and perplexing database, the sight of so many conflicting wonders arouses a desire to enter the labyrinth to try to navigate the elegant maze.

Looking back from the perspective of the computer era, the artifacts in a *Wunderkammer* seem less physical phenomena and more material links permitting the beholder to retrieve complicated personal and cultural associations. Looking forward from the Enlightenment world of apparently miscellaneous pleasures, we discern that scraps of wood, stone, or metal, religious relics, ancient shards, exotic fetishes, animal remains, miniature portraits, small engravings, pages torn from a sketchbook, are the distant ancestors of today's sophisticated software. Resembling the *New Grolier Multimedia Encyclopedia* and Microsoft's *Encarta,* the cabinet or room of curiosities featured hundreds of icons, alluring apparatus, a multitude of mirrors, maps, charts, drawings, instruments, all framed, set apart, and yet asking to be unified in a moment of transporting insight. Such monumental poetic *armoires* also anticipate the diminutive universes of a Joseph Cornell box, filled with ritualized glasses, detritus-stuffed jars, discarded cigarette papers, Victorian greeting cards, tiny penny-arcades.[9] Rarities, assemblage art, personal computer menus, Word and WordPerfect software provoke striking encounters. They are magical conjuring devices impelling the observer to voyage among enigmatic, co-present riddles attractively distributed within an information-rich geography. Treasure chests, mysterious pharmacies, precious packets, allusive hypertext or Hyper-Card function as springboards for the imagination, stimulating it to jump to unexpected correspondences, to leap to unpredictable combinations.

Much as today's students select an icon by touching a keyboard or manipulating a mouse, eighteenth-century beholders of polymathic diversity mentally clicked on a theatrical roster of automata, watchworks, and decorative arts accumulated in a fantastic case. This performative gesture of extending oneself intellectually, psychologically, and emotionally outward to a strange "other" served to bridge the gap between known and unknown experiences. Whether roaming cyberspace or wandering through a densely material collection, according to this interactive view, we remain the producers and directors of knowledge. Nuggets of visual data endlessly and enticingly summon us to collaborate in their restaging.

Such simultaneously entertaining and educational presentations were eventually overwhelmed by textual and systematic approaches to learning. Kaleidoscopic layouts, emphasizing the perceiver's obligation to organize and reorganize cultural or natural remains, appeared to critical late eighteenth-century eyes as unmanaged clutter. The combinatorial aesthetics of collage were supplanted by a cool, linear, linguistic logic stretching from d'Hancarville's museum of antiquities in a book[10] to Gae Aulenti's tunnel-like installation of the Gare d'Orsay. Chronological arrangements of historical material, their separation into distinctive genres and isolated media, discouraged the viewer from making her own connections. Epochs gradually blended into one another, styles smoothly evolved as centuries marched forward to merge with the present. Passive spectatorship was encouraged since the system governing exhibition was both preestablished and concealed from the general public's sight. Coalescence, then, represents a second, lulling approach to information. Consolidation glosses over gaps, disguises the holes in our knowledge to convey a standardized picture of happenings. The viewer shifts from participatory observation to receptive watching. Rather than encountering puzzling, attention-arresting structures, she absorbs "facts" about them. Instead of being delightfully invited to make patterns, the viewer is seduced into the effortless absorption of canned presentations.

To capture this opposition by means of a contemporary analogy, recall Umberto Eco's witticism, recently circulating on the Net, about the friendly iconic revelations of the Macintosh as compared with the abstruse intellectualism of the MS-DOS-compatible computer. In the latter, the operator is always reminded of the implacable machine code driving the system because the program is so taxing. Yet, maddeningly, this text remains hidden from sight and aloof from ordinary comprehension. In the former, mistakes are cheerfully tolerated; the user always gets another chance. This showdown between "Catholic" and "Calvinist" operating systems is modulated in the "Anglicanism" of Windows! I want to suggest another historical analogy. Like the per-

sonal decisions confronting the visitor to a baroque cabinet of curiosities, the Mac player selects from a magical miscellany. Abruptly
juxtaposed colorful icons recall the mechanical dolls, finely crafted
metalwork, and natural specimens with which the seventeenth- and
eighteenth-century beholder conjured. Alluring and mutable shapes
counter the hermeneutic rigidity of MS-DOS and the closed classifications of museum labels. In both the electronic and the material milieu,
objects are easily repurposed in multiple, open-ended, and personal
ways. Importantly, both kinds of viewers, too, operate under the illusion of freedom, since the colorful icons are generated by an unknown
programmer just as *Wunderkammer* possessions were arranged for their
noble owners.

By way of tying past issues more closely to those of the present,
I want to return to my earlier suggestion that serious intellectual implications accompany either description of information. In particular, the
unexamined and quite common opinion of visual presentation as intrinsically coalescent or morphed is, I believe, responsible for giving images
their bad reputation. I have been arguing that there is a special danger
in media that converge graphically because they carry a message devised
by an unseen someone or something. Here we are putting our finger on
a much deeper and older problem. Covert blending, in contradistinction to overt mixing, reinforces the more generalized suspicion that images are inherently tricking or duplicitous by nature. During the
premodern era, fraudulence and corruption tarnished the image of images precisely at those times when they became identified primarily
with one kind of information. As I demonstrated in *Artful Science,* it is
not accidental that those historical moments also coincided with
delusion-producing developments in optical technology. Seamlessly
integrated formats prevented the spectator, then and now, from perceiving how combinations had been artificially contrived or from contributing to their construction.

Given the welter of electronic media and the pull of virtuality,
the imagist of the twenty-first century will have to force homogeneous
data to exhibit its heterogeneity. I think one of our chief professional
duties will be to induce merged information to behave as if it were
linked. Nonstop transmissions can be slowed down to the level of comprehension, just as erased decisions can be rearticulated. The repudiated
flesh of cyberspace can be reincarnated through tangible gestures re-
minding viewers that their actions, not microchips, bring content into
existence. In short, compressive delivery systems challenge us to make

bodies step out of boxes. Who better than artists, architects, designers, scientists, technologists, scientists, and historians of all aspects of the visual working together to demonstrate the masked sutures existing in all patched-together modes of communication? But academics cannot handle this conglomerate alone. Nor are these old terms, concepts, and specializations adequate to the realities of a digital microcosm. The information highway is an immense cabinet of curiosities, a crammed mosaic of disparate technologies and services joining computers, telephones, fax machines, high-definition televisions, and space satellites into a global communications net. Given the sheer quantity and complexity of displayable data, knowing how to make appropriate choices will depend upon astute collaboration among equals across many fields.[11]

I am suggesting that we must also forge an interconnective model of the practice of scholarly interaction itself. True collaboration does not mean emerging victorious in a clash of power among competing interest groups. Nor is it parceling out narrower and narrower tasks to more and more consultants in the era of "dejobbing." Striving for coherent results extends beyond embracing the like-minded to engage broad constituencies. Combined research must cross venerable and entrenched divides, such as those currently separating the arts, humanities, and sciences. Like well-designed multimedia, the synthesizing process is an integrating means for learning contributing to a common purpose, one that respects various expertises and does not consolidate them into an indistinguishable mass falsified under a reductive rubric.

Too often what goes under the name of joint projects or cross-disciplinary ventures is simply a vindication of established hierarchies. These vertical arrangements have led, in universities, to the canonization of literacy as a set of master skills tacitly wrapped up in reading and writing. Imaging's consequent loss of cognitive and cultural stature impedes any serious discussion of its thoughtful, revelatory, and positive role in our society. By reengaging with the human condition, that is, by returning to the material and historical consequences of passive watching or active looking, we can, in Dave Hickey's words, put vision back into visual experience.[12] In order to creatively work with others, we will have to wrestle with why we have allowed ourselves and our objects of study to become so severely compromised. Trying to figure out how to coordinate, connect, or intelligently and effectively collaborate will be the new frontier, not just for data but for people.

29

William Cheselden, *Galen Contemplating the Skeleton of a Robber,* from *Osteographia,* 1735, frontispiece. Engraving by Gerard Vandergucht. (Photo: Courtesy Herzog August Bibliothek, Wolfenbüttel.)

A macabre reminder of violent crime is set in relief by a wild landscape. Legend has it that Galen, during his many travels, unexpectedly encountered a skeleton and stopped to ponder the sublime architecture of the human body, violently stripped bare. In the frontispiece to William Cheselden's landmark study of bones, the Greek physician contemplates the vicissitudes of human life and cruel mortality. This *plein-air* anatomy lesson intertwines the ethical, emotional, intellectual, social, but above all visual realities confronting medicine, past and present.

II   Practicing Vision

Making Images Real

5

While working on *Body Criticism,* I began to reflect on the transformation occurring in those fields that, in one way or another, had occupied themselves with problems of representation. These are confronting the need to shift paradigms in the face of technological dynamism and the changing processes of computerized, digital communication. What light could, say, an art historian shed on the inquiries of a contemporary neurologist or radiologist? What could my students and I learn from biomedical imaging that might open up new, multidimensional areas of investigation for all of us? Venerable western antinomies pitting the immaterial soul against the material body, a numinous internal space against a worthless fleshy surface, seemed to require rethinking in view of spectroscopic "transillumination."[1] At present, researchers can observe veiled phenomena (the beating heart, fetal development, the thinking brain) that formerly could only be inferred (see fig. 4). Optical images capturing biological structures and functions with clarity and in real time stimulated my concern for what we visually adept humanists might bring to the changing ways of doing science. The laboratory as a virtual environment demands an increasing image competence. Conversely, witnessing how doctors wrestled with the potentialities and limitations of looking into hidden corporeal spaces through high-speed instrumentation taught me something that no history or philosophy of art had. This moving encounter with perennial existential questions resulted in two humbling and exhilarating collaborative ventures with the scientific "other."

I joined forces, first, with a broad-minded physicist at the University of Chicago. Robert N. Beck, Director of the Center for Imaging Science, has a special interest in radiology and the whole armamentar-

30

Joyce Cutler Shaw, from the series *The Slow Death of Rose,* 1983–1988. Pen and ink drawing on handmade Japanese paper. ©1988 Hospital Drawing. (Photo: Courtesy Phel Steinmetz.)

Joyce Cutler Shaw, artist-in-residence at the School of Medicine, University of California at San Diego, practices visceral drawing, dissecting the ephemeral self. In *The Slow Death of Rose,* a series of pen and ink studies done between 1983 and 1988, she records the excruciating dying of a cancer-stricken friend. As part of the ongoing epic titled *The Anatomy Lesson,* a ten-year intermedia exploration of the human life cycle from infant to cadaver to the ultimate *Alphabet of Bones,* these raw dramas confront us with the struggles of the sick and old, the powerful presence of the newly dead. The technical brilliance of her craft and the dignity of its source demonstrate that the artist can capture the substance of mortal remains in a way impossible to even the most revolutionary imaging technologies.

ium of innovative visualization techniques. In addition, he was willing to teach a strange art historian about them! Our serendipitous discussions led, in the spring of 1992, to an international symposium, "Imaging the Body: Art and Science in Modern Culture."[2] Three concurrent exhibitions, demonstrating concrete points at which humanistic images and biomedical imaging mutually illuminated one another, were curated by myself and graduate students from studio, art history, and history of science programs. These were installed at the Prints and Drawings Department and the Ryerson and Burnham Library of the Art Institute of Chicago and at the Smart Museum (using anatomy texts from the Crerar Collection of Rare Scientific Books at Regenstein Library). Initially, we had also hoped that new exhibits on medical imaging, displayed at the Museum of Science and Industry and for which Bob Beck had served as advisor, would be ready. They were delayed, opening to general acclaim in September 1993.

Our conference complemented these shows and was meant to be equally unsettling. Interdisciplinarity too often ends up by putting the familiar in contact with the slightly less familiar. This three-day symposium, instead, abruptly juxtaposed radically different fields and specialists: for example, a neurobiologist was paired with a historian of dress, a museum conservator with a reconstructive plastic surgeon, a postmortem painter/sculptor/photographer with a physician/medical ethicist. By leaving ample time for discussion and keeping our overall goal of opening up new areas for exemplary collaboration always in sight, the speakers were able to see the nitty-gritty skills and theoretical assumptions actually determining the performance of very different kinds of work. The foreignness of molecular biology or neurology and the hermeticism of literary criticism or legal theory were punctured at the level of "dirty" practice. While the sense of facing alien experiences did not disappear, participants also expressed a delightful surprise as they began to explore publicly possible ways in which humanistic enterprises and contemporary clinical research might meaningfully intersect at the image level.

Prior to the two years that went into planning the symposium, I had already embarked on a series of pilgrimages to Billings Hospital. What has now become the MacLean Center for Clinical Medical Ethics was, in 1986, a fledgling program invented by Dr. Mark Siegler. While struggling to define early modern cultural representations of the body, I wanted to find out if past modes of visualizing invisible physical and mental processes had any current relevance. Would present-day physicians find it illuminating to know how nonverbalizable states-of-being had formerly been given shape? Could the complex figures and graphic metaphors that surgeons, anatomists, artists, theologians, philosophers, and just ordinary folk had put to therapeutic use in the early modern period to externalize feelings and thoughts fit into contemporary medical practice? Might "old" still or motion pictures and tangible artifacts emerge from history's cabinet of curiosities to captivate and teach today's clinicians about care, sickness, mortality? Could thinking again about the actual practices and social connotations accreting around our western habits of dissecting, abstracting, conceiving, marking, magnifying, and sensing have some relevance for late twentieth-century patients? Surely, concepts such as a personal, durable self, or even a changing identity, are challenged by the virtual slicing and hypothetical fragmenting of the human body by CT, PET, and MRI mapping. In short, I was interested not only in classifying differences but in reusing past perceptions of pleasure and pain, disease and contamination, visible sign and invisible symptom, to reconsider interiority in the age of magical simulation.

Sitting around a long table and listening to doctors speak about individual women and men—analyzing their specific complaints, factoring in public health policy and rising costs, and agonizing over debatable interventions ranging from gene replacement to end-of-life decisions—was an intensely humbling experience. Disembodied scholarship was made flesh. Confronting the reality of the nontextualizable convinced me that the methodological battles raging in the humanities and social sciences chew up too much of our collective intelligence. We are wasting positive energy that might otherwise be expended in pragmatic research on urgent issues.

The cross-disciplinary conversations animating the MacLean Center and the Center for Imaging Sciences have recently prompted me to ask whether there might not be a concrete educational problem around which we could begin to put our different sets of expertises cooperatively to work, both within an institute and as part of an outreach program. Symposia and exhibitions, even when published or accompanied by a catalogue, are of finite duration and suffer through translation into the fixity of writing. Ongoing conversational and collaborative projects are needed to make images thick, dense, real.

So much scientific, medical, and information technology is mediated by imaging apparatus. As researchers find themselves awash in floods of data conveyed through visualizing instrumentation, Plato's critique of the unreal, seductive, and dangerous image has resurfaced with a vengeance. For example, scientists worry about the biopsychological effects of emerging interactive media and the potential for emotionally charged digital imagery to manipulate public opinion.[3] The fear is real. When the producers of electronic signals gain the fiber-optics capability to tailor the presentation of visual material according to the response of the individual viewer, the capacity of the many to mislead the few increases exponentially. Add to this the persuasiveness of certain illusions created by a battery of probes and monitors: the illusion of transparency, i.e., the sense that information is being presented directly without the intervention of fallible devices, and the illusion of familiarity, i.e., an impersonalization and objectification of the body through mapping that makes it easier to counsel invasive surgical interventions.[4] Further, basic image processing techniques needed to analyze digital patterns in a wide range of disciplines make use of potentially deceptive strategies such as smoothing, noise removal, segmentation, correlation matching, and time-variation imagery.

The history of image making is filled with examples of admirable skill and misleading *trompe l'oeil*. The problem is that we have forgotten the conjunction. A massive anti-image bias already exists in much postmodern criticism. The possible immoral ends of art have become the certain abuses of "the gaze." This ancient antiocular rhetoric also fuels the often justifiable denunciations of the television and music-video industry emanating from communications schools. Join to this the vigorous questioning of the role and status of the museum as a contested site for display, and of art history as the fetishization of aestheticized objects. I am not disputing the validity of many of these objections. Nor am I defending some canonical type of art history, an ironical effort, to say the least, since I have always operated on its boundaries. As someone who has spent the last twenty years working in the area of visual culture, I am disturbed, however, by the monolithic and relentlessly negative critique of images coming from all sides. Few arguments surface for their positive role in cognition as well as in society at large. Forgotten is their marvelous capacity to make abstractions concrete, their ability to provide both meaningful direction and delight to the individual thrashing her way through the maze of experience. Surely there is something paradoxical in a profession that despises its objects of research.

In a world literally raining images—whether pouring out of museums, channeled through television, video, software programs, and digital disks, or streaming from multimedia monitors and optical displays—neither traditional nor new art histories have emerged as practical guides. I find that odd. Like our colleagues in other academic areas, we are drenched by visual information. Yet insofar as we constitute a distinctive group of professionals, we have not been looked to for intellectual leadership. No one of political importance, no business director, no college president, no think tank, no prominent social agency, not even the McNeill-Lehrer Report asks for our opinion or finds it to the common good that we apply what we know. Nor, it seems, have we offered. To date, no coherent policies, models, or joint ventures form a visible link bridging the formulation of socially relevant imaging problems within universities, cultural institutions, or humanities centers and the multifaceted public sphere.[5] I am thinking specifically of the urgent need to develop means for educating diverse audiences to the true, false, and ambiguous dimensions of pictures, high and low.

This paradox cannot be brushed aside simply by saying that postmodernism inherently resists any claims to hierarchy, totalizing mastery, or cultural and disciplinary imperialism. Anthropology and literary criticism, respectively, have now long functioned as the implicit or explicit normative ideals for figurative and discursive interpretation.[6]

The advent of global intermediality, enhanced by ultrafast computers, and the return of academe to the primal soup of interdisciplinarity have confirmed that images are too important, powerful, and pervasive to belong to a single class of investigator. Possessiveness can only seem ironic at a revolutionary moment of verbal-to-visual transition coupled with disciplinary disintegration and metamorphosis. Text-based departments such as English, philosophy, history, sociology, and political science that achieved institutional stability and coherence in the nineteenth century are fragmenting, leaving their future appearance uncertain.

On the other hand, while granting this new hybridity and freely admitting that art history finds itself in the same leaky boat, do we collectively know something particular that is useful? Should we, perhaps, resist simply dissolving into some vague and global "literary," "cultural," or even "visual" studies?

It's raining images outside, but we are locked indoors. While English departments scarcely analyze texts anymore because they are so busy examining images, we examine texts. Why not assume an affirmative role as a bridging and orienting discipline centered on our diverse visual aptitudes? Why not integrate the study of art, and more broadly of images and their technology, into the transdisciplinary inquiry developing at the end of this century? Why not demonstrate through concrete projects actualized in short-term exhibitions and symposia, long-term study groups, focused outreach programs, and even a series of white papers dedicated to the challenges of application, that expertise in visualization matters practically? Biomedicine is only one forum for speaking intelligently to researchers struggling with optical instrumentation. The script-bound legal profession, as we saw in the O. J. Simpson trial, could use help in establishing guidelines for the interpretation of videotape, three-dimensional models, and other types of visual evidence now being introduced routinely and without adequate conceptualization into the courtroom. We should also be taking a leadership role within universities. Our specific skills are desperately needed to revise and rebuild the educational infrastructures in which we live. These, too, are changing dramatically under the pressure of the digital revolution.

In sum, I have been arguing that, in addition to whatever else we do, we should also make images real. In addition to being artists, art historians, curators, let's become policymakers, not just policy recipients in our text-based institutions. Let's assist that larger world of doctors, scientists, lawyers, humanists, and general audiences, who might find it helpful to learn what we have to say if only we would stand up and say it. In contributing to other fields and areas as they wrestle to define or identify the impact of optical manipulation and fraud, can we not also begin to design a positive societal role for images as well as for ourselves? After all, historically, graphic objects have given shape to diverse aspects of the human condition, provided complex patterns for living, and given performative expression to otherwise inarticulate states of being.

*Desperately Seeking Connections: Linking the
Internet to Eighteenth-Century Laboratory Life*

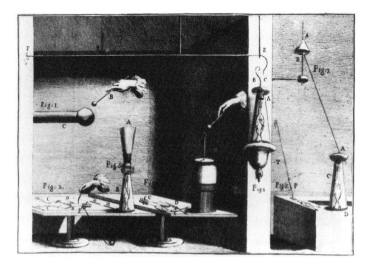

ANCIENTS AND MODERNS

The growing focus on human actions and processes, rather than on exposition of documents, in all branches of historical study still leaves open the question of the proper role of the present in explaining the past.[1] It is a common strategy to model scholarly investigations in accordance with contemporary anthropological, sociological, or literary theories. Yet when an argument is put forward that research can aim both at understanding and at use, resistance sets in. Suggesting that we might learn something now by looking at earlier rituals, ceremonies, practices, manners, mores, or art frequently arouses ire[2] and charges of "anachronism, distortion, misinterpretation, misleading analogy, neglect of context, oversimplification of process."[3]

Admittedly, late twentieth-century categories, objects, and media cannot be seamlessly mapped onto those of the early modern period. Nevertheless, borrowing Nancy Struever's felicitous phrase, I want to "twist the kaleidoscope"[4] so that eighteenth-century spaces of spectacle can gloss current debates about the informatic realm. This essay tries to avoid seeing history as a linear story of ancestors conveniently anticipating us, while attempting to recuperate the failed or forgotten practices associated with chemical manipulations, conjuring tricks, alchemical cookery, and experimental necromancy. Showing visualization at work in four disparate laboratory scenes demonstrates how pictorial strategies of inquiry became morally and intellectually discredited as producers of reliable knowledge in the early modern period.

By exploring early modern episodes in the art and science of demonstration, we may learn something important about our own technological and ecological "theology." Seen in this light, the subjec-

31

Luigi Galvani, *Electrophysiology: Experiments with Frogs,* from *De viribus electricitatis,* 1792, pl. 1. Etching. (Photo: Courtesy National Library of Medicine, Bethesda.)

The pictorial convention of depicting disembodied hands to symbolize experimental procedures was popularized in the illustrations to Diderot and d'Alembert's monumental *Encyclopédie.* Here, Galvani's trials using unpithed frogs demonstrate the voluntary and involuntary reaction of muscles and nerves to electric shock. A ballet of fingers joins scientists to specimens through apparatus. This plate, so evocative of actual and potential connections, is tense with invisible forces about to erupt into visibility.

tive desire to relate to some great unfurling process, whether that of electronic information or cosmic fire, represents a harmonian attempt to bridge such perennial philosophical divides as spirit and matter, humanity and nature, reason and emotion.

Hooked Up

Computer-based communication has been called the "fourth cognitive revolution" after speaking, writing, and printing.[5] Access to a dizzying range of information via the Internet holds out the tantalizing promise of a quasi-mystical connectivity. Technology's growing capacity to facilitate instruction at remote sites through distance learning virtualizes the classroom, so that experiences from a center can speedily travel into peripheral homes and workplaces. Today's worldwide electronic network comprises an estimated 20 to 30 million people hooked up to a matrix of immaterial telecommunications services. A mixture of theology, metaphysics, technology, and physical science characterizes this ostensibly secular quest for far-flung correspondences discoverable while voyaging across a grid or down a well that has no margin or end.

I want to suggest that an unrecognized prototype for our epistemologically open society—one apparently without physical limitations or intellectual boundaries—existed in old-regime France before the rise of professional science. Instead of "knowbots," programmed to be dispatched into cyberspace to find a specific piece of data run aground in the pixelated sprawl, the eighteenth-century popular science demonstrator navigated through an ocean of phantasmagoria mysteriously linked through ineffable analogies. Such a fluid and decorporealized immanence formed a dramatic contrast to the fleshy celestial mythology typical of baroque art. Anthropomorphized spiritual hierarchies, literally chaining together heaven and earth, were staples of Roman Catholic universal histories picturing nature as a passion-filled theater or physical spectacle (fig. 32).[6] After the middle of the eighteenth century, this solidly incarnational image of the world as the body and personified will of a Supreme Being had become transformed into an etherealized sea of diffused influences (fig. 33).[7]

A curious hybrid of engineer-magus, the secular seer of the Enlightenment had the priestly task of promoting intangible ties across vast spaces and so empowering more and more participants by bringing them into emotional contact with one another. In a cosmos increasingly conceived not as a divinized firmament but as an elusive environment crisscrossed by invisible forces, God was no longer adequately meta-

32

Johann Zahn, *Spectacle of the Celestial and Terrestrial Worlds Linked,* from *Specula physico-mathematico-historica,* I, 1696, frontispiece. Engraving. (Photo: Courtesy Herzog August Bibliothek, Wolfenbüttel.)

33

Charles Rabiqueau, *Picture of the True Workings of Universal Physics,* from *Le microscope moderne,* 1781, frontispiece. Engraving. (Photo: Courtesy Herzog August Bibliothek, Wolfenbüttel.)

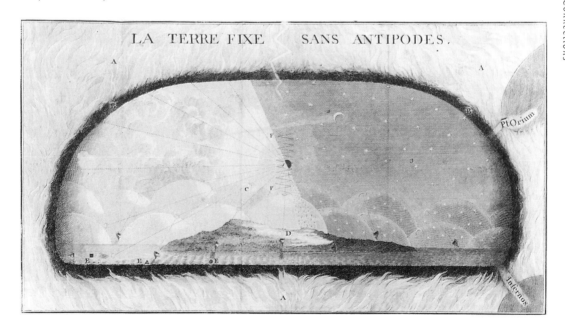

phorized as the author of a static Book of Nature. Instead, His somatic powers were volatilized into a quasi-meteorological atmosphere of equalizing and expanding energies to which even the lowliest initiate might become joined through the right intercessor.[8]

This new, scientized and sacralized ecology of instantaneous connections resulted from the convergence of historically distinct media.[9] Significantly, the coalescence of image, performance, speech, and print, past or present, has been enabled by the latest optical instrumentation. Whether talking of then or now, it is fascinating to note that the supremacy of linear alphabetical or textual literacy became eroded by the push to compact increasingly complex information into seductive tableaux appealing to ever wider audiences. Such sophistic juggling with spectral appearances represented for logocentric high enlighteners all that was most despotic about a papist, baroque oral-visual culture. Neil Postman's jeremiads, hammering away at the electronic gymnastics and fanatical "one-eyed technology" of the television, video, and computer epoch, are an extension of that rationalist critique.[10]

We are witnessing the collapse of precisely those mass literacy drives initiated during the later eighteenth century. Pixels are our movable type. Synthesizable and manipulable images continue to supplant directional narratives.[11] The impulse to display information is everywhere in evidence. Resembling the magic lantern's patched-together light and shadow grotesques, mosaics of picture, word, and sound constitute the playful artificial constructs projected from electronic monitors and screens (fig. 34).[12]

Not unlike our postmodernist era, then, the eighteenth century witnessed the disintegration of congealed categories, the deconstruction of isolated genres, and the stylish collaging of disparate media, permitting everything to interact with everything else.[13] Conjuring with fluid patterns was one way to cope with dynamic phenomena eluding the reductionist thinking that had dominated the mathematical sciences since Descartes and Newton.[14] Just as the simulating computer is both the tool and the metaphor for today's holistic approach to understanding creative processes, optical apparatus and sensually direct demonstrations were the connective means spurring early modern complexity research.

34

J. E. Shenan, *The Magic Lantern,*
1790. Engraving by J. Ouvrier.
(Photo: Courtesy Getty Center, Resource Collections.)

35

Denis Diderot, *Chemistry Laboratory
and Table of Chemical Relations,* from
Planches de l'Encyclopédie, III, 1780–
1782. Engraving. (Photo: Courtesy
National Library of Medicine,
Bethesda.)

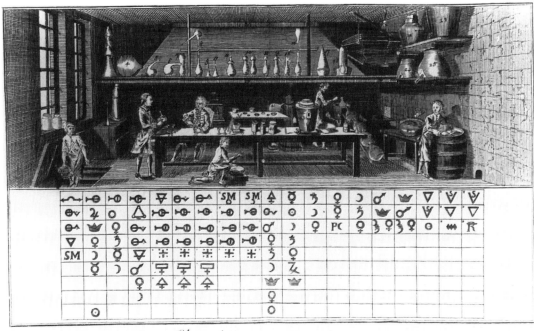

COMMUNICATION VERSUS PSEUDO-COMMUNICATION

Let us consider a scene from the past. The lucid image of the chemistry laboratory as a spacious, silent, well-lit room, stocked with an orderly succession of glass vessels and dominated by a long table sparsely ornamented with regimented utensils, is a late eighteenth-century French invention (fig. 35). The elegant bareness of unadorned stone walls set in relief a choreography of tidy gestures. Diderot and d'Alembert's *Encyclopédie* pictured the revolutionary, Lavoisier-era experimental ideal of material minimalism and measured execution orchestrated by the erudite scientist. The angular neoclassical interior forecast the stripped-down impersonality and automatic routines associated with nineteenth-century bureaucratic architecture: endless hospital corridors, linear prison cells, serial museum galleries. The hygienic severity and emotional restraint, specifically encoding this gray environment as "professional," was surely devised to separate the represented, praiseworthy scene from an unrepresented one that was not. Diderot's vision of well-managed motions enacted by soberly clad technicians, and fully comprehensible only to experts, conspicuously distinguished it from common mystery-mongering.[15] The literal and metaphorical rectitude of the composition precluded any possible comparison to the imprecision of daily life or to the deluding knack of the con man.

The perambulating scam artist, ostentatious charlatan, and theatrical mountebank were enduring features of the European landscape (fig. 36). Rendering natural surroundings artificial, such gawdy outdoor exhibitions stood at the antipodes from indoor rational trials in which the physical world endured abstraction and atomization. Dirck Helmbreker's rustic scene of quacks in performance captured the fair-

36

Dirck Helmbreker, *The Quack*, seventeenth century. Oil on canvas. (Photo: Courtesy Staatliche Museen Kassel.)

ground atmosphere typical of the pre-Enlightenment anti-laboratory. Neither domestic nor institutional in character, this temporary space for manifesting cures and selling nostrums belonged to the provincial domain of the illiterate and the vernacular. While the professional chemist's permanent quarters facilitated an urbane "situated learning"[16] by encouraging commerce among craft, symbolic, and notational forms of knowing, the sharper's collapsible tent and hastily assembled platform did not contain stable objects. Quite the contrary. Poster advertisement, skull, coffer of potions, and falsified documents existed only insofar as they were manipulated, thereby becoming ephemeral events in the life of bedazzled idlers and undiscerning spectators. Significantly, such pseudo-empirical displays, existing somewhere between magic and medicine, were not completely set apart from the town's buildings or from the diversified public existence of its most ordinary inhabitants.

The confined and controlled modern observational environment—literally supported by a schematic table mapping chemical ciphers and their relations—was also at variance with the clandestine alchemical studio, immuring the obsessed seeker within his filthy lair (fig. 37). David Teniers the Younger's frequently reengraved and reissued dark genre pictures, focusing on a solitary operator occasionally accompanied by dimly visible accomplices, evoked these intensely private, cluttered hideaways. The broken jars, jugs, and pots littering the foreground were emblematic of mental disorder and visualized the fitful nature of the dubious great work itself. Consequently, the alchemist's begrimed symbolic ecology[17] was distinct both from the conjuror's seasonal popular appearances in the dusty marketplace and from the specialist's formalized techniques cleanly performed in sequestration.

Teniers's cavernous and phenomenologically dense *Laboratory* provides us with a glimpse of the obscurities of research life before the advent of bright, hermetically enclosed laboratories. Unlike the bourgeois tidiness reigning in Diderot's austere plate, resulting from the assignment of a specific function to a specific place, Teniers's chemist labored at a workbench that functioned flexibly as a smoky kitchen hearth. Dining and living areas, typical then and now of the man or woman without capital,[18] were used informally and nonhierarchically for multiple activities. Strange discoveries thus came into being within a familiar sphere of associations.

While the public performance of science has recently received sustained scrutiny,[19] considerably less attention has been paid to such

folkloric and imagistic dimensions of knowledge production. In *Artful Science,* I interpreted "mathematical recreations," optical apparatus, auto-experimentation, and the old regime's general compulsion toward exhibitionism in light of a ubiquitous "system of imposture." Long before the middle of the nineteenth century,[20] visuality served not just as the model for accurate verification but as a subjective source of faulty, unverifiable, and arbitrary judgments about the sensory manifold.[21] Just as the noble investigators in Diderot's moralized demonstration implied their immoral opposites—the crafty conjuror and the artisanal alchemist—these professionals inhabited contrasting cultural and physical geographies. Legible behavior reproached dirty dealings. Sincerity vanquished insincerity. Stark surroundings leveled an implicit critique against alternative settings in which visual evidence was entertainingly manufactured or criminally tampered with.

EXPERIMENTAL NECROMANCY

I want to turn to a more equivocal situation, one highlighting the paradox that experimental science provides contact with the larger-than-human while relying on an all too human mediator. However briefly, I want to uncover a fourth "information ecology"[22] illuminating the complexities of science popularization during the second half of the eighteenth century. Virtual pedagogy placed a premium on generating ever more convincing illusions. Suggestive of today's high-tech users, jaded spectacle watchers from the well-to-do middle and upper classes

37
___
David Teniers the Younger, *The Laboratory,* 1755. Engraved by T. Major. (Photo: Courtesy National Library of Medicine, Bethesda.)

required increased input from an artificially generated environment to achieve a feeling of the "real." If virtual reality claims to put the observer inside an artificial world, earlier forms of optical projection similarly attempted to bathe beholders in a sea of created sensations (fig. 38). Fanciful mirrors and liquid-filled glass globes, anticipating Jeff Wall's lightbox cibachromes or cyberphotography,[23] also emitted rays and directed them at the viewer. Although not yet William Gibson's data-suffused matrix, such phantasmatic ambients nonetheless encouraged machine dreams and "consensual hallucinations."[24]

Possessing neither the timeless look of the four-square laboratory, nor the transitoriness of a traveling raree show without walls, nor the solitary savant's jumble of curiosities, the illusionist's well-equipped stage unfurled shadow-specters. Ambiguity reigned in this multi-use arcology. It was an assemblage of modish salon, Palais-Royal boutique, Catholic church, entertaining classroom, and technological amusement park. Less concrete site than shifting spectacle of ghostly effects, such extravagantly engineered surroundings challenged even the finest *cabinet de physique*.[25]

Charles Rabiqueau, the eponymous hero of my final scene, encapsulated this new tribe of religious rhapsodist cum theatrical *demonstrateur-en-nouveautés* peopling the capitals of Europe in the second

38

Charles Rabiqueau, *Demonstrations of Reflecting and Emanating Forces,* from *Le microscope moderne,* 1781, part II, pl. I. Engraving. (Photo: Courtesy Herzog August Bibliothek, Wolfenbüttel.)

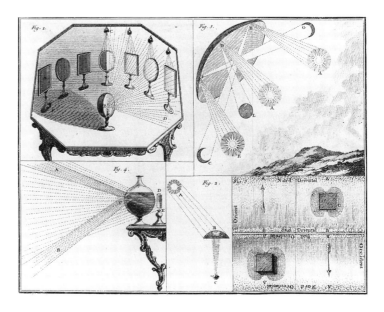

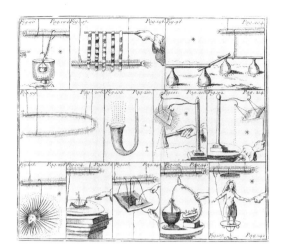

39
Charles Rabiqueau, *Electrical Experiments,* from *Le spectacle du feu,* 1753. Engraving. (Photo: Courtesy Herzog August Bibliothek, Wolfenbüttel.)

half of the eighteenth century.[26] Avowedly Roman Catholic, he reveled in the whole panoply of images, ceremonies, and devotions that were so offensive to the Reformation and Counter-Reformation alike.[27] Presumably basing himself on the heritage of sacramentalism, he was convinced that God's unique powers were sublimely disclosed in the "marvelous universal container" of the sky. The Christian drama of the fall and redemption, however, became metamorphosed into experimental trials, into a kind of empirical mass in which natural forces took on form. Instead of telling the story of how Jesus assumed human shape and came to earth, or recounting the saintly miracles performed in his name, Rabiqueau showed the infinite incarnations of fire when it came into contact with matter.

As educator, entrepreneur, psychic, mystic, sharper, Rabiqueau's heteroclite activities summed up an equivocal breed devoted to exhibiting the latest fads, gadgets, games, and experimental novelties by tapping into the primal instincts of their connection-craving audiences. These communicators traded in their ability to reveal, to make hidden phenomena disclose themselves. Urbane "men of ingenuity," while treading in the well-worn footsteps of Plato's wonder-vending sophists,[28] nevertheless practiced their art in a more self-consciously enlightened and enlightening age. Wandering incongruously from shocking to pleasing topics had to be combined with the semblance, at least, of advanced philosophical criticism.

Defying propriety to raise public awareness has become commonplace in the twentieth century. Antonin Artaud's theater of cruelty, conceptual artist Chris Burden's violent act of having himself nailed to the back of a Volkswagen, or Josef Beuys's confrontation with a coyote no longer startle. Yet Rabiqueau and tribe's antiestablishment happenings in unconventional venues were similarly equivocal, teetering between playful antic, ritual sacrifice, and initiatory rite testing promethean endurance. Whether overtly hooked up to a Leyden jar (fig. 39) or covertly dispensing solar, electrical, and magnetic forces (see fig. 38), the popular demonstrator extended the promise of ever greater attachments to his witnesses.

It was not enough simply to charm one's viewer, following Quintilian's description of epideictic oratory.[29] Providing convincing visual evidence entailed acts of baring, unveiling, maneuvering that went beyond the ostentatious display of the admirable self. Even in its moments of unreason, the Age of Reason demanded that the subject and object of ingratiating performance also seem to be praiseworthy. In light of such flamboyant practices, we need to ask how the operator's appearance, movement, and especially his handling became constituted into irrecusable documentary gestures for an audience? The fundamental paradox at the heart of any methodical strategy,[30] one binding the uplifting teacher to the mechanical scam artist, was that in governing oneself and controlling technology one also controlled or manipulated others.

The eye was central to that long baroque culture the Enlightenment struggled to overturn.[31] *Natura,* for Rabiqueau and his thaumaturgical brethren, was not the grim, abstract *physis* propounded by quantifying scientists. Rather, it was Lucretius's theatrical *rerum natura,* that sensuous kingdom where things dramatically came into being, attracting attention by a continual change of scenery.[32] To understand the technologist's sway over the beholder, we need to contrast the severe view of making science, embodied in the illustration to the chemistry section of the *Encyclopédie,* with the eroticized pagan spectacle disseminated by devotees of *Venus Genetrix* (see fig. 33). Nature's amoral creative and destructive powers were engagingly personified to make otherwise difficult teachings agreeably intelligible to nonphilosophical viewers.

It was this compelling sensory appeal to "lying" surfaces—associated in more recent times with Jesuit rhetoric and "orientalizing" superstition of all sorts—that the *philosophes* excoriated. False images had to be stripped to reveal their bare components, translated into words and numbers capable of declaring the true meaning concealed beneath deceptive figures. Yet, ironically, it is precisely such loosened formats, softened presentation of data, and flexible instructional terrains[33] that characterize today's electronic framing of every kind of information. The popular science demonstrator's interactive modes of encounter were prescient as well of converging media (theater, performance and installation art, video, computer graphics) now expanding the dramatic potential of technology.[34] The practical challenge was and remains how to invent ways in which discoveries can best be thought about.[35]

The body, caught in moments of demonstration, is both a symbol of existing social relationships and the incarnation of the will to control forces transcending the individual and culture. Keith Thomas remarked that historians cannot observe actual bodies of the past in motion.[36] While citing published accounts, formal codes for orators, actors, dancers, monks, legal description, and European fiction as important sources for imagining distant types of self-presentation, he does not mention the scientific conversation generated by natural philosophers in performance. Nor is it merely a question of human actions. As becomes evident by looking at Rabiqueau's synoptic frontispiece to *Le microscope moderne* (1781), even the universe was imagined as a proscenium-framed spectacle where physical mergers were continuously staged for admiring eyes (see fig. 33).

This real theater, however, demanded a virtual theater.[37] A mediating director had to create optical counterparts for the objects or events occurring uncontrollably outside. Producing a simulation indoors meant designing a unified illusion that could only be fashioned within a carefully wrought environment. The virtual laboratory, unlike Diderot's analytical laboratory, was not a fixed site but an ontic place[38] in which phenomena were allowed to remain potential. The late eighteenth-century fascination with all manner of nebulous phantasmagoria stemmed, I believe, from their tantalizing capacity to stay in a transient state for some time before settling into a single pattern. Substitute apparitions were manufactured specifically to mimic the innumerable real drifting and flickering ephemera that swirled above the horizon.

In *Artful Science,* I suggested that this necromantic experimental style appeared "popish" or Italianate to northern reformers because the operator engaged in deft maneuvers and courtly *sprezzatura.*[39] The Protestant culture of English and other forms of puritanism,[40] as well as the iconoclastic continental science being enacted in Diderot's plate, offered an antidote to these artifices by conceiving the production of knowledge more "authentically" and abstractly.

But such religiously motivated strategies were not sufficient to stop the secular commercialization of the self. Merchandise-minded audiences in the age of patronage, just as in the electronic era of Home Shopping, by their enthusiastic response encouraged artists, actors, and writers to sell themselves.[41] Convincing discerning beholders that reliable, replicable, and quantifiable claims about the natural world were being made thus required projecting both an untheatrical and a noncommercial look.[42] Consequently, popular science demonstrators such as Rabiqueau were uneasily caught between two traditions: of natural philosophy as an entertaining performance to advance understanding and as a paid public exhibition enhancing one's personal fame. Ostentatious behavior, attractive commodities, and the exciting prospect of diffusing the latest information were not easily kept separated. Indeed, rearranging the mutable elements of a magic lantern world was synonymous with survival in late eighteenth-century Paris.

"TOUT EST OPTIQUE"

With this derisory phrase, Louis-Sebastien Mercier summarized the *fin-de-siècle* rage for deceptive appearances.[43] *Le nouveau Paris* (1800) simultaneously analyzed and denounced spectacle in all its myriad guises, multiplying uncontrollably from the prerevolutionary to the consular periods. Lamenting the prevalence of a *demi-savoir,* this skeptical biographer of popular culture inquired what was the good of books, academies, institutions of learning, all those waves of philosophical writing spread by the Enlightenment and rendering the eighteenth century so illustrious. None of that movement's illuminating rays had managed to penetrate "the combustible masses." The population remained tenaciously the same, irradiated by the same superstitions that had allowed Mesmer, Cagliostro, and a host of less fashionable *jongleurs* to ply their fanatical trade as sorcerers, diviners, soothsayers, and card sharps.[44]

But it was not the former rue Dauphine (later rue d'Anjou) or the Pont Neuf that managed to crystallize urban depravity into a single, prismatic *jeu d'optique.* The "Palais-Egalité, ci-devant Palais-Royal" was, according to Mercier, the contagious source of that visual "gangrene" infecting modern morals. Its long galleries and shop-riddled arcades not only inspired seditious intrigues, atrocious crimes, ruinous speculation, but housed gambling dens next door to purveyors of

luxuries. This "foyer d'impureté" was also a magical Palace of Armida or Circe, replete with obscene waxworks and metamorphic *Fantasmagorie.*[45]

Mercier was not alone in launching anathemas against the besotting realm of the *imagiste,* that theatricalized ambience where even a respectable domestic interior might become transformed into a loge (fig. 40). In this competitive lens culture, the popular science demonstration was just one *séance* among many. Mesmer's dramatic "cures" had aroused an insatiable appetite for "novateurs." Juggling, "c'est Art de s'en imposer de mille manières," was the derogatory name bestowed on the conjurings of all those operators who pushed nature out of its proper, center-stage position and substituted themselves.[46] Mesmerism, attaining its apogee at the end of the 1770s and the decade of the 1780s, symbolized the pseudo-empirical spectacle par excellence. Dressed in a lilac suit, the medical wizard presided over fashionable, illusion-inducing equipment: wooden tub containing metal filings, movable iron rods, and magnetized water.[47] Induced crises, transmitted

40

Léopold Boilly, *L'Optique* (*Zograscope*), eighteenth century. Engraving by J. P. Le Bas after a painting by Léopold Boilly. (Photo: Courtesy Getty Center, Resource Collections.)

[Noël Retz], *Mesmeric Phenomena,* from *Mémoire . . . de la jonglerie,* 1784, frontispiece. Engraving. (Photo: Courtesy Herzog August Bibliothek, Wolfenbüttel.)

through a human chain of linked fingers, unleashed hallucinations of connectedness. Immoderate laughter, crying, singing, declaiming, and convulsions rippled through the company seated together in a darkened and mirrored salon (fig. 41).[48]

Part fringe psychology and part charlatanism, Mesmer's immensely successful Parisian therapies depended in no small measure on the promise of achieving linkups with global forces. Animal magnetism's adepts touted it internationally as a universal panacea predicated on the existence of a universal ocean inundating all bodies, and so enabling their intercommunication. The magnetizer, so the thinking ran, was particularly predisposed to collect this fluid and direct it at the sick. Significantly, for Rabiqueau's contemporaneous performances this potent liquid was imagined as a vital fire (see fig. 33) intended to inflame the patient and precipitate an attack of nervous ecstasy.[49]

Mesmerism's sensational tactics found their way into the ocular theatrics of legitimate physicians such as Pinel as well as into the apparatus-driven experiments of the popular science pedagogue.[50] In both cases, audiences had grown accustomed to the vividness and sensuous immediacy of spectacle. The alluring or disturbing prominence (depending on one's point of view) given to the eye coalesced with diatribes against religious credulity. The anti-Catholic publicist and *littérateur* Eusèbe Salverte uniformly denounced all opticalized ritual, extending from ancient temple magic to contemporary pantomime, music, fictionalizing poetry, the visual arts, and the "cirque infecte." Everything from nightmares to the barbarism of bullfighting to the ferocity of the Spanish Inquisition was laid at the doorstep of a priestcraft holding an illiterate populace in thrall through a phantasmagorically "delicious spectacle."[51]

THE KNOWLEDGE BUSINESS

The language of theophany, of mysteries conveyed through optical setups and strange rites, returns us to the alternative laboratory of the old regime. In this phenomenological space the perilous empire of the imagination was engaged by means of strange attractors. Here, the sun's reflective and rotational powers could be dramatically enacted, captured in a magical circle of mirrors. Or the magnet's uncanny shaping powers might become momentarily perceptible for anyone willing to pay the price (see fig. 38).

If virtual reality, video games, 500-channel cable television, and computerized animation have raised today's audience expectation for advanced hardware and, more fundamentally, for what constitutes an amazingly real illusion,[52] Rabiqueau's mesmerized spectators were no different. The simple, old-fashioned rabbit-pulling and disappearing-ink routines of fairground mountebanks (see fig. 36) were increasingly upstaged by expensive illusion tricks, just as Siegfried and Roy's Las Vegas Siberian Tiger phantasmagoria makes sawing off limbs, three-card monte, or vanishing acts seem unsophisticated in a slick city milieu. If the working-class magician and itinerant entertainer wowed the villages or worked the back streets, the behind-the-scenes manipulator of fancy devices aimed to please a more urbane viewer. Rabiqueau's customers navigated a vertiginous web of interconnected effects downloaded into complicated anamorphoses, costly camera obscuras, mechanical clocks, doctored prints, and specially constructed tables (*les meubles à secrets*) fitted with mirrors (fig. 42).[53]

Natural occurrences, rendered invisible or bland through habit, could be made technically interesting by recasting them into a visual drama. The curtain went up on prismatic and other emanative processes that had been refocused into artistic scenes, that is, engineered until an intriguing image suddenly sprang into view. For example, light rays were split into two separate beams passing in parallel through a spherical glass vessel. The pull of gravity was envisioned as the reverse tug on a parachute (see fig. 38).

The popular science demonstrator evidently competed in the same cutthroat atmosphere of secrecy and one-upmanship that governed Mercier's kingdom of *l'optique,* where the showman was only as good as his show. Multimedia experiments with electrical "fluid," originating in Musschenbroek's 1746 discovery of the Leyden jar, launched many careers in the lucrative business of *la physique amusante.* This combined information and entertainment industry dispelled ignorance by pleasingly "charging" dolls, toy boats, porcupines, and even the performer himself (see fig. 39).[54] Subtle matter from afar was brought to the polite society attending the "spectacle méchanique *in supremis,*" held daily at the Sign of the Grand Druid Automate.[55] As was the case for Mesmer's and Cagliostro's performances, Parisians in their bourgeois carriages rolled into the rue Bailleul in droves to hook up to Rabiqueau's high-tech *cabinet.* Although it was not yet the telepresence era, seekers could come in contact with elementary fire, Newton's ether, or some other omnipotent virtue supposedly capable of restoring health and balance.

Reminiscent of today's communications revolution, whereby a venerable print world is being overturned by the computer's electronic icons, legerdemain empiricism was being challenged by a technically mediated information economy. The conversion from a traditional, labor-based activity, in which tricks or marvels were literally manufactured (that is, made by hand), to a knowledge-based activity, in which apparatus seemed automatically to project data, carried both old-time necromancy and developing experimental science into the modern age (contrast fig. 37 with figs. 38 and 42). The synoptic plate serving as frontispiece to the chemistry section of the *Encyclopédie* articulated an

42
—
Charles Rabiqueau, *Perceptual Illusions,* from *Le microscope moderne,* 1781, part II, pl. 9. Engraving. (Photo: Courtesy Herzog August Bibliothek, Wolfenbüttel.)

identical upheaval. It showed that the concepts being generated in the laboratory were vastly more important than the anonymous hands busily producing them (see fig. 35).

PAST AND PRESENT

If it is true that our world is wallowing in information but is starved for knowledge,[56] then these four scenes from eighteenth-century laboratory life presage some of the greatest challenges facing contemporary society. Optical jugglers, creating simulation/stimulation ecologies, heralded the breakdown of the authoritative text synonymous with western civilization since the Renaissance. Yet not just written language but all media were destabilized when the record of the physical stages through which a work passed during its production became hidden.

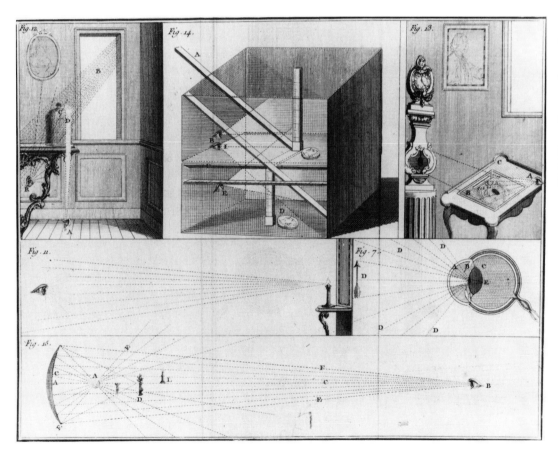

My specific concern, expressed in this essay and elsewhere, is not with all media but with the trivialization, denigration, and phantomization of images from the early modern period forward. In spite of their quantity and globalized presence, for many educated people pictures have become synonymous with ignorance, illiteracy, and deceit. Why? And why should it matter for a knowledge of the past or the present that no other medium (and certainly others are equally prone to manipulation) has been judged so sweepingly as being innately corrupt? These four scenes remind us of what has been suppressed: the negative critique connecting images to the fanatical proselytizing of the Roman Catholic church, to charlatanic performances addressed to the lower classes, to a necromantic optical technology, and to a theatricalized empirical science.

There is no doubt that machine-generated images, like hypertexts, are extremely, even excessively, mutable. If they can be misused, they will be misused. But that is not the fault of the medium. Rabiqueau's virtuoso play with optical technology, well in advance of our dematerialized electronic environment, pointed out the difficulty of separating genuine information from disinformation when the material aspects of making and the character of the maker were concealed or concealable. The Enlightenment taught us that within an increasingly phantasmagoric environment, images have to be shown at work. The no longer evident relationship between the complex form of input and the convergent form of output has to be deliberately exposed. Understanding the historical entanglements of science with pseudo-science intensifies our perception of contemporary fiddling—such as cold fusion—and vice versa.

In our interactive "Age of Blinding Light," in John Callaway's apocalyptic phrase,[57] when potentially every individual can intervene in thousands of political, social, cultural, and scientific decisions by simply seizing the media, we need to transform raw data into wisdom. While desperately seeking like-minded others on the Internet, we might also look for concrete ways to substantialize this dangerous immediacy and to occlude seeming transparency. Reconnecting invisible cause with visible effect will require the construction of intelligent imagery.

The Natural History of Design: Humbert de Superville and Postmodern Theory

7

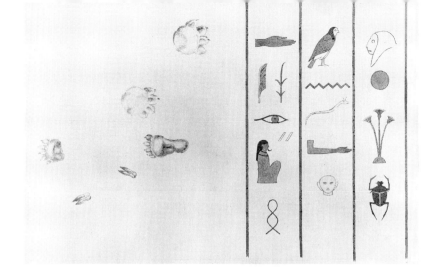

Late twentieth-century thinkers refuse metanarratives and *grands récits,* that is, any general idea unifying social, racial, and sexual differences. At the same time, they hunt after crosscutting methodologies to link far-flung fields and competing theories systematically together. For those of us interested in imaging modalities of all kinds, design studies is rapidly emerging as the exciting focal point from which one might begin to connect a multitude of disciplines, professions, and approaches concerned with the production, reception, and dissemination of visual information.[1] The suppleness of ultrafast computers and the layerings of hypermedia have highlighted the semiotic richness existing within a broad range of pattern-making technologies. Animation, video, and virtual reality possess the unnerving capability of making simulations appear simultaneously as material objects, immaterial processes, natural scenes, and artificial representations.

I want, then, to tell a happier story about signs, symbols, and glyphs. The originality of D. P. G. Humbert de Superville (1770–1849), compared to his contemporary hermeneuticists, consisted in his life-long preoccupation with the creation and interpretation of iconic codes and cultural emblems down centuries, across civilizations, through gender or class barriers, and bridging high and popular art distinctions. An eccentric polymath in an age of polymathy, his investigations adumbrated our contemporary fascination with multiculturalism, ethnic origins, and an evolutionary consciousness. His ruling passion was the drive to uncover a universal grammar of expression, a fundamental logic of forms behind all forms, based on vertical and horizontal symmetry or asymmetry. This Herculean struggle entailed bringing the divided areas of biology, aesthetics, and perception into

43

D. P. G. Humbert de Superville, *Animal Tracks and Hieroglyphics,* 1827–1832. Watercolor. (Photo: Courtesy Prentenkabinet, Rijksuniversiteit Leiden.)

Humbert de Superville interpreted all cultural production as part of a larger order in nature. Animal tracks and human footprints were the originals for the mixed body parts imitated in the earliest pictographs. Such composite glyphs are the ancestors of today's computerized icon-sound-text collages. Primal lines and colors, he believed, were recorded on Egyptian painted bas-reliefs, literally shallow depressions incised into tomb walls that mimicked natural signs. In this analogical system, works of art are evanescent imprints left behind by the passage of living beings. The Dutch polymath ranks among romantics, such as Wordsworth and Blake, who interpreted the cosmos as a network of meaningful correspondences.

conjunction. There is an object lesson here, since present-day etholo-
gists are again opening up the question of whether outward beauty, and
especially the exquisite harmony of mirror-image traits (fig. 44), is a
reliable indicator of underlying health, that is, of good interior design.[2]
For Humbert, determining the maximum possible balance between the
left and right sides of the body in diverse populations was part of a
hermeneutic quest to interpret the perplexing signs and clues left behind by myriad makers and users throughout the world. Aesthetic
judgments about proportion and misproportion, in this scheme, functioned as indicators of what various cultures found appealing or
repugnant.

Far from being a dated concept, bodily symmetry seems to be
intrinsic to nature's plan, even for today's evolutionary biologists. During the early decades of the nineteenth century, however, the cultural
problem of beauty and ugliness was also intimately tied to the larger
anthropological impulse to know the "other." Humbert understood the
sophistications of analogy, that venerable and visionary mode for corre-
lating the mysteries of the human sensory system with the elusive signals emitted by the mind and mysteriously reflected on the face.
Embedding emotion within a psychic matrix led the Dutch enlightener
to devise a transdisciplinary and transglobal semiotic in which mytho-
poetic, religious, philosophical, political, ethical, anatomical, and artistic factors intersected. Such profound correspondences, he believed,
would assist viewers from Europe to Asia in deciphering seemingly contradictory behavior and apparently incongruous customs. So pervasive
is the identification of design with discourse that the *Essai sur les signes
inconditionnels dans l'art* (1827–1832) remains a major theoretical state-
ment on the durable problem of judging from legible appearances.

History has not done justice to this Dutch graphic artist, zeal-
ous pro-French patriot, ardent Kantian, museum founder, mythog-
rapher, semiologist, and cultural comparatist. Belonging to that
international republic of *érudits* growing up just prior to the French
Revolution, his star faded during the doldrums of the Restoration. It
was this generation of *savants* that became the influential teachers in the
nineteenth-century academies proliferating after that great upheaval.
Resembling Quatremère de Quincy, Wicar, Bossi, Runge, and Blake,
Humbert adhered to the idealistic educational goals emerging from Enlightenment humanism. Like these reforming painter-theorists, and
authors such as Winckelmann, Condillac, or Goethe, he wanted to con-
struct a new formal language to elevate the depraved taste of the rococo
era. Part of an activist group bent on establishing guidelines for histori-

44

D. P. G. Humbert de Superville,
Egyptian Colossus, 1827–1832. Watercolor. (Photo: Courtesy Prentenkabinet, Rijksuniversiteit Leiden.)

cal and archaeological exactitude, he militantly argued that the visual arts should rekindle virtue and expose vice. Not coincidentally, the Revolutionary salons were dominated by history paintings claiming to serve morality by offering uplifting examples of virile heroism as antidotes to effeminate, aristocratic *laissez-faire*.[3]

Rather than relying exclusively on the Stoic idiom disseminated by Davidian neoclassicism, Humbert methodically forged an expressive vocabulary rooted in the experience of many intersecting antiquities, whether Egyptian, Chinese, Hindu, Polynesian, Greek, Roman, or medieval (fig. 45). A forward-looking proponent of cultural studies, he sought to develop a comprehensive theory of perception through the codification of human emotions. Somewhat like current cross-cultural researchers looking into the question of what information the face typically conveys, he, too, found evidence of universality in spontaneous reactions as well as in deliberately contrived poses.[4] Humbert's rules for graphic display, then, were both unconditional and culture-specific. What might be termed his natural history of emotions was thus intended to redress Humean relativism, to offer a corrective to the rampantly subjective associationism taken up by British disseminators of the picturesque such as Gilpin, Alison, Knight, and Price.

As in much structuralist and poststructuralist theory from Foucault to Derrida, the body in Enlightenment thought became the prism through which to refract all social rituals and constraining institutions. It was the liminal place where temperament encountered world. For Humbert, too, the body was an irreducible terrain from which all observers, irrespective of their nationality, experienced the primal shock of an individual psychology bumping up against an alien environment. Extending and radically transforming the Cartesian analysis of affect as a manifestation of the passions through corporeal movements,[5] Humbert developed a general science for reading all natural and artificial traces. Belonging to a more rigorous era than Charles Le Brun or Cureau de La Chambre, however, this self-conscious *pédant* wished to demonstrate that the visual arts and the human faculties were grounded in the same formal logic. Graphic design, not muscles, offered the key to interpretation. Lines drawn on a perfectly symmetrical face in repose meet in a single undeviating vertical extending down the nose. The appeal of such regularity, whether in human beings, works of art, or examples drawn from the organic and inorganic kingdoms, consisted in their harmonious impression. This psychological effect of tranquil beauty, he believed, signaled a deeper underlying somatic harmony. Echoing the Neoplatonic system of correspondences, Humbert argued

45

D. P. G. Humbert de Superville, *Comparative Architecture,* 1827–1832. Watercolor. (Photo: Courtesy Prentenkabinet, Rijksuniversiteit Leiden.)

that such symbolic forms presented ontological and epistemological connections between the perceiving mind, the external world, and the thing represented.

The late eighteenth century saw the advent of the art treatise as regenerative manifesto. Criticism was inseparable from neoclassicism's self-designation as the "true" or "correct" style.[6] Thus the intertwining of aesthetic with moral and psychological issues (already apparent at the beginning of the century in the writings of Shaftesbury) was accentuated, at its end, by the high enlighteners' war against corruption.[7] The *Essai*'s habit of talking about architecture (troglodyte), sculpture (Egyptian), and painting (pre-Raphaelite) as edifying examples restoring a lost primitive virtue belongs to this international improving impulse. Further, Humbert's disembodied facial diagrams and somatic schemata should also be seen as part of a larger Enlightenment project of deconstruction. An interventionist pedagogy was to overturn a past school for scandal. All obscurantist claims shoring up the *ancien régime* were to be stripped to the skin. Excess had to be stamped out, irrationalism exposed, fraud extirpated, and superstition expunged. A new conceptual art[8]—Joseph Kosuth before the fact—was to subdue and control entropic matter, wayward imagination, and merely manual skill.

This iconoclastic quest for authentic or pristine forms of experience buried beneath deceptive etiquette, despotic governments, and decadent artifacts shaped Humbert's systematics of corporeal bareness. Innate rectitude or deviance should be clearly legible to the discerning viewer, even if masked by social conventions. It does not seem farfetched, then, to suggest that Humbert's generation bears an uncanny resemblance to the skeptical denizens of our contemporary immaterial culture.[9] While not communicating instantaneously via electronic messages, they nonetheless longed for swift, noise-free transmissions. Spareness was synonymous with directness, with the pure symbol's incarnation of God-like genuineness. It is not surprising that simple and clear visual signs signified truth-telling in contradistinction to manifold lying appearances. Nor is it accidental that an era, accustomed to thinking by analogy and according to binaries, judged hidden moral qualities from surface looks. The antiquarian craze to decipher eroded inscriptions thus merged with an ascetic ritual of reading aimed at penetrating posturing and disguise.

Physiognomics as a paradigmatic interpretive strategy had a major impact on the intellectual and artistic life of the eighteenth century. Marivaux, Hogarth, Lichtenberg, and, preeminently, Johann

Caspar Lavater (1741–1801) drew attention to the legible topography of the animal and human body. "The morally better, the more beautiful; the morally worse, the uglier"[10] was a motto to which Humbert could have subscribed. Extending the semiotic implications of Lavater's spectacularly popular *Physiognomische Fragmente* (1775–1778), Humbert similarly wished to pierce the varieties of dissimulation. On the other hand, he wanted to avoid the impasse of the Zurich pastor's atomistic hermeneutics. Lavater had created an open-ended encyclopedia composed of endless details. A succession of isolated features, excised corporeal parts, even warts and moles, were paraded before the viewer in the hope of establishing a link between invisible depth and visible surface. Humbert's minimalist system, by contrast, cut through this accumulative characterology to establish a radically delimited alphabet of root lines and primary colors.[11]

The Dutch artist's physiognomic intuition that traces of human emotion gave shape to highly delimited moral conditions contributed to his unprecedented admiration of the so-called Italian primitives.[12] Working in Umbria and the Veneto as part of Jean-Baptiste Seroux d'Agincourt's team of young artists illustrating the *Histoire de l'art* (begun in 1782),[13] he rediscovered the *trecento* and *quattrocento* frescoed universe of virtues and vices. Only now is art historical scholarship catching up with his deeply original perception that Giotto's or Orcagna's pairings of malevolent men with virginal maidens represented not a narrative but a *psychomachia*.[14] In the panel paintings and pictorial cycles of the early Italian masters, abstractions became concrete *exempla*. Personifications of mythical archetypes were, simultaneously, historical actors. Such confrontational drama (fig. 46), also typifying the epic heroes and villains found in the Bible, Homer, Dante, Milton, Blake, and Byron, was based on the never-ending cosmic battle between good and evil. Inconstancy or fortitude, envy or charity, despair or hope, were literally and clearly embodied in unstable or steadfast, turbulent or calm shapes, hues, lines.

Journeying in the 1790s with the young British draftsman William Young Ottley, he recorded dichotomized scenes of timeless moral conflict by Pietro Lorenzetti, Nicola Pisano, Taddeo Gaddi, and Masolino. Humbert was struck by the economy of graphic means used by these pre-Renaissance artists, the purity of their abstract linear style prescient of Carstens, Runge, and Ingres. Ugliness and beauty, shiftiness and sincerity, Judas and Christ, devil and angel, seemed to transmit their signals across centuries without equivocation or confusion. By contrast, he felt that modern art—from Rubens to Reynolds—was

46

D. P. G. Humbert de Superville, *Angel and Devil Fighting over a Dead Man's Soul,* 1834. Ink wash. (Photo: Courtesy Prentenkabinet, Rijksuniversiteit Leiden.)

chaotic at the expressive level. Its lines and colors were confused and confusing, lacking precisely those compositional strategies of doubling, reflective symmetry, and antithesis that enabled the beholder to distinguish significant external differences pointing to deeper ethical incongruities. Because the Italian primitives were closer to the beginnings of western painting (i.e., before its flowering during the Renaissance), he reasoned that their works exhibited more explicitly and in an unsullied fashion the natural signs from which they had been constructed.

Humbert's never-completed *Essai,* whose truncated version intrigued David d'Angers, Charles Blanc, Charles Henri, Georges Seurat, and Charles Signac, attempted to uncover those pristine conditions in which the world's myths, rituals, and art had once arisen and from which its present-day manifestations measurably departed. Signs, both natural and artificial, posed a double problem to the late eighteenth-century semiotician. They could have referents in two directions. The downward, upward, or horizontal lines traced on the faces and gridded into the bodies of Egyptian colossi, Hindu gods, Greek herms, Easter Island sculpture (fig. 47), or Giotto's saints and sinners evoked or provoked, on one hand, the sorrow, joy, or tranquillity felt by the modern observer who perceived them. On the other hand, these axes and their corresponding black, red, or white colors were also universal symbols. As hieroglyphics, originating at the beginning of recorded time, they signified actual cosmic cataclysms and subsequent historical revolutions transcending the sensorium of any individual viewer.

External occurrences and ephemeral emotions could thus coincide when past experiences collided with current events. On occasion, objectivity intersected with subjectivity. According to Humbert, we are able to intuit the meaning of ancient or foreign monuments because their physiognomy reflects common somatic reactions that, insofar as we are human, we still respond to and, however dimly, still understand. We apprehend and react to select lines and colors because they reawaken a succession of tribal memories of terror, happiness, and peace deposited in our collective unconscious. Humbert believed that the faint traces of the traumatic beginnings of humankind (involving death by water or fire, a miraculous resurrection, and the restoration of social harmony by wise legislators) registered on the *corpus* of archaic works continue to move us. These eloquent signs rekindle the primal sensations or environmental shocks once felt by a frail and endangered psyche.

When the laws of January 24–25, 1790, were passed in France, creating a museum in each of that nation's eighty-three departments, a model was put in place that, eventually, would be extended by Na-

47

D. P. G. Humbert de Superville, *A Herm of Easter Island,* 1827–1832. Watercolor. (Photo: Courtesy Prentenkabinet, Rijksuniversiteit Leiden.)

poleon to embrace his conquered countries.[15] Humbert's neoclassical (and even Jacobin) exaltation of great men, commemorated by colossal monuments housed in secular "temples," link him to that new exhibition-creating generation associated with Quatremère de Quincy and Alexandre Lenoir.[16] These devisers of moral "repositories" to house an edifying patrimony untainted by the luxury and corruption characterizing the *ancien régime* were the French fine arts administrators who set in relief Humbert's failed sculptural, architectural, and painted projects. The Netherlander's uplifting civic arena, Gothic grotto, museum of plaster casts, and gallery of transparencies exist only as drawings. Yet they were intended to be built, public spaces, real sites for elevating the debased arts. The Hebrew, Egyptian, Greek, and seventeenth-century Dutch juristic "bienfaiteurs de l'humanité" were to serve as guides. Timeless authorities, including Moses, Lycurgus, and Socrates, joined ranks with more recent historical figures such as Grotius, Du Guesclin, and William of Orange. These lawgivers, Humbert argued, transcended their tumultuous epochs to become symbols of justice, ethical awareness, and rational behavior under duress.

In line with eighteenth-century cosmologists and mythographers like Burnet and Dupuis, Humbert conjectured about a sublime geological and astronomical cataclysm that, at first burned and then flooded the earth. The Bible (especially the *pseudo-epigrapha* and the book of Job), the Koran, as well as records of Zoroastrian funerary rites, Mithraic purification rituals, even Hindu caste marks, Peruvian knots, South Sea Islander tattoos, and Celtic pictograms, were interpreted as forming part of an ageless semiotics attesting to the lasting and pervasive effects of that catastrophe on the impressionable minds of primitive people everywhere.

Not just high art monuments, but a truly ethnographic range of material cultural remains symbolically commemorated the collision of the earth with a comet's tail. Comprising a lexicon of globally felt emotions, similar designs diversely signified pain, joy, and tranquillity as a common response by the survivors to a succession of generally endured events. Designating families of emotions, each type in the triad of lines and colors evoked a nexus of related affective states. Moreover, the dominant characteristics shared by all members of an emotion family (black, white, red) were personified, according to Humbert, in mythology and cosmology. For example, Athena and Pan stood for classes of serene or animating experiences. Analogously, the heroes Humbert wished to commemorate in his museum were precisely those who, time and time again, rescued humanity from the anarchy and anguish of recurring unenlightened epochs. Their noble and composed features embodied the quiet fortitude required to wrest social order from civil unrest.

This performative dimension of Humbert's theory extends its range beyond semantics, the logical and linguistic dividing of data into discrete units, or the merely *structural* dissection of preexisting meaning. He raised the eighteenth-century fascination with analogy and metaphor into the creation of a forward-looking hermeneutic tool.

The utopian design thinking governing the *Essai* had an important afterlife in Charles Eastlake's call for simple shapes and the honest representation of materials, in Herbert Muthesius's summons to create an industrial form language, and in Adolf Loos's hostility to ornament.[17] On one hand, as a manifesto for conceptual clarity, schematic distinctness, and a radical economy of visual means, it adumbrated modernist formalism: the bare style of Le Corbusier, Mies van der Rohe, and Mondrian. On the other hand, as the philosophical matrix from which to develop concrete projects, the *Essai* bears eloquent testimony to the increasing split between theory and practice in the contemporary world. A mountain of manuscripts, housed at the Leiden Prentenkabinet and the Royal Library of The Hague, brim with ideas for aborted projects. Doomed by historical factors, these visionary drawings and folios set in relief the book's incompleteness. The treatise is thus paradigmatically postmodern in its melancholic fragmentariness.

Conceived under the long shadow cast by the French Revolution and shrunk to its current epigrammatic proportions during the wars separating Holland from Belgium, the *Essai* is not just about the Neoplatonic precession of immaterial ideas. It offers poignant material evidence concerning faltering European economies, the post-Revolutionary shattering of aesthetic consensus, and the thwarting of universalizing aspirations by a bureaucratic reality. The vicissitudes of the corporeal world and the prosaic commodity interests of nineteenth-century European bourgeois society proved increasingly at variance with the elite, metaphysical, sign-induced speculations of the published text.[18]

This evolutionary awareness of the fragility of human creations, coupled with the realization of their eternal recurrence, moved Humbert's theory simultaneously toward Rorty's neopragmatism and Chomsky's Cartesian linguistics.[19] The performative and socially engaged dimension of his work extended it beyond both the confines of a hermetic logic or Derridean semantics and the Foucauldian structural dissection of preexisting meaning. Further, he raised the eighteenth-century fascination with origins to an interpretive tool in the analysis of truly fundamental emotions.[20] Certain exemplary buildings, sanctuaries, human and animal sculpture, hieroglyphics, blazons, and clothing were viewer-centered speech acts, not passive codes, waiting to be retrieved through decipherment.[21]

The Dutch artist's sophisticated grammar of signs, prescient of Saussurian linguistics, deconstructed artifacts and images into pure signifiers. A succinct alphabet of irreducible linear vectors and corresponding primary colors, abstracted from their tangible contexts, constituted a Leibnizian *ars combinatoria* or basic visual language from which the varieties of found or invented communication might be deduced. Yet, simultaneously, these designs were historical records picturing the psychological frame of mind of beholders faced with the anarchy and anguish of chaotic times. An ardent Kantian, Humbert believed in a priori moral laws, but he was also interested in the rules of art and technique that are based on experience and applicable to it. When compared to the contemporary critique of colonial discourse as dependent upon the unnuanced concept of fixity and to poststructuralism's celebration of instability, Humbert's quest seems all the more pertinent.[22] His labyrinthine pursuit of sameness in otherness and otherness in sameness revealed an unchanging order as well as prevailing disorder. Avoiding the merely stereotypical in the search for deep connections between natural and artificial domains continues to be a pressing issue today. Conversely, resisting the reification of the detail, the radically individual, the tribal, the nationalistic, similarly calls for a more embracing and international perspective.

In sum, steering between the poles of essentialism and relativism, hierarchy and marginality, nurture and nature, theory and practice, Humbert struggled to establish a concrete bioaesthetics. General graphic formulas, he argued, corresponded to personal attitudes and specific situations as well as reflecting more common habits of response to the environment. This pragmatic milieu theory claimed that the physical and ethical dimensions of human beings were inseparable from the material habitat and cultural setting in which they originated and evolved. The *Essai*'s author would have been capable of uttering the words of the great American logician and pragmatist Charles Sanders Peirce: "The rational purport of a word or other expression, lies exclusively in its conceivable bearing upon the conduct of life."[23]

An Image of One's Own

ILLUSIONS OF INTERDISCIPLINARITY

The current enthusiasm voiced by academics of all stripes for multidisciplinarity, crosscutting cultural studies, and transcategorical investigations has obscured a disturbing fact. Higher education in this country is experiencing not only a liberating intellectual interdisciplinarity, but a compressive fiscal interdisciplinarity as well. Although a long-standing advocate for the need to incorporate diverse areas of humanistic, scientific, and technological knowledge into art history, I am troubled by the unanalyzed rise and proliferation of potentially reductive "area studies."

Who, surveying the shipwreck of departments ranging from geography to sociology to studio occurring in major universities around the country, has not noticed that the surviving flotsam usually accrues to the already most powerful and largest units in these institutions? For example, the English department is now routinely the site for literary, colonial, media, film, and, most recently, "visual culture" programs. In our laudable desire to encourage scholarship and promote exchange, have we imagists been putting ourselves out of business?[1] To put the question another way, can people who are self-selected for, and who are committed to, textual issues be willing and able to support the intent and repeated confrontation with physical objects and to value the skilled making necessary for a truly visual approach?

After apocalypse, that is, after the drastic retrenchments visible daily on the outside strike with equal force inside the walls, what and who will remain? I predict that we will be left with the mega-trinity of literary studies, cultural studies, and visual studies, i.e., all-purpose vast containers into which national languages, varieties of history, etc.

48

Edmé-François Gersaint, *Art Collectors and Connoisseurs,* from *Catalogue raisoné des diverses curiosités du cabinet de feu M. Quentin de Lorangère,* 1744, frontispiece. Drawing and engraving by Charles Cochin. (Photo: Courtesy Getty Center, Resource Collections.)

Edmé-François Gersaint captures the intensity of close, discriminating, and passionate looking as it was practiced by well-to-do eighteenth-century collectors. Intimately examining paintings, studying drawings, and discussing prints was a social and civilizing activity. Beyond the intrinsic worth of seriously interacting with works of art lay the additional value of refining those perceptions and empathetic responses needed in everyday exchanges. This knowing attachment to well-designed things, nurtured through conversation with friends and colleagues, developed an awareness of the communal importance of paying attention.

will be swept. Without a compelling *raison d'être*, then, is it logical to expect territorial generosity from colleagues similarly threatened by dwindling resources? Could, would, or even should universities permit the simultaneous existence of art history departments, studio art, design schools, *and* a visual studies program? It is not reassuring that, to date, the politics of identity and difference has tended to be monological, not dialogical.[2]

I am not disputing the accuracy of the proposition that fields defined in the nineteenth century require redefinition and reconfiguration at the end of the twentieth.[3] Rather, I am asking whether the undiscussed and unmonitored collapse of an eclectic plurality of specializations will not lead to the tyranny of the homogenizing few within the beleaguered liberal arts curriculum. Think of how the breakdown of single corporations in the business world has produced a handful of global megaconsortia driven by the economics of expedient consolidation. Building bridges among diverse disciplines is a design problem,[4] not the automatic result of the ideology of hybridity nor even of dire budgetary realities. More specifically, I wonder what the twin pressures of conceptual amalgamation and financial downsizing in our colleges portend for those of us whose expertise has consisted in the historical/theoretical illumination of visual topics, graphic practices, display strategies, and beholder responses in all their varied and rich forms.

ATTENDING TO IMAGES

It is not as if the politics of differential recognition (i.e., the administrative perception that being numerically smaller also signifies cognitive inferiority vis-à-vis larger, mentally superior departments) were the only impetus behind inappropriate mergers. Not enough attention has been paid, I believe, to the marginalization of imagery of all kinds in our society as an intellectual form of communication.[5] No one seems to deny that we inhabit a visual universe. Yet, especially among media critics, the quantitative presence of electronically generated images drowns out the recognition of their qualitative capability for informatively shaping knowledge.[6] In spite of the multiculturalists' new tribalism and the social constructivists' respect for alterity, it is depressing to see to what extent postmodernism still privileges the single criterion of the text.

Rigorous self-scrutiny is standard procedure in all aspects of our culture wars. Textuality and reading, however, retain their quasi-ontological status as unquestionably good goods, in opposition to supposedly innately deceptive and irrational "commodified" representations directed merely at the eyes of besotted consumers. Many literary critics seem unwilling to consider that neither the essence nor the function of imagery is exhausted by simulation. The awareness that artificially produced patterns are, by definition, made or crafted experiences[7] should not doom them to the nonreflective realm of simplistic sensation. Good design gives value to visually encoded information.[8] Imaginative, engaging, appealing, and truthful ordering lifts forms, lines, and colors to the sphere of sophisticated intellectual creations.

In view of the overwhelmingly negative trend to debunk vulgar, voyeuristic, violent, and vapid mass media, perhaps we should accord some sympathetic attention to the ocular objects of our research. An emergent integrative design discipline, adequate to the compacted shape of future education, must remetaphorize debased physical appearances and deflated material phenomena. If we ever hope to overcome the hierarchical structures ruling contemporary academic and public life, we have a responsibility to present a more comprehensive, affirmative paradigm of picture and artifacts. It does not seem mere Polyannism, then, to suggest that experts in visualization should assume leadership for providing society with glimpses, at least, of good images.[9]

Making visible the complex work of creativity can occur only through a reciprocally enlightening relationship among partners. In the innovative design discipline I see emerging, individual members would prismatically refract different, but complementary, aspects of the image. My criticism of the current text-driven visual studies trend is that it implicitly reifies old power bases and verbal biases under the explicit and fetching slogan of intellectual coherence. This is evident in the tendency to discount historically situated, concrete looking in favor of abstractly theoretical readings.[10]

What is missing from the visual culturalist's preconceived laundry list of perceptual "pathographies," to adapt Joyce Carol Oates's term coined for the recent fashion in gratuitously dysfunctional biographies,[11] is disciplined training in, and respectful attention to, sensory knowing. Simone Weil suggested that love of the other depends upon accurate apprehension.[12] Visual objects, too, it seems to me, are deserving of that just, effortful, and loving gaze directed upon any particular reality we wish to understand fairly. Fusing the historical study of the arts and crafts, studio, museum displays, traditional graphic processes, and advanced computer modeling would permit us to see all design efforts as part of a complex technical, formal, psychological, and critical continuum. Such an exemplary union is justified by the evidence coming from visual science showing that the major sensory systems, while executing different functions, share a remarkably similar organization.[13] From our various vantages, we need to work together to show how the results of our modular analyses yield synthetic cognitive percepts. With one eye cast backward to distant precedents, models, examples, and another eye cast forward to contemporary production, we could start to behold, comprehend, and interpret more perspicuously our phenomenological condition as generative human beings. While recognizing that cultures and styles of existence are different, we might begin envisioning practical and nonreductive ways in which they could become commensurate. What better means for demonstrating that visual knowledge is indispensable to the competence of every educated person?

AFFIRMATIVE ACTIONS

The difficulty of constructing an appropriately nuanced image for images in our postdisciplinary climate (borne out by the rarity of the attempts) is further exacerbated by the swelling scholarly critique of technology.[14] The condemnation of much optical apparatus— "mindless" video games, "isolating" virtual reality entertainments, and "controlling" television signals—shores up the epistemologically and morally driven bias that to approve of instrument-manufactured imagery is tantamount to supporting falsehood. The attempts by Bataille, Foucault, and Derrida to destroy bourgeois secular humanism by praising death, violence, and rebellion further renders it almost impossible to conceive of an acceptable icon. For Marxists, as well, the aesthetic, as a purely formal tool wielded by money-grubbing capitalists to confine, control, and passify the masses, resembles a deluding machine, not a promising model for living.[15]

The collapse of the many into the even bigger few, the persistent taint of delusion surrounding visual media, the nihilism of postmodernism, and the massive replication facilitated by technology: all these educational and ethical issues pale when compared to the disappearance of the job market. There is a revolution erupting in American higher education, and it is called technological restructuring. Personal desktop computing, on-line services, data banks, and high-speed global networking magnetically draw students not into mortar and brick ivied walls but into virtual classes, or even into full-degree programs transmitted electronically. Wireless technology and digital imagery have made long-distance, off-campus learning a reality. Moreover, this fundamental pedagogical transformation is coupled to a growing sense that doctoral programs individually are producing too many Ph.Ds, and a grudging acknowledgement that we have generated too many graduate programs given the paucity of openings.[16]

Consequently, who we are educating and for what purpose has become a more unavoidable issue than ever. An orienting and united design discipline with a strong sense of social responsibility and a common purpose might better be able to counter the purely negative strategies of folding less dominant fields into conventionally more authoritative ones, outright curricular axing, and arbitrarily shutting down the production of doctoral candidates. We need to make the case that a truly cross-categorical, many-cultured, and focused field concerned with manifesting the intelligence of imagery is *the* place to study nonverbal and composite forms of communication. Indeed, both as nucleus and locus, this type of praxis should form the intellectual agenda and be the guiding spirit behind all academic projects concerned with imaging. At the existential level such a design discipline, because of its conceptual richness and unique capacity to train people in a broad range of spatial skills, could offer the requisite flexibility for coping with career erosion in an ongoing economic recession. Our students should be prepared to respond to the diversity of employment opportunities in a dwindling world market, using their distinctive flexible expertise in the multiple facets of visualization to solve real-life problems as well as engage in imaginative *Gedanken-Experimenten.*

In sum: I have been arguing that those of us centrally concerned with graphicacy should pool our resources and skills for a positive and constructive endeavor. Against the denigration of the visual, let us put forward as a group of intellectuals the liberating counterargument that to understand images and the intricate processes of imaging is to understand a deeply connected body of nonverbal knowledge with specific cognitive and formal properties, rules and techniques, that need to be learned. A distinctive and powerful image of one's own makes it possible to reach out with dignity to other fields and professions from a position of appropriate strength.

49
___
Rembrandt van Rijn, *Jacob's Bless-ing,* 1656. Oil. (Photo: Courtesy Staatliche Museen Kassel, Gemälde-galerie alte Meister.)

Rembrandt presents the moral di-lemmas surrounding the theft of primogeniture (Gen. 27:22–29). Through the plotting of Rebecca, the blind Isaac mistakenly blesses the smooth and handsome younger son, Jacob. Perhaps unconsciously, the patriarch pushes away the right-ful heir, the rough and unkempt Esau, to favor the beautiful usurper. The painter subtly immerses us in a tragedy that looks and feels differ-ent according to the greedy, oppor-tunistic, ignorant, or bereft points of view of its actors. The ethics of aesthetics emerges as the capacity to exhibit the inflections of human mo-tivation and nuanced desire from multiple intersecting and individ-ual perspectives.

III Aesthetical Ethics

Medical Ethics as Postmodern Aesthetics

9

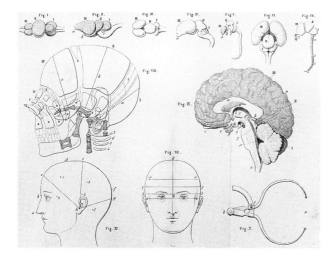

For over a decade, medicine has focused with almost preternatural intensity on a single organ, the brain. Neuroscience is among the fastest growing areas of biotechnology, spurred on by exotic new drugs and a sophisticated and rapidly advancing imaging science. As a powerful learning machine, the brain is emerging as an evolving, not static, body part. PET, MRI, and CT scanners reveal the cerebrum to be a constantly changing mass of cell connections. From the outset, scientific rhetoric has also yielded a remarkable number of metaphors, images, and visual theories transposed from the realm of aesthetics onto therapeutic practices.

Conversely, the new technology driving the neural sciences raises broad epistemological implications for nonscientific disciplines as well. Medicine's focus on the transparent head is postmodernist in its drastic *reformulation* of information about a formerly opaque body and its rupture of any utopian ideal of corporeal wholeness or sensory coherence. If to be modernist meant constructing a formal vocabulary that was clean, streamlined, in which representations looked abstract and were reconstructed from geometrical forms, to be postmodernist implies the figure-ground ambiguity of virtuality and the inter-twistings of hypervisible collage. William Gibson's science fiction novel *Neuromancer* (1984) anticipated the culture of the artificial and the patently false simulation now characterizing the global communications process in which the computer is the generating medium.[1]

Given the drifting and separating of organ from limbs, art historical perspective seems vital to a full understanding of brain research conducted in the era of opticalized media permeating the postmodern workspace, home, and hospital.[2] Although interfaces may resemble the

50

Karl Gustav Carus, *Frontal Hemisphere of the Brain,* from *Grundzüge der Cranioscopie,* 1841, pl. 1. (Photo: Courtesy Department of Special Collections, University of Chicago Library.)

Karl Gustav Carus, the physician-friend of Goethe, stimulated the nineteenth-century craze for morphological studies of all kinds. The physiognomic assessment of invisible mental powers from the visible face stretches back to antiquity. But calculating the mind's impact on the external geography of the head is a relatively recent phenomenon. From the Enlightenment onward, measuring intelligence became a matter of craniological and, eventually, physiological computation. Will MRI, CT, and PET scans similarly apply digital "calipers" to specific regions of the brain to predict its function and misfunction?

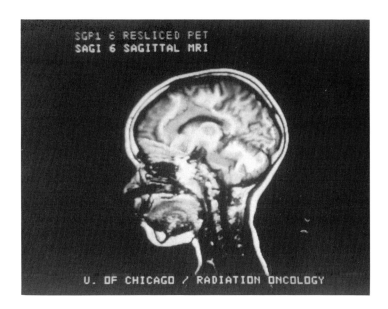

real world and apparently duplicate it, they only approximate physical actuality. Doctors and patients, like the rest of us, will need to make informed judgments about how the electronic information they increasingly rely upon only partially mimics somatic experience, even though it *looks* as if it is indistinguishable from that experience. Three related areas spring to mind where an art historical perspective might prove helpful to neuroscientists. First, the divisiveness of postmodernism has infused neuroscience with its fragmenting and distancing deconstructions of the body carried out with the aid of visualization apparatus. Electronic medical scans fetishize isolated parts of the anatomy (fig. 51). Second, mounting new economic pressures are affecting medical research in the postindividual era. As operating costs rise for health care agencies and health maintenance organizations, the value of the single consumer of such services becomes contested. Is there still room for the romantically autonomous person in the potentially alienating realm of global insurance corporations? Third, the loss of physician control over data, and the concomitant rise of "patient-centered measures of quality," is specifically linked to the accessibility of clinical records and statistics made available in visual form. What is an original or a copy, an authentic or inauthentic portrait of a suffering person? The ubiquity of reenacted information housed in public databases evokes the telling comparison to the perennial problem of forgeries.

51

PET image: sagittal view of the head. (Photo: Courtesy Maurice Goldblatt Magnetic Resonance Imaging Center, Department of Radiology, University of Chicago.)

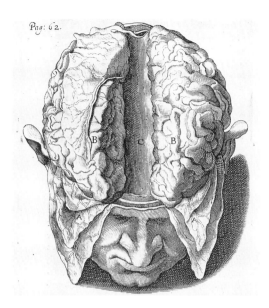

SHATTERED INSCAPE

Turning, first, to the beautiful but broken and polarized inscape projected by means of postmodern medical probes, the art historian sees not only the piling up of information but its contradictory clarity. The unsettling optical "amputation" of the brain from the torso leaves the mind strangely adrift, a chaotic sea of signs floating above an absent scaffold. This ironic dislocation of the control center from what it controls poses a fundamental and still unresolved question. What constitutes a balanced relationship between the body and the mind? Reconstructions apparently without internal life, bereft of recognizable evidence of anguish and pain, either remove the mind from its material circumstances or make the body immaterial.

Historically, anatomists from the Renaissance forward plumbed nature's depths by examining its individual elements. Peter Paaw in his engraving of the *Anterior Portion of the Brain* achieved the illusion of three-dimensionality by carving out a channel in the cerebrum (fig. 52).[3] This Vesalian technique of opening a severed head, removed from the pathos of the total human subject, continues in present-day MRI scans (fig. 53). Significantly, whereas the Dutch anatomist peeled back the skin to offer a glimpse of serene features, modern scientific setups excise or obliterate the face through an insistent transparency. The external envelope becomes overwhelmed by its internal components (see

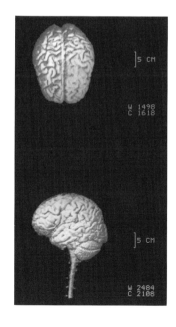

54

William Cowper, *Muscle Man,* from *An Anatomical Treatise on the Muscles of the Human Body,* 1724, pl. 12. Engraving. (Photo: Courtesy Department of Special Collections, University of Chicago Library.)

fig. 51). Then and now, technical mastery in scrutinizing and reproducing single organs raised questions about the absent corporeal context and how it might be included in a veristic depiction of the body. The British anatomist and surgeon William Cowper's etched *écorché,* or flayed figure, demonstrates one way in which brain and sinews could be integrated into a single living form (fig. 54).[4] Captured in full stride, the muscle man displays limbs and tendons in harmonious motion obviously coordinated by a directing intelligence.

Nonetheless, the question remains whether we are still heirs to a Cartesian dualism. Do we privilege the global sphere of concepts or abstractions and demote the significance of material physiology? At its extreme, as Ronald Dworkin has construed it in his analysis of "brain death," the empty body is identified with "the vegetative state" or "bare biological existence."[5] So in Alzheimer's disease, the dead nerve cells are associated with the higher cortical functions contributing to the human personality, leaving untouched the "vegetative" physiological functions. But consciousness cannot be so simplistically dualistic, since physicians often cite the courageous *physical* struggle of their patients when speaking of the horrible progressive atrophy of motor neurons in ALS. This subjective sign of nonbiological spirit, emotion, or will in the effort to move the lips, to breathe, to be understood suggests coordinated behavior that transcends the conventional dichotomies of an isolated brain and a disposable body.

VANISHING WORTH

To the initial, alienating issue of splitting apart mind from body can be added a second problem. What are the social values attached to these domains of immaterial thought and inanimate matter?[6] The term *value,* frequently used offhand, is an ambiguous concept. It covers etymological connotations of arcane mathematics, high finance, aesthetic worth, and profitable economics. Since the eighteenth century, value as a quantifiable property has dominated the realms of both ethics and aesthetics. Drawing, as an incisive medium for separating clear from confused, worthwhile from worthless phenomena, contributed to the dream of the mechanization of knowledge and the urge to compute cognition. Straight and curved lines possessed the normative imperative of statistics. Geometrical shapes were employed to create proper or improper models of mind. Deviance was pictured as the literal veering away from rectitude into obliqueness and diagonality. An antinomy was thus established between formal perfection and imperfection, measuring human value in graduated and quantifiable steps.[7]

The positing of reasonable states of mind can easily slide into norms made to transcend the merely subjective. Johann Caspar Lavater's *Essays on Physiognomy* attempted to establish a one-to-one correlation between the fixed anatomy of the face and intangible intelligence (fig. 55).[8] His twelve outline profiles of *Idiots,* like the illustrations to nineteenth-century craniological texts, theorized that the brain was the organ of the mind. In subsequent phrenological lucubrations, mental and emotional functions became localized in specific regions throughout the skull. Physiognomics had popularized the notion that hidden capacities could be "read" with great precision from the minute variations registered on the somatic surface. The legacy of these two pseudosciences continues today in talk of "structurally wrong" brains that presuppose an anatomically "normal" prototype. Stuart Yudofsky, formerly of the University of Chicago, foresees a developing genetics of schizophrenia permitting cellular and, eventually, molecular chemical and biological mediation. In this new neuropsychiatry, just as in Lavater's graphic diagnosis of idiocy or Gall's and Spurzheim's subdivided cranium, the danger looms that quantifiably "deviant" looks—whether external or internal—may be used to divine character, intelligence, and the propensity to genetic health or illness.[9] The implicit assumption is that clinical judgment can decide which human beings are valuable and which are not.

The specter of discrimination may well come to haunt the decade of the brain. The idea that one can picture the contrast between mental health and diseased or deformed thought is not farfetched. Indeed, the analogy colors the suggestion that medical imaging technologies reveal how brains, as embodiments of particular minds, are as unique as faces or thumbprints.[10] Scientists now suggest that bad parenting "stamps" an individual for his or her lifetime, not only in terms

55

Johann Caspar Lavater, *Twelve Faces of Idiots,* from *Essays on Physiognomy,* 1789–1798, III, pl. 1. Engraving. (Photo: Courtesy National Library of Medicine, Bethesda.)

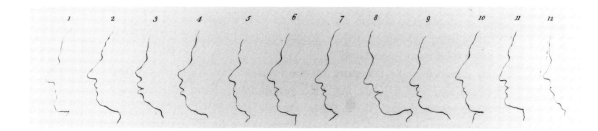

of a child's future behavior but literally in terms of the predisposition to disease. Brain research's redefinition of the roles of nature and nurture in learning disabilities is disturbingly couched in language reminiscent of physiognomic and phrenological theories.

A similar predictive component is found in the idea put forward by child development psychologists who claim that bad things like depression and epilepsy can be learned and are passed to the physical structure of brain cells. Far from abandoning Lavater's premise, they are suggesting that "different" brains, caused by poor environmental conditions, have a high risk of leading to a variety of cognitive, environmental, and emotional problems.[11] The identification of brain-impaired children within the first five years of their lives holds out the promise of interventions that "can change their brains right then and there." The ghost of Lombroso stands behind assertions that brain-imaging devices should be used to look for specific patterns of mental organization that may predispose a child to crime.[12]

Taking averages and calculating somatic deterioration or mental "deficits," as if they were commodities, erases the variations so crucial to individuality. When we think in multiples, it is easy to confer on the greater sum a reality that outweighs its variable and pathos-laden parts.[13] Significantly, today's ethical, epistemological, legal, and artistic fields are increasingly coming to resemble one another in the desire to save money. Enumeration is at the heart of a general process of monetary exchange. In the current climate of advertisement and consumerism, of countable dollars and finitely divisible goods, to ask what mental disorder or destruction costs is an equivocal question. Given the enormous complexity of medical decisions, specialists in health policy and management foresee a future in which physicians will have increasingly to think quantitatively. They must weigh explicitly the costs of procedures in making decisions and in formulating guidelines about whether to perform them.[14] There are already signs that such prophetic calculations are becoming a reality. Considerations of age, gender, and the genetic likelihood of a genetically induced disease are entering into employment and insurance decisions.

Questionable Originality

Computable relationships, entailing the loss of power over our lives, raises the issue of personal worth in another context.[15] The art historical concern with true or original works of art as opposed to bogus copies is pertinent to the examination of what constitutes a valuable, cohesive, and coherent human experience. The visibilization and projection of the interior of the body made possible by the new imaging processes enables the physician to discriminate authentic from counterfeit goods. The neurosciences also possess their connoisseurs, or masters of visual detection. They, too, judge healthy or diseased organisms through a process of mediated and mechanical observation susceptible to transformation and manipulation.

Information is now available to doctors at the touch of a keyboard, but it will also be used by expert panels of the future to analyze the pros and cons of different strategies and the medical entitlements of diverse claimants. The art historical dialogue concerning forgery[16] is instructive in this regard because biomedical specialists and, increasingly, sophisticated consumers will be asked to judge differences in visual evidence. It is all the more important, then, to realize that computers do not make objects; they process information. Any reproduction, whether of a work of art, a human being, or a natural object, fails to capture some properties of the original. Chérubim d'Orléans's *Observation of the Lunar Disk,* which depicts instrument-armed *putti* measuring, inscribing, and drawing the pocked face of the moon, offers poignant testimony to the slippage between desired accuracy and actual record (fig. 56).[17]

56

François-Saneré Chérubim d'Or-léans, *Observation of the Lunar Disk,* from *La dioptrique oculaire,* 1671, pl. 37. Engraving. (Photo: Courtesy Herzog August Bibliothek, Wolfenbüttel.)

It is precisely those nontransmittable qualities, the other side of the moon of all phenomena, that may prove vital to their understanding.[18] Furthermore, the scanned, screened, or electronically probed human body and its segmentable parts are serial images or replicas. As marvelous as the noninvasive modern imaging procedures are, we should remember that the virtual person—reconstructed from his or her digitized, "sliced," and "resliced" simulations—is the descendant of a venerable print world and its reproductive practices and analogies. This modern graphic commerce, as in Chérubim's engraving, made multiple representations out of a unique object, and flat impressions out of a volumetric body. On the positive side, however, since people are organic processes, not physiognomical or phrenological fixities, a sequence of digital images in real time may offer a better graphic modality than photographs for capturing complexly evolving human beings. Like a print series, PET and MRI scans are capable of registering developing persons caught in a changing cognitive space.

METAPHORS OF REPRODUCTION

The brain enjoys some metaphorically interesting bedfellows. What has made it amenable to tropes of anonymity, such as Stuart Yudofsky's rebaptism or reconceptualization of schizophrenia as a neutral "brain illness" rather than as a stigmatizing "mental disorder"? Then there is the rhetoric of industrial management, talking about the head's control of inner and outer spaces. This corporate language separates the mind from the body, painting a picture of the brain as a lofty, hierarchical, and bureaucratic command center issuing orders to the lowly physiology through a system of ever more far-flung networks. The negative picture of mental failure, breakdown, and dissolution seems based on the same model. The brain as a superior regulator exists above or apart from the body it regulates (see figs. 51, 53). Reflecting the global language of multinational business, the computer-mind is also conceived in terms of high performance and tireless productivity.[19] Perhaps most strikingly, in biogenetics and the new birth technologies, the brain and the fetus have recently emerged as public spectacles—as prime examples of the computer's power to turn the body inside out—taking the most private and intimate of inward recesses (the center of the mind, the cavity of the uterus) and displaying them openly. The comparison is not farfetched. Childlessness and infertility have aroused the same diagnostic expectations of, and provoked analogous social pressures on, the medical profession as have those surrounding mindlessness and conceptual infertility.

Gulielmus Harveus
de
Generatione Animalium.

57

William Harvey, *The Cosmic Egg,*
from *Exercitationes de generatione ani-*
malium, 1651, frontispiece. Engraving. (Photo: Courtesy National
Library of Medicine, Bethesda.)

Hubert Markl, president of the Deutschen Forschungsge-
meinschaft and professor of biology at the University of Konstanz, drew
attention to the shared root of the words *gene, genus, gender, generation,*
and *genius.* As an international spokesman for more humanistic biosci-
ences, he connects such terms to "the actual enlivening principle, the
genuine core of any being."[20] Indeed, the old pun on "concept" and
"conception" plays on the relation between the authentic "child of the
mind" and the precious fetus in the womb.[21] The analogy is based on
the belief that thought propagates our most personal and original substance, if not our very identity. Similarly, as the famous seventeenth-
century epigeneticist William Harvey recognized, every birth releases
a new, genetically unique organism into the stream of history (fig. 57).
Zeus cracks the cosmic egg from which all animals symbolically issue.

As Leon Kass eloquently wrote, living things "seek to transcend
their own isolation, particularity, and impermanence, through awareness, communication and, above all, through reproduction."[22] Creative
thought and physical procreation, then, return us both figuratively and
literally to the idea that people are complexly intertwisted spiritual and
physical beings. Metaphors that marry the activities of the mind with
those of the body serve, in the face of reductive efforts, as reminders of
the fact that we are compounded of psychology and biology, of thinking
and feeling matter. We are ideas incarnate or thoughtful flesh.

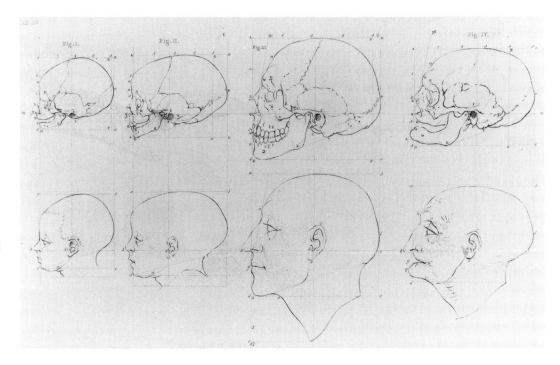

While the specter of desubstantialization and decontextualization haunts the neurosciences, denaturalization imperils biogenetics.[23] Arguably, just as we have an ideal in our society of a flawlessly executing brain, we also have expectations of a premium baby. Markl cautions against a new fundamentalist biologism that seeks to attribute to the genome the essential and almost mystical capacity for predetermining the emergent organism.[24] Here, again, the early modern period provides a pertinent instantiation of his fear. The great Dutch anatomist Petrus Camper's measurement of the facial angle in diverse races and at various moments of biological development (fig. 58) led to nineteenth-century racist speculations.[25]

Markl's caution that the human being is more than the sum of his or her genes is thus apt. We could say the same about the autonomy of the brain. Think about the broad relevance of the distinguished biologist's observation at the most practical laboratory level. *In vitro* fertilization separates the egg and sperm from their natural containers, just as the head and its internal hardware seem increasingly removed from their originary site in modern neuroscience. IVF, artificial insemination, embryo freezing and transfer, and gamete intrafallopian transfer depersonalize us in the most personal areas.[26] Embryonic sex selection, polymerase chain reaction, and preimplantation genetics peer into the more minute and fragmented microdomain of preconception. These prenatal procedures isolate reproduction from natural behaviors and seem to offer tantalizing, if unanalyzed, dreams of fashioning future populations. Gene splicing, computerized prosthetic systems, and cybernetic implants also raise the specter of eugenics. In the quest for the best or the perfect person, science risks bypassing nature and its practice of mixing up genetic material to produce human beings that are uniquely different.

These technologies also conjure up the atomistic schizophrenia of postmodernist culture, in which living people are metamorphosed into Duchampian readymades. In a postbiological utopia, where the contents of a person can be downloaded into a robot, human beings might well become fragmentary assemblages of engineered parts. These bits might collide with one another but never form an integrated whole. Norman Cook, in *The Brain Code,* exposes the unarticulated values of mastery and dominance adhering to phrases such as "split-brain" research and "hemispheric specialization." Cook attacks the autocratic and uncooperative image of the brain as the repository of all thoughts, noting that such a polarizing paradigm stretches back to the seventeenth-century theories of Descartes and Willis. But he finds equally objectionable the contemporary hierarchical two-brains, two-selves view. According to this model, the superior left hemisphere deals with the realm of abstract thought, while the right hemisphere remains locked in its sensory field and directs the inferior nonlinguistic skills.[27]

Needless to say, for anyone dealing with images as a serious source of cognition, Cook's argument that verbal-spatial dichotomies are not only unhelpful but inaccurate is refreshing![28] He has suggested that the corpus callosum, the largest single nerve track in the human nervous system, not only connects the cortices of the two hemispheres but aids in the integration and flow of information between the two. His larger aim, developed more recently by Jerre Levy, is to tie together psychological and physiological data according to a model of an intact and collaborative brain.[29] Cook is optimistic that a unitary paradigm can transcend the dualism that has characterized thinking about our brains and bodies. Future investigation, he argues, ought to look toward the horizontal and complementary intercortical aspects of brain function and ask how the hemispheres interact.[30]

58

Petrus Camper, *Facial Angle in Children and the Elderly,* from *Dissertation physique: Traits du visage,* 1791, pl. 5. Engraving. (Photo: Courtesy National Library of Medicine, Bethesda.)

59

Honoré Daumier, *A Superstitious Father-to-Be,* n.d. Hand-colored lithograph. (Photo: Courtesy National Library of Medicine, Bethesda.)

METAPHORS OF DECONSTRUCTION

Cook seems in his work to be raising a more general cultural and educational problem, involving science and not just medical science. In spite of our information-oriented society, no one appears to see the whole anymore.[31] Myriad health care agencies, plural insurers, multiple specialists, armies of lawyers, and a spate of replicating technologies have parcelized and caricatured the identity of the patient. He or she provides a map of competing scientific expertise, a picture of the uneven distribution of power and knowledge in which no one wishes to assume responsibility for the totality. Like a Daumier "charged" lithograph or "loaded" drawing, in which a single feature or trait is exaggerated at the expense and even annihilation of the whole (fig. 59), the picture of the patient in modern medicine depends on the point of view of the expert: to the neurosurgeon, we are all brain; to the geneticist, an alphabet of microscopic genes and spliceable DNA; to the obstetrician, a womb pregnant with monstrosity. Daumier's freakish family, visiting the ape cage at the Parisian Jardin des Plantes, visualizes the hazards of reproduction, the abnormalities that depart from an ideal norm.

The vanishing relationship between corporeal segments and coherent whole is also mirrored in the increasing commodification of body parts. The marketability of dismemberings is accompanied by the growth of regulation and the loss of personal control; we store, retrieve, and purchase somatic fragments in the belief that they can regenerate life and thought. Our computerized culture has not resolved the formal problem, familiar to the early history of writing, of the relation of excisable disparate data to its original source, and the potential for manipulation, or even erasure, of bits and pieces of information.[32]

METAPHORS OF ELUSIVE AUTHENTICITY

I conclude with an example of the nearly universal phenomenon of artistic faking. The medical lesson to be learned from optical deception in the visual arts consists, I think, in the revelation of a common psychological reaction. When exposed, bogus pictures are often dismissed as nothing more than superficial likenesses.[33] In retrospect, the phony simulation is judged to lack intellectual depth, the inexpressible or invisible properties of the real thing shaped by an original mind. Subjective visual judgment is called into question by supposedly objective machinery. In scientific visualization processes, whether used to probe the pigment layers of a painting or the flesh and bone of the human body, attention is transferred from the recognition of visible surface qualities—now deemed deluding—to penetrating devices assumed to be free of illusion. Technological testing, regarded as if it were uncontaminated by human consciousness and history, forms a stark contrast to earlier, and admittedly imperfect, forms of clinical practice that relied on the physical observation and tactile examination of suffering communicated through gestures, body movements, and deformity (fig. 60). By contrast, reason-extending apparatus supposedly ferrets out questionable aesthetic and biological signs invisible to the unassisted and fallible eye.

Underlying this depreciation of optical surfaces was a system of metaphysical values that condemned the pride of expert craftsmen in their tangible handiwork. Skilled artisans, like clinicians and physicians, possessed the manual ability to restore damaged or impaired

60

Cornelis Stalpart van der Wiel, *Physician's Office,* from *Observationum rariorum,* 1687. Woodcut. (Photo: Courtesy National Library of Medicine, Bethesda.)

works retrieved in mutilated condition from the past. Restoration, with its occasion for sleights-of-hand, suggests an additional comparison. There is a fundamental analogy between the absence of touch found in mechanically mediated works of art and the practice of projecting human beings on screens. To distinguish the false from the real, the variant from the type, the copy from the original, we require ever finer and brainier analyses that dismember the work into smaller and smaller parts. As in the notorious Rembrandt Project, a battery of assaulting tests, not unlike those plumbing the pathology of the hospitalized patient, search for reliable symptoms of authenticity in Rembrandt's disputed corpus of paintings. Considerations of facture and content disappear in the hyperinflated and expensive mechanical dazzle.

This quest for certain evidence of the hidden mind of the artist, or the concealed and elusive cause of a disease, returns me to my initial question concerning the overestimation of the cerebral. Microscopic ultraviolet- or X-radiograph examination, infrared reflectography, thread counts, material and isotropic analyses, and dating by radiocarbon, dendrochronological, and thermoluminescent methods all perpetuate a distrust of appearances. These apparatus are dedicated to unearthing the invisible mark of falseness that proves the visible work a fake. Does this quest for abnormal signs not resemble the scanning of brains for deluding structures and specious functions masquerading as health? "Intelligent" equipment, however, cannot prevent us from taking something for what it is not, whether in art or in medicine.[34]

Picturing Ambiguity

10

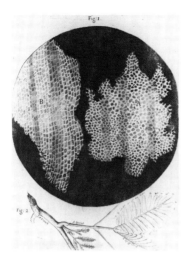

Magnification drives to the center of a major aesthetic problem faced by all natural history description. What do you do with beings that are neither one thing nor the other? To the eighteenth century, a bizarre geography of "betwixt and between" seemed particularly characteristic of the universe observed in its greatest vertical descent. Microscopic organisms, as literal pictures of ambiguity, opened an enticing realm of equivocal biota to scholarly and popular audiences.[1] Their liminality was conveyed in entertaining transparencies and slides (fig. 62). As I hope to show, much of the Enlightenment understanding of the complicated processes of growth, nutrition, and reproduction depended upon dynamic representations of tiny biological systems. These animated molecular "no-bodies" could not be effectively described in words. The paradox posed by complex and contradictory "invisibles" was that their intricate, and obviously compounded, look rendered them apparently unclassifiable. This meant that illuminating metaphors had to be drawn from supposedly better demarcated epistemological areas.

Conspicuously mixed microorganisms were regarded as living grotesques (fig. 63). Their ill-assorted animal and vegetable components helped in the long run to break down the conceptual hegemony of the integral human body and loosened the grip of anthropocentrism. By their incongruity, they startled the spectator into paying attention to aspects of reality that had formerly been taken for granted or ignored. This trend toward the dissolution of a standardized or normative organic coherence was offset, however, in the second half of the century by a neoclassical emphasis on the strict examination of the perplexing separate parts. Like the human countenance in physiognomic scrutiny,

61

Robert Hooke, *Microscopic "Cells" of Cork,* from *Micrographia,* 1667, observ. 18, p. 112. (Photo: Courtesy National Library of Medicine, Bethesda.)

The microscope subverted the norm of lucid, coherent, and stable bodies. While this popular instrument transformed ordinary items, such as Robert Hooke's magnified cork cells, into mysterious and beguiling images, it could as easily explode attractive forms into repugnant or nonresembling patterns. The equivocal nature of information gleaned from optical apparatus, rendering the insignificant significant and the worthwhile worthless, also reveals how easily the observer's perception might become confused. What appeared clear and distinct to the naked eye was exposed as chaotic or flawed under the lens.

62

August Johann Rösel von Rosenhof, *Frogs' Eggs and Tadpoles,* from *Historia naturalis,* 1758, pl. 2. Hand-colored engraving. (Photo: Courtesy Department of Special Collections, University of Chicago Library.)

63

John Ellis, *Actinia or Animal-Flower,* from *Natural History of Zoophytes,* 1786, pl. 1. Engraving by James Kirk after Georg Ehret. (Photo: Courtesy Department of Special Collections, University of Chicago Library.)

or the brain in phrenological analysis, minutiae were parcelized into their specific organs and functions.[2]

The anthropologist Victor Turner remarked that the study of such confusing phenomena in mid-transition, before the imposition of a definitive structure, exposes the basic building blocks of the culture to which they belong.[3] Retooling that hypothesis, I find that the examination of these kinetic shapes in which a coincidence of opposites can be discerned allows us to enter a past, and otherwise inaccessible, mentality. Research into heterogeneous zoophytes, minute creatures that were neither this nor that, revealed the distress of their investigators. Natural philosophers were constantly obliged to revise definitions, establish new orders, or extend old ones to accommodate recently discovered organisms, especially of the marine variety.[4] But the more outrageous and improbable they were, the greater the delight these denizens of an apparently impossible world provoked in a public hungry for "recreative philosophy."[5] Microscopic images belonged to a new and amusing sensory technology dedicated to the creation of optical illusions that strained credibility. Magnifications joined sorcerer's mirrors, concealed magic lanterns, and machines for projecting phantoms on smoke in making things appear as they were not.[6] Paradoxically, by placing such "visual lies"[7] in the hands of everyone who could afford them, these enlightened technologists hoped to unmask perceptual fraud.

There was an important class of illustrated popular science compendium—stretching from della Porta and Ozanam in the seventeenth century to Guyot, Ledermüller, and Hooper in the eighteenth—whose purpose was to offer "instructive entertainment" by transforming mathematical, physical, or abstruse learning into seductive spectacle. For these educational reformers, knowledge was "not dull, tedious, and disgustful, not rugged and perplexing, not austere and imperious, but facile, bland, delightful, alluring, captivating." According to the English physician and translator William Hooper's *Rational Recreations* (1774), "sober philosophy" must be led by "the hand of the sportive nymph Imagination, decked in all the glowing evervarying Colours of the Skies."[8] A common theme of such literature was rational enlightenment through the pleasing demonstration of the uncertainty of the senses.

Like many of the popularizing microscopic manuals, such works were intended for "the rising generation." (But neither did they exclude "the jaded, those who have given themselves up to the passions, sensuality, or wretched hankering of enjoyments [they] can no longer attain.")⁹ Even more conventional and overtly "serious" pedagogical treatises extolled the visualization of knowledge¹⁰ as best appealing to, and fostering, the curiosity of children. The Scottish moral philosopher George Turnbull's *Observations upon Liberal Education* (1742) reminded the teacher and parent that the young were mental "travellers." These innocent voyagers are "newly arrived in a strange country, and . . . it is cruel not to give them all the information we can, and much crueler still to deceive and mislead them."¹¹ Consequently, he recommended coming "down" to the level of their capacity. His opinion that children were pleased and delighted with knowledge supported the ends of the popular science text. The latter, too, was dedicated to the prevention of youthful abandonment to silly pastimes that would eventually lead to adult indolence.

I

For Turnbull, all human inquiry was reducible to two questions. What is it? What is it for?¹² These quintessential queries return us to the consideration of an infinity of tiny animals invisible to ordinary eyes. Louis Joblot's typically multiple-purpose production, the *Descriptions et usages de plusieurs nouveaux microscopes,* was completed in 1718 and reissued in a revised, posthumous second edition in 1754.¹³ It was intended to introduce a broad and mixed public to the strange but appealing dimension inhabited by infusoria. This professor of mathematics at the Parisian Royal Academy of Painting immodestly proclaimed that both his lenses and his observations would prove useful and enjoyable to doctors, surgeons, physicists, anatomists, chemists, as well as painters, engravers, manufacturers of mathematical instruments, jewelers, medal-casters, antiquarians, epigraphers, and clock and spectacle-makers! The first in a long line of distinguished French microscopists,¹⁴ he had been inspired by Huyghens and Hartsoeker's Parisian demonstrations of their optical instruments before the Academy of Sciences in the summer of 1668. Joblot's significance, however, was not limited to making improvements on existing Dutch technology. His true importance, as the intellectual precursor of Pasteur, lay in the study and illustration of protozoa. The *Descriptions,* accompanied by twenty-two plates engraved by Lucas, was the initial treatise devoted to these novel and singular "animalcules" growing in cold infusions (fig. 64). He himself drew, with the aid of a *porte-loupe* of his own design, this multitude "walking, creeping & swimming in prepared liquors, & even in those that were not."¹⁵

64
Louis Joblot, *Infusoria and Infusion of Royal Anemones,* from *Descriptions et usages de plusieurs nouveaux microscopes,* 1718, pl. 6. Engraving by Lucas. (Photo: Courtesy Department of Special Collections, University of Chicago Library.)

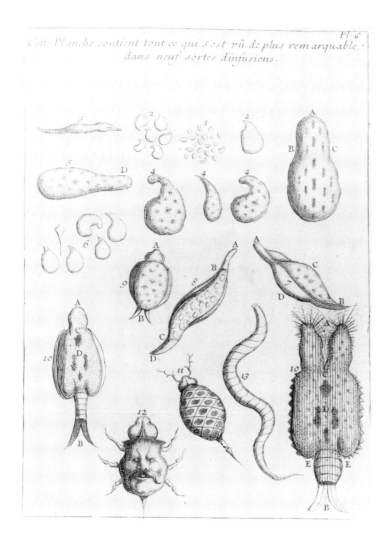

Cett Planche contient tout ce qui s'est vû de plus remarquable dans neuf sortes d'infusions.

The early date of Joblot's publication is significant, for it allows us to witness the beginnings of what would become a continual struggle with nomenclature. The sensational aspect of infusoria, such as a colony of *Royal Anemones,* spawned a visual encyclopedia of witty monsters and an ingenious rococo vocabulary of decorative hybrids. Joblot's terminology revealed a quiet desperation. The elusive and mixed-up nature of what he beheld was captured in such Watteauesque objects as "Bagpipes," "Ovals," "Aquatic Caterpillars," "Tufted Hens," "Kidneys," "Blindmen," "Pirouetters," "Gluttons" (*les Goulus*), "Vacillators" (*Inconstants*), "Buffoons," and "Swells" (*Elégans*).[16]

But it was an international group of midcentury microscopists who transformed this ornamental miscellany into a kind of art botany under the lens. Henry Baker's research into "the minutiae" was part of an educational campaign to get the investigation of "numberless species" of imperceptible creatures out of the hands of the "very Few." The latter had made "a Secret" of the microscopic, and had "endeavoured all they could to keep it to themselves; and when it became a little more publick, the Price was fixt so high that the most Curious and Industrious who have not always the greatest Share of Money could not conveniently get at it."[17] Although, now, the expense was less, the natural historian worried that many people were still frightened away by thinking it required a great skill in optics. The *Microscope Made Easy* (1742) thus took pains to be short, "intelligible and pleasant," in order to guarantee that the book would not be laid aside. The populist image of the microscopist that Baker conveyed was not of Joblot's aristocratic orchestrator of a comic *fête galante,* but of the pedestrian botanist gathering specimens in an ordinary field. "Living Wonders," or equivocal "Invisibles," were collected in the scum floating on pepper-water, in the slime of ditches, ponds, and "almost every Puddle." Rural tropes of a swarming and fertile terrain were also extended in a downward perspective. To a nativist and regionalist eye, the concave glass reveled the tiny and indigenous tenants of a miniature farm in a sort of miniature English landscape. Baker trained his gaze on the "surprising" animalcules that Leeuwenhoek had originally discovered adhering to the roots of duckweed, a humble vegetation that floated on the surface of stagnating pools in summer. He was amazed to see its tiny and rapacious parasite—in the form of bells, sheaths, or cases—incongrously festooned with "wheels." The latter were equipped "with a great many Teeth or Notches" that could be withdrawn at the least touch.[18]

Such hybrid metaphors were also deemed necessary to explain phenomena considered, under normal circumstances, to be inherently stable. When, for example, the "invisible particles" in *Amber Salt Crystals* were heated and magnified, they metamorphosed into a succession of combinatorial views (fig. 65). Baker charted the serial unfolding of a Gilpinesque topography in which "pretty Shootings," sprigs of fir or yew, and the downy feathers of a bird divided and subdivided until they painted "a Winter Scene of Trees without Leaves."[19] Before Ruskin, then, Baker devised an "aesthetics of the vegetable world"[20] that he transposed onto fundamental, but ambivalent, animate and inanimate structures.

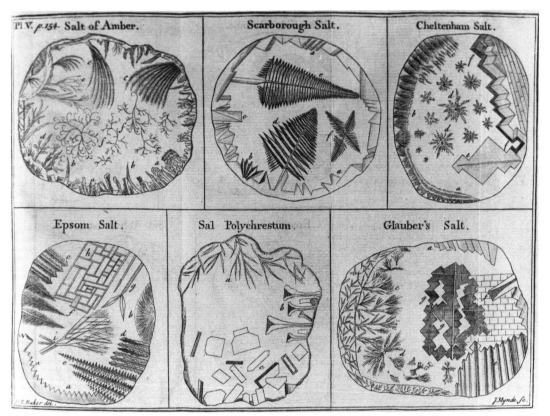

65
—
Henry Baker, *Salt of Amber and Other Crystals,* from *The Microscope Made Easy,* 1744, II, pl. 5, p. 154. Engraving by J. Mynde. (Photo: Courtesy Department of Special Collections, University of Chicago Library.)

This strategy of unframing, or of liberating substances from the confines of their categories, was by no means unusual. The Austrian microscopist Wilhelm Friedrich Gleichen-Russworm, active at Schloss Greifenstein, made the observation of crystal formation central to the study of the processes of fertilization in plants and animals. The *Dissertation sur la génération,* first published in German in 1778, introduced the use of phagocytic staining to render invisible tissue visible (fig. 66).[21] In order to study the feeding of a colony of ciliates, he added water dyed with carmine to an infusion of oats and observed the subsequent coloring of the food vacuoles. Connected to this desire to see complex imperceptible patterns were his equally unusual observations made on dried sperm taken from a wide range of animals (fig. 67). When the transparent globules evaporated and clotted, he remarked that the "spermatic animalcules" assumed, under the enhancing glass, the floral organization of ammonia and salt crystals.[22] This flow of transformations from one domain into another can be illuminated by Gleichen-Russworm's investigation of drifting pollen. The continuous release of minuscule, fecundating particles must have convinced him that the design of the genetic world was similarly botanical, and depended upon analogous male "germs" circulating in the blood and fertilizing the female.[23]

Supporting the underlying notion that all hard-edged boundaries might be dissolved was the theory that all things were related and thus could be transformed into one another. In this Leibnizian and Neoplatonizing philosophy, everything was in a state of becoming, and change merely affected the appearances of bodies, not the unknowable bedrock of their essence. Macroscopic and microscopic life alike was developmental, easily turning from solid to liquid to gas. Generation was continuous motion from seed to bud to blossom to dust, or from unformed to formed and then back again. John Turberville Needham, a major warrior in the polyp controversy of the 1740s, actively proselytized on behalf of this vitalistic principle of universal analogy. Microscopy convinced him that there was much uniformity throughout nature's ascent and descent, embracing "the whole Scale of visible Beings . . . but also the Subordination of Worlds." In his *Account of Some New Microscopical Discoveries* (1745), he declared that, if observations into the minute realm advanced, his hypothesis of cosmic similarity would be confirmed. In time, we would come to see "that the peculiar Inhabitants of several Portions of matter often bear a near Resemblance to each other, tho' they differ extreamly in Magnitude." The likeness

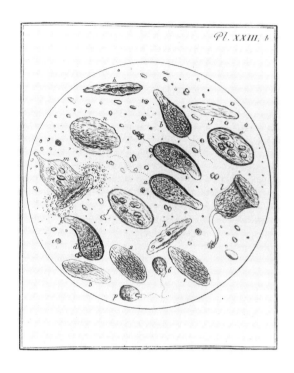

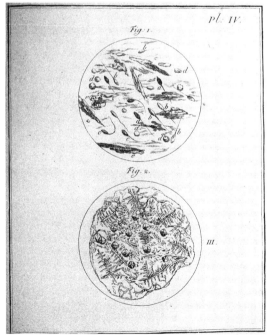

66
―
Wilhelm-Friedrich Gleichen, called
Russworm, *Phagocytic Staining,* from
Dissertation sur la génération, 1798–9,
pl. 23. Hand-colored engraving by
Rose. (Photo: Courtesy Department
of Special Collections, University of
Chicago Library.)

67
―
Wilhelm-Friedrich Gleichen, called
Russworm, *Fresh and Crystallized
Asses' Sperm,* from *Dissertation sur la
génération,* 1798–9, pl. 4. Hand-
colored engraving. (Photo: Courtesy
Department of Special Collections,
University of Chicago Library.)

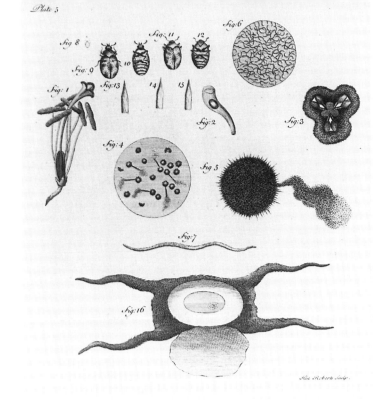

68

John Turberville Needham, *"Foerina Foecundans" in the Common Lily and in the Eggs of the Thornback Fish,* from *An Account of Some New Microscopical Discoveries,* 1745, pl. 5. Engraving by Henry Robert. (Photo: Courtesy Department of Special Collections, University of Chicago Library.)

between animal and vegetable (fig. 68), and its supposed source in an "identical Point of Matter," spurred him to colonize an empire that was not yet accessible to sight. Although the extremes of large and small were "immensely distant" from one another, he thought it not unreasonable to suppose "that the whole Sphere of our Knowledge from known Objects of the greatest Dimensions to the minutest microscopical Animalcules, a Million of which are less than a Grain of Sand, would appear but a Point, if it could be compared with the real Bounds of Nature, as much as a little Ant-Hill in the supposition of reasonable Emmets would appear to the Inhabitants upon Comparison, an Infinitesimal of the terraqueous Globe." [24]

This sense of endless cycle, of eternal brooding, and of a teeming earth also characterized the work of Needham's contemporary, the zoologist and botanist John Hill. He claimed that microscopy taught him "that every cavity in every solid body lying under water is a recess for some animal or another; and many to a thousand different kinds." Hill exhorted the reader of his *Essays in Natural History and Philosophy*

(1752) to remember that "the several Folds of the Oyster-Shells, the spiral Hollowings of the Wilks, and other turbinated Shells, the longitudinal Furrows of the Cochlea and the very Species of the Murex, which have Them foliated and hollow, are all while the several Shells are in the Sea inhabited by Numbers of Animalcules."[25] His medical training impelled him to examine that fraction of the universe wherein he could discover not "the Forms and Outsides only of Things," but their ordinarily hidden "internal Qualities." Hill's preferred field of vision encompassed those ambivalent sea substances now confounded with animals, now mistaken for vegetables or minerals. Relying on a geographical metaphor of vertical expansion, he declared that the conchineal, polyp, and kermes, watched through the aggrandizing lens, brought "unbounded Treasures" into sight, and allowed the explorer of the subvisible to "step into the most distant Tract of its Territories."[26]

But the foremost student of such perplexing sea organisms as corals, sponges, millepores, and madrepores was John Ellis. This distinguished scientist and Fellow of the Royal Society came to the examination of the minutely segmented and celled creatures dwelling in the world's oceans through an interest in botany. Not coincidentally, Sir Joseph Banks was responsible for having his monumental *Natural History of Zoophytes, Collected from Various Parts of the Globe* catalogued by Daniel Solander and published posthumously in 1786. Ellis's earlier accounts of coffee, designed to "encourage the consumption of that article," and of the mangostan and breadfruit trees, printed "with the view to introduce them into our own settlements,"[27] anticipated the creation of this subscale and underwater florilegium. His discovery that several subjects arranged by natural historians under the title of "Marine Vegetables" were, in fact, "Animal Productions," dated, however, to 1756. In that year, he composed the popular *Essay towards a Natural History of British and Irish Corallines,* which was immediately translated into French. After this initial success, he continued to dive "deeper into the hidden treasures of nature" and was supplied, through the king's agents, with specimens form the West Indies, the Pacific, and "from the most distant Countries."

Significantly, the dispute as to whether corals and keratophytes were animals or plants decentered both kingdoms by calling any hard and fast boundaries between them into question (fig. 69). The margins of both domains dissolved and the identity of the inhabitants literally fell apart, the one centrifugally intruding into the looks and the behavior of the other. These living ambiguities obeyed William

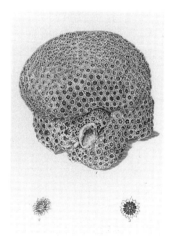

69

John Ellis, *Madrepora Rotulosa,* from *Natural History of Zoophytes,* 1786, pl. 55. Engraving. (Photo: Courtesy Department of Special Collections, University of Chicago Library.)

John Ellis, *Madrepora Cineracens,* from *Natural History of Zoophytes,* 1786, pl. 43. Drawn and engraved by James Barnes. (Photo: Courtesy Department of Special Collections, University of Chicago Library.)

John Ellis, *Madrepora Lactuca,* from *Natural History of Zoophytes,* 1786, pl. 44. Engraving. (Photo: Courtesy Department of Special Collections, University of Chicago Library.)

James's "law of dissociation," whereby what was first associated with one thing and then with another tended to become dissociated from either, and grew into a separate object of contemplation.[28] It was Cuff's aquatic microscope that enabled this relocation from one realm to another, convincing Ellis that corallines should be ranked among animals, not plants. But when he followed the method of preservation invented by the famous Berlin botanist Buttner, and spread some especially beautiful specimens on white paper "such that they formed a sort of landscape," he discovered that they could be described only through botanical analogies. Pine, sea moss, fern, cypress, thistle, lily of the valley, daisy, fig, and marigold had to be imported from the level, so to speak, in order to do justice to the subtlety of the submerged animal-plants, with their myriad filaments and ramifications (fig. 70).[29]

The *Natural History* was filled with equivocal beings ranging from the common *Hydra vulgaris,* or freshwater "polyp of the Ditches," gaily bedecked with a riot of "flowers," to the exotic blooms of the *Cellaria,* that "animal growing in the form of a plant." Then there were those zoophytes known as "Bird's-Head" coralline, and picturesque madrepores, sending forth their progeny in the shape of branches or lettuce (fig. 71). The underside of the *Asterias echinites,* or starfish, when magnified, revealed thorny spines resembling those of the rose, and locked into similar sockets (figs. 72–74).[30] This submarine Eden, however, also had its grimmer features. The mottled and spotted surface of some varieties elicited darker, dermatological tropes that further decontextualized the object under scrutiny. Thus *Flustra,* or *Teges,* the sea mat (fig. 75), had formerly been called *Eschara,* a term used in surgery, signifying the crust on the flesh arising from the wound of a burn. (In renam-

72

John Ellis, *Asterias Echinites,* from *Natural History of Zoophytes,* 1786, pl. 60. Engraving. (Photo: Courtesy Department of Special Collections, University of Chicago Library.)

73

John Ellis, *Underside of the Asterias Echinites,* from *Natural History of Zoophytes,* 1786, pl. 61. Engraving. (Photo: Courtesy Department of Special Collections, University of Chicago Library.)

ing it, Ellis rebaptized this pathological lamination into a pleasing silken weaving or basketwork.)[31] Nevertheless, there were other examples testifying to the persistance of a cutaneous semiology of sprouts, dots, and points.[32] Growths, such as Sea-Hair, Bottle-Brush, Sea-Beard, Sea-Bristle, vied with "Pimpled," helmet-shaped "bullae," or "Dodder-like" excrescences.[33]

These descriptive and graphic efforts to grapple with the diversity of rough texture and stigmatization encountered in the exploration of the deep were a reminder of the contemporaneous struggle to standardize the language of skin disease. The eighteenth-century founders of dermatology drew upon a monstrous garden of pustulance to fashion the image of an antiparadise, the painful and disorderly geography of contagion (fig. 76). Somatic flowers of evil were the uncontrollable staples of this perverse agronomy. Metaphors of miscultivation aided Robert Willan in his heroic attempt at classifying the bewildering tangle of epidermal disorders. His *On Cutaneous Diseases* (1798), the first illustrated book devoted to the subject, was a terrifying *corpora* of sponge, scurf, and scale, of the body's rank and weedy vegetation. Patches, maculae, crescents, horseshoes, and rings of psoriasis, efflorescences of prickly heat, lichen of papulae, exfoliations of scabs, eruptions of red rashes, welts, and tubercles, constituted a grotesque botany of the deviant and deformed plane.[34] Ellis's pocked and pitted marine organisms certainly did not possess the morbid aspect of Willan's speckled human integument (fig. 77). Yet, importantly, their variously figured and uneven casings posed a problem similar to that faced by the categorizer of mottled appearances.[35] Moreover, like the invisible or subcutaneous funguses that were the source of visibly peculiar skin

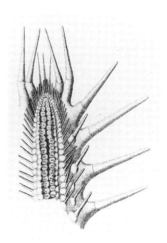

74

John Ellis, *Magnified Spine of the Asterias Echinites,* from *Natural History of Zoophytes,* 1786, pl. 62. Engraving. (Photo: Courtesy Department of Special Collections, University of Chicago Library.)

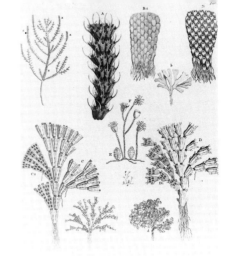

75

John Ellis, *Sea Mats,* from *Natural History of Zoophytes,* 1786, pl. 4. Engraving. (Photo: Courtesy Department of Special Collections, University of Chicago Library.)

76

Thomas Bateman (after Robert Willan), *Psoriasis Gyrata,* from *Delineations of Cutaneous Diseases,* 1815, pl. 12. Colored engraving. (Photo: Courtesy National Library of Medicine, Bethesda.)

Psoriasis gyrata

77

John Ellis, *Madrepora Fascicularis,*
from *Natural History of Zoophytes,*
1786, pl. 30. Drawn and engraved
by James Roberts. (Photo: Courtesy
Department of Special Collections,
University of Chicago Library.)

marks, these bizarre underwater forests also beckoned the scientific
traveler to dip below the obvious tide. Consequently, and obeying the
ubiquitous eighteenth-century law of analogy, botanical terms and
images helped to coordinate the more established study of microscopy
with the developing science of dermatology. Both supremely visionary
endeavors depended upon an optical roaming over unusual and discontinuous physical territory. Both required the interpretation of singular
scenery witnessed superficially and, then, pierced *in profundis.* This
halving of the visual field into exterior and interior was predicated on
a horticultural model of overt bud and covert root.

II

The tolerance for mediating links in the Great Chain of Being was, like the Chain itself, not to last. Scientists increasingly abandoned a world constituted along the plan of "as if," or "not yet," for that of "either/or." The assault on those natural historians who believed in hybrids came from self-proclaimed exacting observers who were not fooled by the allure of the initial aspect. Thus the Abbé Dicquemare's aptly entitled "Dissertation sur les limites des règnes de la nature" (1776) denounced the advocates of the animal-vegetable collage. Deceived by mere looks, they thought "imperceptible nuances" supported the existence of novel, in-between beings. According to the aesthetics of the neoclassical era, to which he evidently subscribed, the idea that the three kingdoms added up to a harmonious whole was not incompatible with the fact that they consisted of separate and distinct parts. Dicquemare mocked those amateur naturalists sitting in *cabinets,* that is, in private chambers that were nothing but "the delicious confection of the interior decorator."[36] It was these unprofessional gapers who metamorphosed oysters into plants! Harbinger of a progressivist positivism, the stern French scientist declared that, as microscopes became better known, "& the more we observe, the less we shall have of the equivocal."[37] This bifurcation between the supposedly shallow viewer and the profound investigator spurred the development of tidy organizational charts for the use of public lecturers in natural history. In such neat schemes, no creature was so ambiguous as to be consigned to the penumbra (fig. 78). The great French anatomist Vicq d'Azyr's synoptic *Table* (1774) abbreviated or epitomized the animated universe so that it might become accessible to the searching glance. He even designated a logical spot for microorganisms (Buffon's *molecules organiques*) before they vanished from the edge of the page.[38]

In such clearcut outlines, there was no room for the radically different, or for the incoherent uniqueness of grotesque and ambivalent entities. The late-Enlightenment trend toward systematization opposed careless inspection, or merely passive ingestion of the spectacle. Belief in conspicuous mixture, the basic tenet of a "romantic," eighteenth-century materialism, was also cast aside. As espoused by Buffon, Diderot, or Needham, this doctrine had glorified the infinite divisibility of an inherently composite and autonomous matter. In this combinatorial chemistry, both the human body and the tiniest animalcule visible under a microscope were chimerical, derealized modes of

78

Félix Vicq d'Azyr, *Table,* from Rozier's *Observations sur la physique,* 1774, IV, p. 479. (Photo: Courtesy Department of Special Collections, University of Chicago Library.)

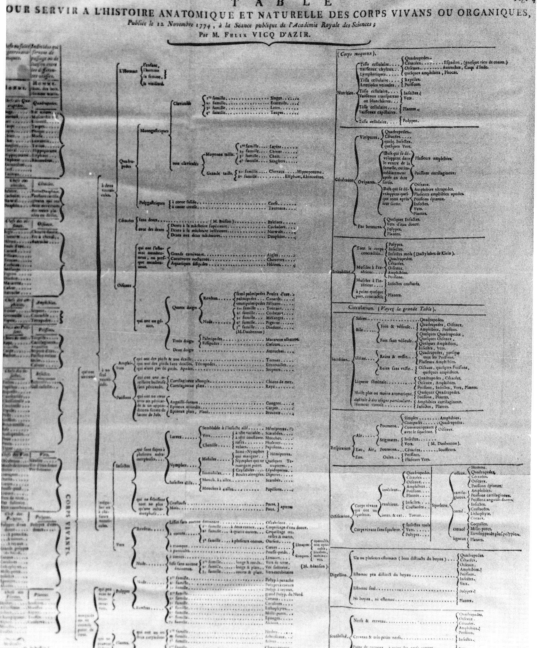

TABLE

POUR SERVIR A L'HISTOIRE ANATOMIQUE ET NATURELLE DES CORPS VIVANS OU ORGANIQUES,

Publiée le 12 Novembre 1774, à la Séance publique de l'Académie Royale des Sciences ;
Par M. Felix VICQ D'AZIR.

Picturing Ambiguity

changing perception. They depended, not on a fixed, external space but on shifting and mixing subjective points of view.[39] Contrary to received opinion, the growing rigorous quantification of the experimental sciences did not make them any less mystical or metaphysical. Instead of appealing to a common, and entropic, physical energy as the material origin of all creation, they reified an immaterial, purely mental, or transcendental abstraction.

Let me end with a telling, early example of how taxing method grew to compensate for the uncategorizable Proteus of reality. Pierre Lyonnet, the Leiden-trained theologian, jurist, and art collector, was among the revolutionary microscopic "correctors" working to advance the cause of intelligibility. His painstaking *Traité anatomique de la chenille* (1762) was inspired by Réaumur's monumental, but incomplete, encyclopedia of insects.[40] Characteristically, whereas the celebrated French entomologist had presented the whole panorama of insect life, the Dutch researcher zeroed in on the single species of caterpillar infesting willows (fig. 79). The preface announced his project of intellectual mastery through precise mapping. Contrasting his own immensely detailed drawings and engravings—requiring two and one half years of intense labor with the burin—to the sloppiness of the Swedish microscopist Charles de Geer's renditions,[41] Lyonnet stated his observational credo. The moment when the draftsman became content with generalizing what he beheld was also the moment when "the false mingled with the true, & disfigured the whole."[42] Consequently, copying involved repeatedly staring at the tiniest lobe of fat, the most minuscule ganglion, the least folding and refolding of flesh.

Combating those ancient materialists who turned the universe into a "chaos of extravagance and atheism," as well as those modern "Don Quixote revivers of a peripatetic philosophy," Lyonnet was decidedly uninterested in the superficial.[43] Transformations, he declared, were not limited to external, visible form but affected internal, normally invisible morphology itself. He ushered in a revolutionary, objectifying scrutiny—based on close and reiterated inspection—that adumbrated nineteenth-century positivism. This led to the proud (and one must admit, just) assertion: "I pushed accuracy to such a point that I do not think it can be exceeded." His targets were those absurd "Novels, Dreams, or philosophical Deliria" spun by the materialists. He scoffed at their unsound speculation that the dizzying variety of insects was the result of the chance concourse of variously compounded monads, atoms, or organic molecules.[44] In Lyonnet's scientific practice,

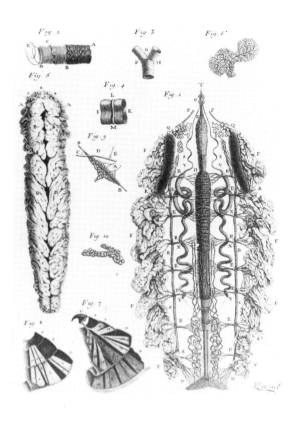

then, we can detect the inception of the modern, distanced and dispassionate model of quantitative vision.

Rather than validating the shifting perspectives of multiple viewers, or the existence of an odd *mélange* of fickle beings, Lyonnet posited the invariability of the typical. The maddeningly intricate physiology of the lowly caterpillar seemed to demand the imposition of a lofty, unconditional or absolute *ligne idéale* (fig. 80). This artificial element or organizational principle was, of course, the foundation stone of every kind of neoclassical minimalist abstraction.[45] It was but a short step from the *homo perfectus*, constructed by the famous Dutch anatomist Bernard Siegfried Albinus, to the perfected caterpillar. Already in the 1720s, this professor of anatomy at the University of Leiden had sought to establish a universally representative or average skeletal type free from abnormalities. A standardized male figure was composed from a heterogeneous collection of specimens derived from different bodies,

79

Pierre Lyonnet, *Dissected Caterpillar,* from *Traité anatomique de la chenille,* 1762, pl. 5. Engraving. (Photo: Courtesy Department of Special Collections, University of Chicago Library.)

80

Pierre Lyonnet, *Dissected Caterpillar Showing the "Lignes idéales,"* from *Traité anatomique de la chenille,* 1762, pl. 6. Engraving. (Photo: Courtesy Department of Special Collections, University of Chicago Library.)

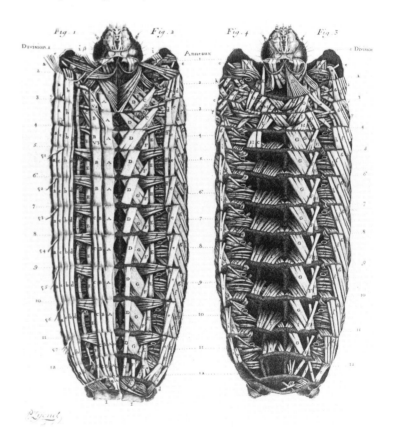

but determined by an a priori set of proportions.[46] The long shadow of Albinus's grid also touched Lyonnet's Leiden-trained contemporary, Petrus Camper, a Dutch surgeon and virtuoso executant of anatomical drawings who became famous throughout Europe for the invention of a body calculus ruled by the "facial angle."[47]

Lyonnet's efforts at the measurable clarification of uncertainty must, I think, be interpreted against this common background of the mathematization of perception. Pushing microscopic examination to its then limits, he decreed it both absurd and impossible to give names to the "ten thousand" things he witnessed. The strict empiricist enterprise, therefore, ironically necessitated symbolization. Since, paradoxically, it was confusing to identify all the minute fragments dissected, or rationally put asunder, the researcher had to have recourse to "ideal lines." Salvation from disorder was to be achieved through the external superimposition of regularity and symmetry onto internal animal complexity. Imaginary constructs tamed phenomenal wildness, redeeming both the shortcomings of the observer and the uncontrollable excess of life.[48] According to Lyonnet, these higher schemata were devised in order to give an "exact idea" of "an extremely composite object." Their merit lay in legibility and immutability, in the stereotypical encasement of illegible and changeable bodies.

This essay began by looking at how certain major eighteenth-century natural historians coped—through a diversity of metaphor—with equivocal and vexing microorganisms. It concludes with a glimpse into a critique-ridden future when such oddities would become annihilated in the name of an elevated truth or orderly design. Lyonnet's daunting project illuminated the dilemma accompanying any study of romantic singularity in which individual intricacy seemed to require, in the end, the introduction of simplifying symbols. If there is an imperial tendency to be discerned in this theoretical enterprise, it lurks in the powerful and relentless grip of a superior and separate intellectual order, and in the institutionalization of a higher and distinct class of interpreter. In the early modern period, the failure to resolve this dualism further dichotomized those ancient antinomies, noumenon and phenomenon. As we know only too well from our current vantage, it succeeded in making rebellious second-class citizens of all those inferior things deemed to require methodization.

Difficult Content, or the Pleasures of Viewing Pain

11

Introduction: Exhibitionism

Continuing political outcry over purported cases of pornography and the desecration of national symbols such as the American flag have focused attention on a venerable, if intractable, quandary. The unstated charge, I believe, against artists, museum curators, and art historians is that they have committed an obscenity even greater than Robert Mapplethorpe's *X Portfolio:* the uncritical preoccupation with the merely visual. "Thoughtful critics" find problematic the commercialism of the gallery scene. Blockbuster expositions,[1] as well as makers and scholars of imagery, tend to be judged by their linguistic colleagues as equally dedicated to the mindless activity of looking without thinking. For a substantial portion of the academic and nonacademic public, art and exhibitionism seem to have become inseparably linked.

This dubious conflation brings me to the center of my topic. For the division between a pleasurable or merely curious watching and a rational, language-driven observation arose during the eighteenth century. I want to examine this rift in the context of one of the most popular lens-using eighteenth-century sciences. The problems associated with microscopy as a paradigm of instrumentalized looking will illuminate the diversified exhibition strategies of natural history museums. By examining the dilemmas of display in another area, that of early modern science, we can learn to see our own field anew.

Before proceeding, I will itemize key points. First, microscopes—like many present-day photonic gadgets—fulfilled the long-standing human yearning to visually enter entirely different realms. Experimentation on vanishing entities, in particular, popularized disengaged and disembodied witnessing (fig. 82).[2] Strange scenes occurred

81

Georg Eberhard Rumphius, *Gazing at Shells,* from *Amboinische Raritäten-Kammer,* 1766, title page. Engraving by August Zenger. (Photo: Courtesy Herzog August Bibliothek, Wolfenbüttel.)

The word "display" now routinely provokes pejorative comments: about mindless spectacle and an imperial or subjugating gaze. The title page to Rumphius's collection of conchological rarities, gathered by the celebrated German marine biologist on Amboina in the Moluccas, alludes to both the pleasures and pains of an optically acquired knowledge. Natural History, personified as an intently observing female figure, registers the seductive power of an array of enticing phenomena. Flanked by Eros, she invites us to join in the intent examination of and the desire to possess shells.

82

Louis Joblot, *Porte-Loupe and Specimen,* from *Descriptions et usages de plusieurs nouveaux microscopes,* 1718, pl. 13. (Photo: Courtesy Department of Special Collections, University of Chicago Library.)

at the bottom of an optical instrument and were surveyed distantly from the top of a tube. In addition, eighteenth-century improvements, such as the solar microscope, made possible the projection of the sub-visible. Beguiling dimensions, unknown to earlier generations, were thrown on a screen for the diversion of an audience, no longer just for the distraction or edification of a solitary viewer.[3] Significantly, the content of these slides was difficult, often showing either the cruelty of voraciously feeding mites or the almost sadistic violence and indiscriminate promiscuity of reproduction (figs. 83, 84). Vision thus became an even more problematic or immoral activity than it had historically been. Many Enlightenment educational pleas for the packaging of natural history information both as a type of home entertainment and as a form of useful instruction were made, at least on one level, to escape the charge of detached and empty voyeurism.[4]

Second, the connection between the magnified diminutive natural image in the round (fig. 85) and the compressed or abbreviated artistic composition (fig. 86) was more than coincidental. Both sorts of framed insignificant creations depended upon seeing patterns without being able to touch them. Metaphors of "tiny scenes" and of minute landscapes, mixed from the weird infusoria and slimy minima found in dirty ponds and ditches (fig. 87), were negatively associated with unedifying grotesques, while the engraver's artificial and scurrilous "little pieces on walls" or monstrous grylli on gems (fig. 88) were derided by neoclassical critics in contrast to great themes and imposing murals. Yet both biological and artistic miniatures initiated the early modern drive toward the compact (fig. 89). Thus Goya's hybrid *Los Caprichos* (1799) and Grandville's mixed and metamorphic *Un autre monde* (1884) were examples of that romantic inclination toward making ignoble *bizarreries* (figs. 90, 91). These conventionally trivial images, filled with "Figures of little Men" fit to make "a proper Frontispiece for the Memoirs of Lilliputia," deliberately spurned high-minded "large Capital Pictures."[5] On the other hand, unlike ignoble grotesques, microscopic minima managed to achieve a positive status within deistic thought. In physico-theological treatises, even the most insignificant of God's works—a spider's web or a grain of sand (fig. 92)—was deemed superior to the rude bungling of the grandest man-made imitations. Microscopic transparencies, then, constitute an important chapter in that still unwritten history of the vogue for the small picture.

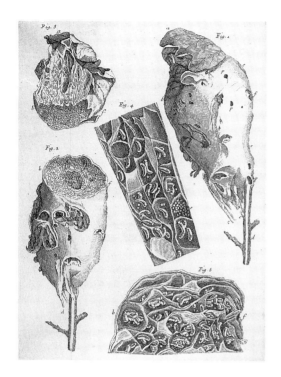

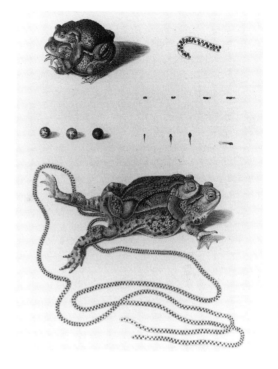

83

R. A. F. de Réaumur, *Magnified Caterpillar Larvae,* from *Mémoires des
insectes,* 1734–1755, II, pl. 6. Engraving by Philippe Simonneau.
(Photo: Courtesy Department of
Special Collections, University of
Chicago Library.)

84

August Johann Rösel von Rosenhof,
Frogs Mating and Laying Eggs, from
Historia naturalis, 1758, pl. 20.
Hand-colored engraving. (Photo:
Courtesy Department of Special Col-
lections, University of Chicago
Library.)

85

Henry Baker, *Animalcules in Semen,*
from *The Microscope Made Easy,*
1744, I, pl. 12. Engraving. (Photo:
Courtesy Department of Special Collections, University of Chicago
Library.)

86

Anne-Claude-Philippe, Comte de
Caylus, *Symbols on Ancient Intaglio
Gems,* from *Recueil,* 1752–1767, fig.
133. Engraving. (Photo: Courtesy
Department of Special Collections,
University of Chicago Library.)

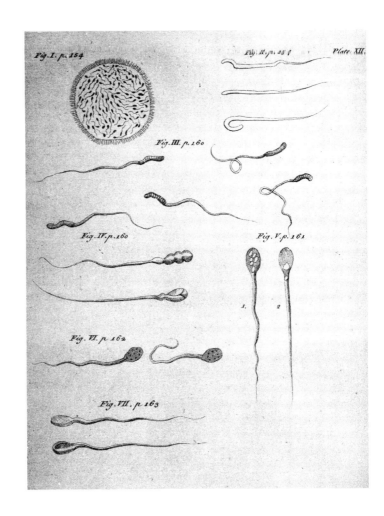

un Pied une Mouche un Caducé

134

Hercule portant le Monde

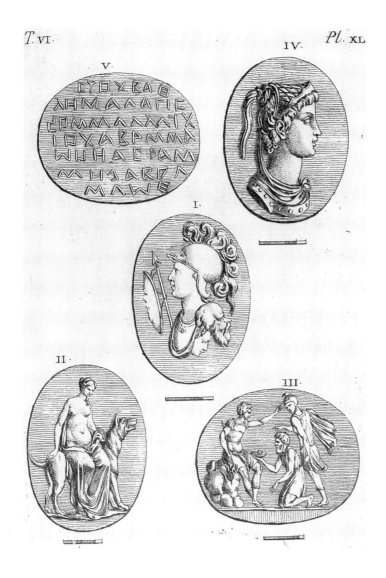

87

August Johann Rösel von Rosenhof, *Frogs in Their Habitat,* from *Historia naturalis,* 1758, title page. Hand-colored engraving. (Photo: Courtesy Department of Special Collections, University of Chicago Library.)

88

Anne-Claude-Philippe, Comte de Caylus, *Grylli,* from *Recueil,* 1752–1767, pl. 40. Engraving. (Photo: Courtesy Department of Special Collections, University of Chicago Library.)

89

Henry Baker, *Pocket Microscope and Slider,* from *The Microscope Made Easy,* 1744, I, pl. 1. Engraving. (Photo: Courtesy Department of Special Collections, University of Chicago Library.)

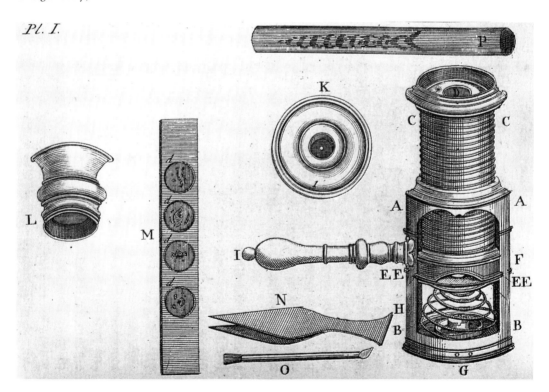

90

Francisco de Goya, *Tale-Bearers—Blasts of Wind,* from *Los Caprichos,* 1799, pl. 48. Etching and aquatint. (Photo: Courtesy National Gallery of Art, Rosenwald Collection, Washington, D.C.)

91

Grandville, *Masked Ball,* from *Un autre monde,* 1844, p. 41. Hand-colored engraving. (Photo: Courtesy Library of Congress.)

92

Martin Frobenius Ledermüller, *Magnified Grain of Sand,* from *Amusemens microscopiques,* 1768, pl. 4. Hand-colored engraving. (Photo: Courtesy Department of Special Collections, University of Chicago Library.)

BAL MASQUÉ.

Third, microorganisms contributed to the growth of a new and visual form of education heralded by the publication of scientific "amusements," physical "recreations," and "useful toys."[6] Delightful optical demonstrations with soap bubbles and flimsy cards—such as those stocking Chardin's paintings of the 1730s and 1740s—were invented to conjure up concretely the realm of the invisible. Our contemporary interest in playful learning, in computer sketchpads, and in video games relying on children's fascination with electronics was already predicted in eighteenth-century interactive technology. Similarly, mysterious animalcules with unexpected powers could not only be watched under the enlarging lens but controlled and directed. Cabinets and museums of natural history provided an additional impetus to this generalized turn toward exhibitionism.

Lurking beneath the surface of various attempts to make scientific training graphic and attractive was the much broader polemic concerning the right or wrong presentation of information. Long before the onset of nineteenth-century positivism, arguments were mustered for severing enjoyable watching from exacting observation. This dichotomy was promoted by the rise of the logocentric critic as rational censor, external to the inferior sensory field of inquiry being judged. In examining facets of this historical debate, we might keep in mind the question: do we currently need aesthetic ethicists rather than critics?

Microscopy and the Nanotechnology of Suffering

Was microscopy a scientific enterprise or an aesthetic one? What happens when moral concerns come into conflict with exploratory curiosity, or the desire just to see? In the case of a group of English investigators and one notable French researcher, the seer's task entailed not only the careful presentation of empirical observations but the sensational recreation of the actual experience of witnessing them. In the absorbing illustrated narratives of Henry Baker, John Hill, and René-Antoine Ferchault de Réaumur, the diminutive picture functioned as an efficient image-storer for the violence of the macrocosmic world. Using the analogical method, these authors vied with their engravers in conveying the vivid impression that life down under the lens was even more bloody and rapacious than life above it.

Henry Baker was in many ways a typical natural historian of the eighteenth century. His interests ranged widely, including the publication of valuable work on the teaching of the deaf and dumb, the collection of antiquities, and the study of crystal morphology. He was particularly famous, however, for *The Microscope Made Easy* (1742). This popular book ran to five editions in Baker's lifetime and was translated into several foreign languages. Its avowed purpose was to woo everyone who had the inclination and opportunity, not just the wealthy few, to make experiments. This mission he thought would be accomplished by rendering them "easy, intelligible, and pleasant."[7] As "a philosopher in little things," Baker evinced a keen and pious interest in the wonders of nature, especially in minute water creatures. Shocking to our twentieth-century sensibilities, however, was the deeply religious Baker's not uncharacteristic production of, and absorption in, numbing destruction. Havoc was deliberately created with the praiseworthy intention of seeing in order to understand. His practices served as a potent reminder of the gruesome role animals had already played in the seventeenth-century vivisectory experiments of the Royal Society: as often as not, in that institution, beasts were looked upon as Cartesian "machines" bereft of feeling souls.

With microscopy, however, the pleasures of viewing pain became associated with an ever finer optic and a literally lengthening perspective. Baker, like a host of his contemporaries,[8] trained his attention on the circulation of blood in a live frog. The scopophilic text simulated a succession of natural events induced by the experimenter.[9] The description was construed as an unfurling, or cinematic, spectacle. Baker dispassionately explained how the animal's limbs were extended and fastened onto a frame. Then the skin of the belly was slit from the anus to the throat and stretched with fish hooks in front of the microscope. This transparent view "presented on the Screen a most beautiful Picture of the Veins and Arteries in the Skin." The scientist enthusiastically reported that he could plainly perceive the blood stopping and starting in the arteries, while in the veins it "rolled on in a continuous Current." After considering this spectacle as long as he thought necessary, Baker sliced open the abdomen and spread the muscles before the lens. With the aid of a projection cast by the solar microscope on a cloth, his audience also "had the Pleasure of viewing their Structure." Then, he "gently" drew out the mesentery and brought it up to the microscope. "No Words can describe the wonderful Scene that was presented before our Eyes." The magnified circulation of the blood "appeared like a beauteous Landscape, where Rivers, Streams, and Rills of running Water are everywhere dispersed."[10] This living topography persisted until, eventually, the creature grew languid and expired.

The transubstantiation, by metaphorization, of bodily suffering into an inanimate landscape painting was a technique for distancing the beholder from the awareness of how what he beheld had been contrived. Baker seemed to rely on the voyeuristic fiction that the object agreed to its exhibition.[11] The onlooker—bereft of emotional and moral contact with the observed—aptly metamorphosed the amphibian into its watery habitat (see fig. 87). This picturesque *tableau vivant* was literally suspended, or hung for viewing, in the gallery of the laboratory. Baker's story about the life and death of a frog highlighted the enduring difficulty of meshing purely curious, or aesthetic, watching with high-minded, useful scrutiny.

No text, however, better embodied the conflicting project of natural description or more cogently posed questions about its fundamental purposes than the *Essays in Natural History and Philosophy* (1752) by the apothecary John Hill. Hill's many writings included works on Linnean classification, vegetable remedies—uncharitably termed "quack"—medicine, zoology, mineralogy, and especially botany. He is of interest to us because, along with the unillustrated *Essays,* the third volume of his illustrated *General Natural History* (1752) studied those animals "too minute for unassisted sight."[12] He coined lasting names, such as "paramecium," for those invisibles that "had none before." Less respectable than Baker, who was a member of the Royal Society, Hill with even greater assiduousness devoted himself to the confection of popular accounts of microscopic examinations. He, too, pleaded for the "Combination of the useful with the entertaining in these Studies." His approach gave the illusion of looking in on a private world. More of a scopophiliac than his contemporary, Hill took tiny entities and subjected them to a controlling gaze. This obsessive watching veered toward perversity by forcing a change in their customary environment and behavior.[13] The "allurements" of natural history, which "astonish our Eyes."[14] were presented in the *Essays* through a series of sensory impressions so melodramatic, perhaps, precisely because they were not accompanied by plates. Moreover, the narrative made things happen, as in the movies, one after the other, and as if right there in front of us.

Sanguinary metaphors of microscopic wars humanized Hill's tale of a heretofore unknown insect inhabiting the hollow joints of a species of coralline. Because events were seen close up, they took on the brilliance of flickering patterns beheld in a dark room. The sensational account of subscale combat unfolded as part of his overarching argument for the reclassification of this species from the pacific, vegetable to the violent, animal kingdom. Removing a tiny specimen from its cell, he at first placed it in a drop of its native sea water. Hill claimed that there was no species of animal "so rapacious as those minute Creatures, which are not visible to us except by the assistance of the Microscope." These "Minims of Existence" were more destructive than birds or beasts of prey. No sooner had he introduced fresh fluid, taken from a field pond, into the concave glass than he was "entertained with a Sight" to which he wished he had "a thousand Witnesses." Suddenly, the preparation was teeming with animalcules and the experimenter was amused "with seeing them following and preying on one another, and with tracing the Chace of a larger after a smaller." The "Discovery made by the Eyes" was of a scene of comic horror. The larger kind pursued the smaller pursuers, and all fell upon each other and gorged themselves in a frenzy of feeding.[15]

Hill abruptly interrupted his watching with the disjunctive interjection of a philosophical meditation: "Various are the Arts of Death, not only from the mischievous Inventions of Men, but from the Provision of Nature for its several Productions. Such a Scene of Butchery, so universal, so varied, and so hurried in all Parts, human Cruelty itself never offered."[16] Significantly, the natural historian admitted that the miniature slaughter was contrived by himself, thus linking knowledge to pain. While it would not have been easy under natural circumstances for these "little Legions" to escape their enemies, the creation of an artificial, or laboratory, ambience altered the odds. "Devourers [were] brought as it were from Another World, and Assailants against whom no Form of Defence had been concerted."[17]

After this brief, meditative interlude, Hill returned to gaping. The fascinating spectacle hinged on the various forms and sizes of the predators and their victims, and the varied means of death they incurred: "Every one of the hungry Inhabitants of my coralline seemed like a *Briarus*, crushing different objects at one Instant in his different Arms, and dealing out Destruction several Ways at once." He methodically classified the types of violent seizure: pressing, clapping together, crushing. With a mixture of anguish and surprise, he beheld twenty or more animalcules "dealing Destruction so many Ways at once among an innocent and defenceless Race." Nonetheless, he asserted that in order to understand this voraciousness, the area of observation had to be narrowed and focused upon with even greater powers of magnification. Consequently, he trained his lens on one coralline "wearied of Slaughter," only to see it killing still.[18] The implication of this procedure was that the animalcules became epistemologically and narratively interesting only insofar as they engaged in aberrant visual behavior. The experimenter's controlling intervention organized decimation, thus constraining the invisible to surface. The inferior physiognomy of instinctual drives and appetites were revealed to a superior, if sympathetic, gaze.

Such graphic descriptions of unequal combat were not unique to the ambiguous world of aquatic plants and animals. They functioned as a new kind of mirror for the reflection of amoral, but rationalizable, zoological behavior. Torture could be explained and justified by the all-knowing design of God. The law of the survival of the fittest seemed to have been specifically formulated for the world of insects. Hill was not unusual in singling out the troubling generation of a species of ichneumon fly. In this case, the barbaric occurrence was natural, not contrived. The observer, like a peeping Tom, merely "witnesses the helpless caterpillar assaulted" as it insouciantly rolled along on a leaf. He watched as the tender flesh was cruelly stung "more than fifty times" by its tiny tormentor. Creating a sort of empathetic natural painting, a precocious Humboldtian *Naturgemälde,* Hill emphasized both the aesthetic aspect that tugged on the feelings of the spectator and the scientific enterprise that simultaneously distanced him from the horror studied. Rescuing the hapless victim from other vicious flies, Hill's experimental urge soon prevailed. He took it, the mulberry leaf, and the attacker home for further observation. Soon he realized that both fly and caterpillar, predator and prey, were female, and that the "sting" was a means for depositing eggs. This evidence of purpose allayed his fear that here, at last, was the exception to the divine dictum that brute creation never hurt its fellow in wantonness.[19]

The subject of generation, in particular, was conducive to the coupling of feminine behavior with the pathological and the sadistic.[20] It released a flow of innocent pity from the male scientist—freed from complicity—and allowed him to indulge in the pathetic fallacy. The latent voyeur quickly overcame the moralist. The caterpillar, we are told, passed the first two days after the infliction of the wound in ease. But thereafter, she spent her time "in the most violent agitations." On "examining her nicely with magnifying Glasses, I could at any Time during the last Day and a Half, distinguish the motion of living Animals under her Skin." On the evening of the fifth day the caterpillar ceased to eat. On the following morning, she tried to spin the escaping web that would transform her into a chrysallis and then a butterfly. But it was to no avail. Already on the fifth day, there had been abundant evidence of the "Fly's having laid her Eggs in its Body." Hill inspected the damage as if he were located at a great height. He recounted how the young "gnawed" their passage through the back and sides of the creature, and often chewed holes much larger than necessary to make their exits. In short, they "had eaten their Way out in their full Perfection on the very Day of the Death of the Caterpillar, and were now prepared for Metamorphosis."[21]

These masculine metaphors of conquest and weaponry, these tropes of sexual abuse, penetration, and violation—does contemporary television possess a more equivocal mixture of sensational docudrama with egregious titillation? And all accomplished through imagery and in the name of images. Scanning frames of indiscriminate feeding, killing, and multiplying was not unlike staring at pornographic photographs or films.[22] Both activities constituted an eroticized perception without the involvement of touch or a contact with social responsibility. In exhibition for exhibition's sake, the spectator was volatilized into a disembodied self distilled into pure vision.[23] By the persuasiveness of their visual rhetoric, Baker and Hill urged us to devour more or less unreflectively with our eyes, just as what we saw was being devoured.

Unlike the two English researchers, Réaumur attained international stature as the foremost entomologist of the eighteenth century.[24] It is to this polymathic geometrician, physicist, and composer of an industrial encyclopedia that we must look for the most perspicuous reflections on why natural history in general, and microscopy in particular, became transformed into a spectator sport. The monumental, but incomplete, six-volume *Mémoires pour servir à l'histoire des insectes* (1734–1742) frankly tried to make zoology popular by resorting to the imagery of *sensibilité*. Like Hill, Réaumur humanized the description of nature, but with the specific purpose of encouraging its study. Thus he claimed that even "the most hideous spider" enclosed its eggs in a small silk box from which it was inseparable. When the young were born, the devoted mother carried them stacked on her back as she raced about at top speed. He also confessed to being "touched" by the care that bees and certain wasps lavished on their offspring, feeding them with miniature beakfulls several times a day. This anthropomorphism led the French scientist to marvel at how certain insects born with tender skin made "clothing" from wool, silk, or leaves (fig. 93). Others even knew how to lengthen their garments when they became too short, or

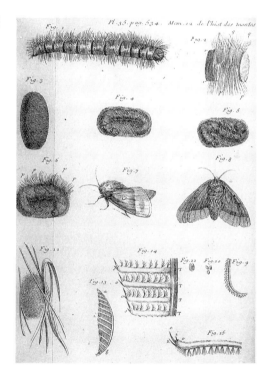

Pl. 35. pag. 534. Mem. 12. de l'hist. des insectes

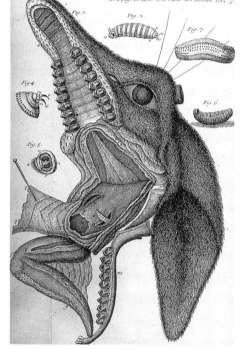

Pl. 9. pag. 60. Mem. 2. de l'hist. des insectes. Tom. 5.

to weave entirely new vestments. The prodigious morphological diversity and behavior of all classes and genera offered "a grand spectacle to him who knows how to consider it." Réaumur's emphasis on the wonderful, and even the shocking, was always intended to lure the future investigator to search for what was still absent or invisible. The interior of tiny structures remained elusive, and the microscope was continually dangled before the would-be discoverer as an inducement to see more than skin-deep.[25]

Education in this scheme, as Charles Bonnet indicated in his *Essai de psychologie* (1755), depended upon a kind of material sensationalism. For this Genevan biologist and self-styled "intellectual son of Réaumur,"[26] learning was tied to the reproduction of images and the multiplication of motions in the sensorium. The constant stimulation of the brain's fibers by strong external impressions meant that curiosity, or watching, was essential to the generation of ideas.[27] The technological revolution of the microscope had thus allowed Réaumur to bring stunning, if frequently cruel and destructive, sights to jolt the escapist spectator out of a relaxed or passive viewing. In the *Mémoires,* there was no emphasis on the human body perfect, on good looks, or on beautiful people. Caricatural images demonstrated that real life was closer to nightmare or hallucination. The grotesque engraving by Jean-Baptiste Haussard of a *Dissected Head of a Stag,* anticipating Jean-Baptiste Oudry's paintings for Louis XV recording deformed antlers, did not minimize the fleshy pouches under the tongue filled with concealed worms (fig. 94). In this instance, too, parasitical eggs were laid in living flesh, raising tumors and causing unspeakable suffering when they developed into spiny and pincered maggots.[28] Nor was this an isolated case. Volume IV of the *Mémoires* chronicled the ferocity of the *Oestrus* or gadfly that fed on grazing herds. Its larvae were deposited in the cracks of cows', sheep's, or horses' throats, in the slits of their nostrils and anuses, subjecting them to indescribable torment.

The universal ravages wrought by omnivorous insects must have caused real discomfort also to the wealthy French *curieux,* or collector, whose money derived from agriculture or manufacture. Réaumur cleverly provided large-scale views of moths "occupied with chewing two pieces of cloth." Surely his intention was to agonize the sluggish visual consumer at the magnified sight of holes gnawed in an expensive fabric or fur (fig. 95)! The youthful reader, or future physiocrat, would similarly awaken to a need for active engagement with the world he inhabited when shown a mangled bunch of linden leaves attacked by

93
R. A. F. de Réaumur, *Metamorphosis of Hairy Caterpillars and Cocoons,* from *Mémoires des insectes,* 1734–1755, I, pl. 35. Engraving by Philippe Simonneau. (Photo: Courtesy Department of Special Collections, University of Chicago Library.)

94
R. A. F. de Réaumur, *Dissected Stag's Head,* from *Mémoires des insectes,* 1734–1755, V, pl. 9. Engraving by Jean-Baptiste Haussard. (Photo: Courtesy Department of Special Collections, University of Chicago Library.)

95
R. A. F. de Réaumur, *Moths and Holes Chewed into Cloth,* from *Mémoires des insectes,* 1734–1755, III, pl. 6. Engraving by Philippe Simonneau. (Photo: Courtesy Department of Special Collections, University of Chicago Library.)

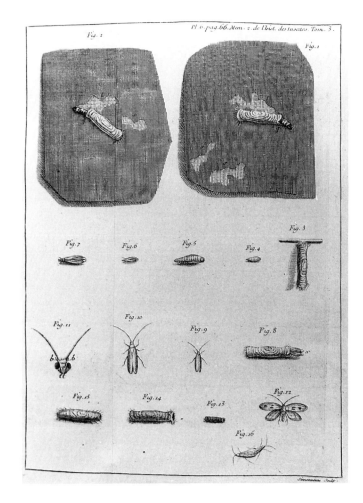

96
R. A. F. de Réaumur, *Lice and Distorted Linden Leaves and Stems,* from *Mémoires des insectes,* 1734–1755, III, pl. 23. Engraving by Philippe Simonneau. (Photo: Courtesy Department of Special Collections, University of Chicago Library.)

97
R. A. F. de Réaumur, *Pear Leaves with Lice and Galls, and Currant Bush with Tubercles,* from *Mémoires des insectes,* 1734–1755, III, pl. 24. Engraving by Philippe Simonneau. (Photo: Courtesy Department of Special Collections, University of Chicago Library.)

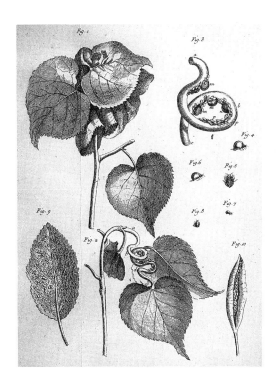

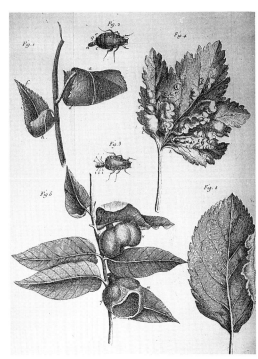

crippling tree lice (fig. 96). The additional enlargement of the contorted spiral, in order to make the greedy beasts more clear and distinct, was a summons to the no longer disinterested beholder to get up and take on the demanding chore of prevention. Indeed, there followed a rapid succession of harrowing plates illustrating plum or pear trees, and currant bushes, swarming with mites and riddled with galls (fig. 97). Leaves were curled, crumpled, or swollen in a display of conspicuous pain.[29] No viewer could remain inert or uninvolved as his or her worldly possessions succumbed to the ubiquitous crunch of miniature marauders. My point is that Réaumur—in a way that Baker and Hill did not—introduced complexity and intellectual demands into his deliberately unpleasant images. They were compelling invitations to action, to the effort-filled structuring of experience, not an excuse for facile voyeurism.

The "philosophical" observer—sailing to the limits of the visible and traveling to the extremities of the microcosm—was not born, but created.[30] Réaumur belonged to that strand of Enlightenment pedagogical thought believing that people explored unexamined intellectual terrain both because it challenged their skills and because they intensely enjoyed the search. Thus a leitmotif of the *Mémoires* was that the discovery of something useful was often preceded by visual delight, or "pure curiosity." After all, he declared, humanity was "not just interested in utility, but in what pleases, amuses. . . . The taste for the marvelous is a general taste, it is this taste that fosters the reading of novels, short stories [*Historiettes*], Arabian tales, Persian tales, and even fairy tales, rather than true histories."[31] Yet, as he himself so amply demonstrated, nowhere can one find so much "de merveilleux vrai" than in the history of insects. He criticized the tedious cataloguing of caterpillars by John Ray, bereft of illuminating plates. But he disapproved as well of the beautiful albums by Maria-Sibylle Merian or the watercolors of Eleazer Albin because they provided no explanation of the figures.[32]

Spectacle of Nature/Museum Display

Significantly, Réaumur's unlikely model was the aptly entitled encyclopedia of stunners, the *Spectacle de la nature* (1732–1750) of the Abbé Noël-Antoine La Pluche.[33] Addressing the curiosity of the young as well as the young at heart, these eight illustrated volumes were speedily consumed by the public, sold out immediately upon publication and subsequently reprinted in fifty-nine editions. The zoologist profitably wedded La Pluche's habit of epitomization, the extraction of admirable scenes, with the scientific memoir and report. Ordinary or common phenomena were made to appear singular. Visualization techniques were put at the service of the mass popularization of natural history. The biology of living creatures was shown to be both entertaining and the source of lifelong learning and intellectual fulfillment.

In place of the venerable catalogue, or classical form of natural history itemization,[34] La Pluche invented the written "spectacle." This key text for the eighteenth century allows us to glimpse the beginnings of a remarkable shift in emphasis, a turning away from the older painstaking method of presentation that was condemned as being exhausting to the reader. The influence of mellifluous English descriptive poetry was evident in the heartfelt exhibition of a series of physical *tableaux.* Such unpedantic verbal pictures displayed only "the exterior or that which strikes the senses."[35] La Pluche, holder of the chair in rhetoric at the University of Rheims and a successful private tutor, evidently conceived of the project as an enormous, summarizing textbook. Its purpose was to expose what was common to mankind, what was intelligible to all ages, and what everyone had to know. It functioned as the eighteenth century's manual of cosmic literacy. Significantly, La Pluche openly dichotomized the act of looking. He stated that the labor of "delving" into the universe's deeper mysteries must be left to a superior order of genius. His arena, instead, was that of touching sights and "the outside of nature." His general public was intended to remain at the level of "the exterior decoration of this world and of the effect of those machines that make up the spectacle."[36]

This deliberately chosen form of superficial watching—content with striking representations that forcefully filled the senses and brain with pictures—was intended to attract a broad and well-to-do range of consumers. Based on his experience among the *beau monde,* La Pluche was convinced that this fickle audience was easily tired or bored by more taxing mental exertions. The spectacle form, this deist asserted, was devised to chase away the blues. His readers had no need to inspect the "engine room" of God's creation. They were content with the cheerful excerpting of a succession of scenes. Anyone involved with any aspect of present-day art education has encountered the afterlife of this conviction that the distasteful and the scholarly are synonymous. Rather than the tedium of a continuous treatise (*un discours suivi*)—such as Réaumur's—or a series of fatiguing dissertations, he selected the dialogue style.[37] La Pluche thus unintentionally reinforced the dangerous, and even pernicious, assumption that the enjoyment of views was predicated on an absence of work: that there were categories of images that made no demands on the beholder, and that intellectual labor was inherently displeasing and painful. Such an opinion clearly went against the grain of eighteenth-century practice, in which even amateur naturalists toiled until they dropped. Surely they must have found both a special pleasure and happiness in their arduous perceptual exertions.

Yet Réaumur, too, was struck by this antinomy between professional observers and unprofessional spectators. La Pluche's conversations in the countryside, taking place among three *personnes du monde,* shaped the zoologist's own novelistic style. He must have concurred that the ordinary reader did not have to expend as much mental energy to understand a *chevalier,* a *comte,* or a *prieur-curé* as he did to comprehend famous scholars. La Pluche had claimed that when one wrote for savants, no subject was too paltry, no discussion too lengthy, to try their patience. Indeed, he slyly commented that such experts would be content with Réaumur's history of insects, founded on a rigorous method and filled with minute distinctions. Consistent with his conviction that entering into particulars would be repugnant to his broad audience, La Pluche "improved" the second edition by pruning even more detail.[38]

This radical prying apart of deep from shallow looking, of investigation from gaping, continued apace as the century unfolded. Charles Bonnet's *Contemplation de la nature* (1764), for example, explicitly declared that it was not intended for the learned, although he hoped his readers might become so.[39] How did the laudable intention to communicate difficult information to a nonspecialist audience become converted to the attitude that almost every particle of matter should offer "an Entertainment"?[40] How did the impulse to create "reasonable and useful amusements" end up by opposing the rational to the irrational?[41] The natural history cabinet as the museum for an epitomized creation or spectacle incarnate was, I believe, the source for this spectacularization of experience. Moreover, the conflicts over its nature and function, and the tensions between a supposedly serious linguistic system of ordering and the merely appealing exposition of images, has a distinctly contemporary ring. The unsigned article on the "Cabinet d'histoire naturelle" in the *Encyclopédie* distinguished such public spaces from the "Cabinet," or solitary study. The latter was a place for seclusion, for withdrawal from the world for purposes of personal prayer, meditation, nap, toilette, or the private perusal of precious paintings, bronzes, books, and curiosities. The natural history cabinet, on the contrary, was a suite of open rooms teeming with collections under glass. Taking up

an apartment, it was meant to house "a spectacle," with "all sorts of animals, plants, & minerals present . . . gathered together in the same place, & seen, so to speak, at a glance."[42]

Significantly, the author of the entry converted the three-dimensional objects located in this gallery into a compact painting, or into a multivariate and nuanced *tableau* much as slides for microscopes had (see figs. 85, 87). Furthermore, the fact that this motley assemblage was itself an abstract, an *abrégé,* specifically tied it to the essence of the pictorial. Images could miniaturize, compress, and combine complicated information while displaying it simultaneously within a small area. The analogy to be drawn, however, was not to just any type of painting. I suggest that in the ensuing discussion over Daubenton's organization of the *cabinet du roi* at the Jardin des Plantes, the laborious, lexical, or neoclassical classification of disparate treasures was pitted against a rococo parade of merely pleasing show (fig. 98). This polarization between learned scientific asceticism and ignorant sensuality mirrored the criticism then current concerning the grotesque. These attacks were leveled against "false Ornaments and affected Graces of mere Pretenders";[43] such small "florid and shining" decorations "nauseated" austere and simple tastes by their visual surfeit. According to the censure of the Scottish moral philosopher and art critic George Turn-

98

Augustus Charles Pugin and Thomas Rowlandson, *Microcosm of London: Vauxhall Gardens,* 1809. Hand-colored aquatint. (Photo: Charles Deering Collection, The Art Institute of Chicago.)

bull, they gratified and flattered the senses of the unlearned public "by a various mixture of gorgeous Colours."[44]

Louis-Jean-Marie Daubenton categorized the royal collection of naturalia depending on the kingdom to which each item belonged and its genus and species. But was there a more grotesque collage of incongruities than the assortment reconstructed under the rubric of the *règne animal?* Crowded into a limited space were bones, notable for their sections, fractures, deformities, and diseases; dried, wax, or injected anatomical preparations; fetuses in various stages of development; other "singular" pieces preserved in alcohol; parts of mummies; stones removed from human organs; skeletons of quadrupeds; and, of course, innumerable shells and insects gathered on land and sea.[45] This freakish *ars combinatoria* was the obvious source of the quandary plaguing natural history description. To whom was such a farrago meant to appeal? In the lengthy extract from Buffon's and Daubenton's *Histoire naturelle* included in the *Encyclopédie* article, the problem of multiple audiences and the incompatibility of method with aesthetics loomed large. In brief, the fundamental difficulty with the installation of a cabinet of natural history was that, paradoxically, it could not mimic nature's order. Unfortunately, according to Daubenton, the latter was more of a chaotic heaping up of phenomena, or a "désordre sublime." Perforce, some kind of artificial system had to be imposed on the unruly universe. Here, however, was the rub. Since such exhibitions attracted visitors from all walks of life (Daubenton estimated that 1,200 to 1,500 "spectateurs" per week strolled through the *cabinet du roi* alone), did one arrange the collections for the amusement of *gens du goût,* for the easy instruction of *amateurs,* or for the rigorous researches of *savants?*[46]

Daubenton's startling, if somewhat depressing, conclusion was that the pattern that pleased the mind was almost never the one that proved most attractive to the eyes. His solution, like that found in many of today's art museums, was a compromise. The major holdings were to be rationally laid out so that each glance became instructive, revealing the real characteristics of the object and its relations to those surrounding it. But the surplus, the reserves, the grotesque marginalia, if you will, might break ranks and be combined and recombined in favorable viewing locations. In fact, as the engraving shows, they were "skied": as intellectual lightweights, or subjects solely for voyeurism, they were used to compose "an ensemble agreeable to the eye." Varied in form and color, these manipulable or retouchable images had no cognitive import and were not constrained to obey a strict logic.[47]

Although this proposal was mocked by Réaumur's staunch apologist, the Oratorian Joseph-Adrien Le Large de Lignac,[48] Daubenton defended painless spectacle. He asserted that it functioned as a form of protection against the dangers of overweening and painstaking method. But moralizing critics of a sterner age, like Lignac, claimed that Daubenton sacrificed his scientific principles of order to charm the eyes of the spectacle-craving public, substituting elegance and beauty for purposeful training, lowbrow emotional practice for high-minded theory.[49] Lignac's condemnation derived, in part, from what he took to be Daubenton's preferred viewer. His pleasure-loving and pain-avoiding audience was made up of wealthy amateurs who arranged their natural history collections according to diverting or provocative contrasts. Unlike Réaumur, this monied leisure class bought their expensive specimens from the debris auctioned at public sales. The lazy lack of initiative, characteristic of unprofessional watchers, stood at the antipodes from the strain and suffering endured by true observers. The trained investigator actually went into the field, and possessed "eyes that [knew] how to see."[50] If La Pluche relied on facile sights to achieve science literacy in a broad public, Daubenton saw them as a needed corrective to the excesses of systematization. For Lignac, however, the worst method was preferable to layouts that were merely visually attractive.

As mentioned, Daubenton's defense of imaginative recompositions was based on the epistemological perils attendant upon always observing things that were deliberately placed. He feared that, under such overly structured conditions, the beholder's responses would become predetermined by the all-powerful and stultifying method. Rather than piquing the viewer's curiosity to explore and discover the world, the system blunted his desire to study the objects themselves. Interestingly, the natural historian forecast our postmodern condition. Already by the mid-eighteenth century, nature was losing its authority to the lure of the disembodied and artificial reconstruction of reality. To avoid this irrevocable division between matter and manner, Daubenton urged the observer not to abandon himself uncritically to the critical inquiry of conventions that had little to do with the entities under scrutiny. He reminded his readers that all systems were arbitrary, and so imperfect or defective. They provided an index only to the specific collection for which they had been designed and should not be reified into absolutes. Ceaseless acquisition, in addition, demanded the flexibility of constant rearrangement and displacement. Finally, there were those equivocal entities that seemed to fit nowhere, that evaded any standard categorization. In sum, for Daubenton, "a little art"—embodied in pleasing patterns—was the antidote against an excessive rage for rational order.[51]

FROM VERBAL CRITICISM TO VISUAL ETHICS

This essay has explored some of the historical roots of an unsettling contemporary dualism. That dichotomy pits a trivial, mediocre, and obscene spectacle without discipline against a regulating, schematizing criticism. Manifold entertainment, thoughtlessly sucked in by the eyes, is separated from those nonvisual and informative methods that supposedly convey truths to the mind. It can be said that pictures, in the words of George Turnbull, have now become exclusively identified with that "which neither convey[s] into the Mind Ideas of sensible Laws, and their Effects and Appearances, nor Moral Truths, that is, Moral Sentiments and correct Affections." Many contemporary media analysts would concur with the British author that unphilosophical and nonlinguistic images "have no Meaning at all: They convey nothing, because there is nothing to be conveyed."[52]

Criticism was minute philosophy. Since the eighteenth century, the concepts of dissecting calculation and of exact gauging have been central to the computing regimen of "the Criticizing Art." This moral microscopy discerned in artistic productions incompetence, decadence, and controversial opinion that were not accessible to the unassisted eye. Its lofty and restrictive task was to prevent the untutored public from being "imposed upon" by the fabricators of visual sham.[53] Today, while a flood of electronic spectacles purvey pleasure, often through the infliction of pain, a rising tide of language-based criticism threatens to destroy any awareness that there is such a thing as a responsible image. By responsibility, I do not mean something intrinsic to the subject matter, but a quality integral to the style of presentation. Thoughtful exhibitions provide a context; indeed, they create it. Ethical modes of creation do not eliminate or conceal from the viewer the signs of how the display was made. Just as there is an artist or designer conspicuous, and therefore accountable, behind such work, I think the artistic practitioner should be visible in the aesthetic theory. Art, like life, is fundamentally about ambiguity. Unless we forge an ethical aesthetics sensitive to that innate lack of measurability, the absence of numerical and discursive precision will continue to be taken as a sign of corruption. Or, worse, it will invite more external, correcting "Censors of

Manners, and Criticks of a higher Degree [who] disdained not to exert their Criticism on the inferiour Arts, and claimed it as the indisputable Right of true Philosophy to give Laws to them All."⁵⁴

Is Turnbull's Platonic vision of bringing the arts and sciences under the reconnaissance of legislating magistrates so different from what is being contemplated today for the National Endowments for the Arts and Humanities? The neoclassical critic expressed the hope that pictures might become "moral Magnifiers." Such illustrations, or "Samples" and "Experiments" in philosophy, signified "that the Laws and the Arts might speak with the same Language, and These [the arts] might not be employed to pull down what Those [the laws] were intended to build. And What honest Man and true Lover of the Arts, doth not heartily regret that ever They should be alienated from Virtue and prostituted to give false Charms to Vice?"⁵⁵ If we do not wish outside regulation, let us cease placing the responsibility for our judgments, decisions, and even reputations in other hands.

Finally, much postmodernist method has fostered the identification of imagery with sham bricolage, or with faked sex, lies, and videotape. The decade of the 1990s has seen no abatement in the manipulation of the manipulable. The result of this mercenary exploitation is that the common perception of our medium and of our discipline has become synonymous with sensationalism and the deliberate manufacture of fraud.⁵⁶ And now there is the alarming general perception that the "arts community" is "foreign to everything the rest of the country stands for." To many eyes, artists (and, one could add, academics) are no longer us "with a difference," with a creative gift that makes them interesting; rather, they seem to be contemptuously signaling that the rest of the citizenry is not welcome, while demanding money from those very people.⁵⁷ What additional humiliation will it take for those of us professionally concerned with images to be moved by pity for their plight? Learning from the Enlightenment, we imagists might do well to remind the disaffected public that art is neither detached voyeurism nor a mirrored hall of methods.

99

Nina Levy, *Ferris,* 1995. Polychrome resin and steel. (Peter
Miller Gallery, Chicago; photo courtesy the artist.)

Nina Levy's ravishing polychrome
resin and steel sculpture functions
as a situational analogy. The lurch-
ing, swaying, unexpected stopping
and starting of a ferris wheel provocatively allude to the medieval wheel
of fortune whose rotations unseated
rulers, ministers, clergy, the rich,
powerful, and famous. But *Ferris* is
slung with anonymous, gender-
ambiguous, alternating forward-
and backward-facing, naked bodies.
These translucent figures have no
discernible character or rank nor can
they be confused with fairground
joyriders strapped into place. Seeing
the likeness in unlike things, the
viewer is challenged to conjecture
about the ups and downs of human
fate, to speculate on the similarities
and differences between the operations of naturally or technologically
induced chance in the past and
present.

Conclusion: Analogy in an Age of Difference

So it is a wolf looks like a dog, the one a most fierce, the other a most tame,
animal. But a careful person should always be on his guard against resem-
blances above all, for they are a most slippery tribe.
—Plato, *Sophist* (231 a)

Writers have long pondered the relation of fiction to the appearance of
reality. Characters in a novel, as Nadine Gordimer recently snapped, are
connected with actual persons encountered through sight, sound,
touch, whether or not the author is aware of this.[1] But description, she
argues, is not literal replication since it is impossible to perceive the
whole of anything, the depth of anyone. Although, it has to be con-
ceded, Flaubert, Zola, Edmond de Goncourt, and a host of nineteenth-
century realist writers championed lengthy itemization. In their
voluminous works exhibiting the ethics of labor, exposition became a
sort of department store inventory in which every object was accounted
for.[2] This *galerie de glace* method of presentation tends to flatten exhaus-
tive detail. It is the inverse of Primo Levi's "metaphysical mirror" in
which no two images coincide. Unlike a normal looking glass, the at-
tachable "Metamir" strapped to the spectator's forehead secretly harbors
reflections of persons and things. In defiance of the rules of conventional
optics, this unnerving surface reproduces one's own shifting image "as
it is seen by the person who stands before you."[3] Timoteo, Levi's allego-
rist mirror-maker, also confected Arcimboldesque shards that divided
the figure into a multiplying mosaic and crafted undulating panes to
enlarge, diminish, or distort any individual who dared stand before
them.

As fascinating as serial description or metonymic fragmentation are, I want to explore the recesses of another mirror. Forgotten or, if remembered, despised analogy ingeniously coalesces realms usually kept separate in obedience to the laws of a linear physics. Although he would have resisted the suggestion, analogy is a good example of Foucault's "arthrology," a term he coined for a science of the "joints" between forms of discourse within an overall epistemological configuration.[4] But the Foucauldian thrust is always to underscore disjunctures, while analogy, on the contrary, seeks to bring about liaisons. The long hermeneutic shadow cast by deconstruction and poststructuralism has meant that both the Balzacian amassing of observations and the Baudelairean glorification of kaleidoscopic transformations continue to receive critical scrutiny. Within the current intellectual climate celebrating diversity and difference, not surprisingly, little if any value is attached to the rhetorical practice of focalization, that amatory process that intensifies and relates discrete objects. Yet after thirty years of mining the theories of Foucault and Derrida in this country, who can deny that those theoretical veins have thinned, that the arguments have grown stale? It's time to craft new methods, invent new subjects, launch other initiatives.

In an era of ever-expanding and unfolding information, why and how apparently alien things become sympathetically joined remains a conundrum. Marrying opposites, as Van Gogh remarked, belongs to an alchemical chromatics of love. Bringing complementary hues from opposite sides of a color wheel into contiguity points to a larger project. Today, not only has similarity vanished from the academic, cultural, and social spectrum in the single-minded drive to reify separateness, but the very concept has become eclipsed by postmodernism's embrace of a "logic of decay."[5] Adorno, in his anti-Enlightenment *Negative Dialectics* (begun in 1959), emphasized that philosophy could no longer hope to grasp the whole. He set in motion an intellectual program of renunciation in which all aesthetic, epistemological, and political attempts at embracing a greater unity were tainted with smugness, falsehood, futility. The dispiriting result has been a kind of "moral dandyism" denying the power of the imagination to identify with situations, places, and people we have never seen.[6]

The conviction that differences cannot be honorably reconciled is one of the most tenacious legacies of the Frankfurt School's critical theory. Its contemporary instantiation is visible in the rhetoric of oppositional politics, ethnic, generational, sexual wars, totalizing imperialisms, and ideological polarities. Oddly, if dialectics was intended as a form of discovery used to open up questions that had not previously been conceptualized, the one area to which its adherents have not been open is the mind's positive tendency to discover affinities. Unlike its Hegelian transcendent prototype, Adorno's dynamic interrogation of unequal subject-object relations was intended to purge the tyranny of unity. But where have acrimonious strategies of resistance, coercion, contradiction, and absolute heterogeneity landed us? As the art critic and writer Dave Hickey wryly observed about Norman Rockwell's and Johnny Mercer's generously inclusive painterly and musical populism, "[now] we do statistical demographics, age groups, and target audiences. We do ritual celebrations of white family values, unctuous celebrations of marginal cultural identity. . . . But what we don't do is collect all these incongruities around us and make sure everybody gets their solos."[7]

What we also don't do is try to fit our limited local perspectives into a bigger picture of humanity. By way of suggesting an alternative epistemology, I want to propose an old model for binding microcosm with macrocosm, one that provocatively intersects with a new understanding of consciousness. Considering analogy together with the emergent sciences of sentience could help explain why people are capable of both subtly differentiating and nonreductively integrating perceptions into compact sensory arrays. Investigating the galvanizing force of creative association, its empathetic drive to find and fuse—without disfiguring—the likenesses in unlike things, extends my earlier attempts to put a positive account of visual perception into circulation. This pursuit logically led to the latest research on the brain, that supreme organ of communication and guidance, which deploys and manipulates the images shaping our thoughts. Iconophiles should be cheered by the neurological fact that we share our image-based concept of the world with other human beings who make comparable images and so permit us to imagine ourselves into their lives.[8]

Heart and conscience (*conscientia* in Latin; *syneidesis* in Greek) are historically linked. As a private knowledge that touches us personally, its dialogical structure helps individuals "to know with" someone or something.[9] Especially important to philosophers of the Middle and Late Stoa, conscience became conscious as an inner voice, intoning the higher morality of the cosmos. For the prophets of the Old and New Testaments, it was *vox dei* whose troubling murmurs attested to the divine source of human nature. Only with the skeptical moderns, with

Descartes, Spinoza, and La Mettrie, did the body become disensouled, emptied of the divine authority that had once beaten in the pulse.

The religious debates formerly swirling around conscience have now turned into the secular polemics raging around the nature of consciousness. Given the highly contested question of what is truly distinctive and strange about the human mind and its imagery, I predict transcategorical analogy will come into its own again precisely because it reveals how the brain actively synchronizes its baroque activities. In addition to "the neuroscientific revolution" [10] pondering the knowledge that lies in ourselves but also inferable in others, the so-called second Darwinian revolution is exploring the selectivity, even the intentionality, of individuals within a shifting environment. Rethinking changing yet continuous species has had the effect of highlighting one of the most remarkable aspects of our universe: the puzzling fit between one biological system and another, the adaptation of some aspect of an organism to some aspect of the environment. Such congruences demonstrate a degree of complexity not easily ascribed to chance, whether one is speaking of an already achieved fit (adapted) or as something learned, our ability to achieve a new fit (adaptive). Remarkable instances range from the molecular arrangement of mammalian cells to the subtle adjustments made by the brain as seat of knowledge to the vagaries of the world. [11]

If John Searle is correct in stating that the most important problem currently spanning the biological sciences, philosophy, cognitive science, and artificial intelligence is how, exactly, the myriad, localized neurobiological functions in the brain cause coherent awareness, [12] then seeking cross-cortical ties becomes a major issue. Ironically, with a few significant exceptions (Hofstadter, Lakoff), the disciplines concerned with the historical and humanistic praxis of imaging have not been looked to by the cognitive science community as potential guides in the illumination of this fundamental dilemma. Conversely, art, architectural, or design practitioners and historians—centrally concerned with the production, reception, and interpretation of sensory stimuli— have, to date, shown little interest in learning the neurobiological processes from which well-ordered inner states of being arise.

Certainly, the problem of consciousness is too important to leave to philosophy and the natural sciences alone. Since thinking involves scenography, the staging of a flow of perceptions and a warehouse of memories into the spectacle of ideas, shouldn't its study also be aestheticized? Percepts, as the visible remains of our day, are constantly being reconfigured into a compressed exhibition that unifies free-floating, decontextualized icons. Moreover, the stream of thought becomes a perceptible bodily sensation precisely in those heightened moments when the work of art makes us aware of the intricacies of experiencing.

Let us consider, first, how display as a paradigmatic *bridging* activity offers clues to the operation of this mysterious, private, and qualitative phenomenon occurring in human beings and higher mammals. Neither the mechanistic metaphor of the brain as a digital computer nor of consciousness as a computer program[13] is adequate to the collecting, arranging, and showing of differences that gets done when ideas are triggered. Happily, a more holistic view of thought claims there are many ways in which people make sense of things by linking them into concepts possessing an overall *Gestalt*. As George Lakoff noted, every time we categorize something in a way that does not mirror nature, we are using general human imaginative capabilities.[14] His abstract comments about classification can be situated concretely within a pictorial framework. Juxtaposing the strange with the beautiful or putting the distant into play with the familiar uncannily describes the visionary coincidence of opposites occurring when the viewer confronts a cabinet of curiosities. Here, too, flashes of intuition create momentary mental proximities by knitting together antithetical species, antipodal geographies, and farfetched artifacts. I am suggesting, then, that the problem of qualia bedeviling researchers into consciousness has as its aesthetic analogue the multisensory problem of how to correlate the divergent feelings aroused by a partitioned assemblage of artful objects.

Throughout the sixteenth, seventeenth, and eighteenth centuries, princely *Wunderkammern* exhibited exotic animals, strange seashells, oddly shaped stones, pictures of rare flowers. A secular extension of religious relics, these visual aids were viewed in terms of analogy. *Naturalia,* bearing striking patterns, embodied signs placed by God in the world to illustrate his omnipotence. This ancient doctrine of sympathetic signatures also played an important medical role. God benevolently endowed nature with flora and fauna assisting a fallen humanity in finding healing therapies for all that ailed it. Based on a venerable theory of correspondences operative in the imitative talismans and protective amulets used by the Greeks and Romans to draw down astrological powers, signs of restorative properties were similarly impressed on plants and animals so that they might be recognized and used in treatments. Like mended like: headaches were alleviated by the application of shelled walnuts, eye disorders were improved by the placement of *abrus precatorius* or small red fruits with a black dot resembling the pupil in the center of the iris.[15] Unfortunately, such extravagant and fanciful claims for kinship gave the discovery of resemblances a bad reputation.

But the fact that people can and do leap to false comparisons does not mean they cannot properly conjecture about appropriate connections, those justified by context and judged by more than personal assent. The treasures collected in a compartmentalized case could stimulate just such an art of conjecturing. Behaving like material object hypotheses, they invite the beholder to explore the analogies evoked by their inventive arrangement. Freewheeling speculation, however, remains controlled by a conceptual framework. Further, this art historical example of visual coordination across multidimensional domains could provide critics of the computational model of cognition (such as Edelman, Flanagan, Lakoff, Penrose, Varella)[16] with an alternative, iconic paradigm showing that embodied minds have more going on inside them than the manipulation of abstract codes. Specifically, I am suggesting that this minority group could muster more compelling arguments if they drew on the research of humanities-infused imaging disciplines. Surely Roger Penrose is right in claiming that robots cannot save this troubled world and that mind (arguing against the strong AI position) is more than merely the extreme complication and organizational sophistication of our material brains. Nevertheless, to make this point effectively science must come to value a more humane ingredient in human mentality.

Here, the Benjaminian vision of the collector as sandwichman, *Lumpensammler,* and *flâneur* proves helpful. Looked at as a physical assortment of potential ideas, visual oddments gathered into a case can lead to knowledge. Consciousness of an evocative macrocosm of physical things goes hand in hand with consequent intelligence, the distillation of an untidy empirical amalgam.[17] *Wunderkammer* collage thus incarnates a dream of connectedness, the encyclopedic will to comprehend remote or farfetched things by bringing them within the intimate grasp of our very being. Conversely, the clean mind-as-machine paradigm is predicated on a clear brain-body, text-image dualism. According to this fleshless neo-Cartesianism, the mind is a massive Turing machine running digitally on alphabetical and numerical symbols that apply only to discrete, not continuous, systems. There may be input from the sensory organism, but thinking belongs to the disembodied noumenal sphere engaged in hermetic operations divorced from biological functions.

Taking the metaphor of mechanized cerebration too literally has been given a boost by the expansion of the so-called sciences of complexity (nonlinear dynamics, molecular biology, artificial life, cognitive science, fuzzy logic, computational mathematics, material science, ecology). These, too, depend on the capacity of high-speed computers to find fits between nonlinear interactions. Just as the objectivist view reifies the brain as the place where all the encoded thoughts are, so attempts to characterize contingent and chaotic systems have led to the deconstructive tactic of merely juxtaposing diversity—from genetics to linguistics to cultures—rather than looking for new modes of conjunction. Similarly, poststructuralist theories of representation as subjugation have radically denied to the artist the possibility of imaginatively identifying with marginalized "others." Craig Owens, for example, indicts such connective mental leaps linking different cultures, genders, and races because they serve as the "primary agent of their domination."[18]

These are not the best of times, then, for seeking principles of kinship or for placing the arts and sciences of the mind in relation to one another. Yet a key concern preoccupying cognitive scientists is how people manage to make sense of the vast amount of raw data bombarding them from their environment. The heart of human perception—like the collector's subtle ordering of his possessions—consists in shaping this prismatic and mutable blur. At this point, we need to consider a second and nonbiological issue, namely how traditional epistemology tried to account for "wit," the mind's nimble capacity to see correlations among dispersed, disordered, or random elements. In classical theory, analogy was an art of discovery (*ars inveniendi*), not a rigorous method of demonstration. In the *Topics* (I 12, 105 a 13), Aristotle discussed it as a type of imperfect induction expressing reason's progress from particular to general ideas.[19] In a syllogism, its position was that of the middle term, mediating between many particulars and a single common category. Of special significance to us are certain eighteenth-century developments. Kant, influenced by Reimarus's discussion of *Witz* or imagination, drew an important distinction between mathematical and philosophical analogy. In mathematics, formulae expressed the conformity of numerical proportions to each other. In philosophy, however, statements of similarity were not about quantitative characteristics but about qualitative properties. These judgments could only be imperfect or uncertain, since they drew conclusions from known quantities in order to discover something about an unknown entity.

Kant also separated induction from analogy. The former described a mental operation that moved from the one to the many, to conclude that a specific property belonged to all. The latter saw the many in one, so this one was also common to many others.[20]

Analogical thought—as a similarity-creating power—is profoundly intertwined with meaning-producing high-level perception. As imaginative *insight,* it recognizes in something unfamiliar, alien, something familiar; a correspondence, not a comparison. When people make analogies, either they perceive some aspects of two different structures as similar or they perceive one situation in terms of another.[21] Sensing affinity goes beyond vaguely intuiting resemblance when the viewer can demonstrate the existence of a reciprocal proportion between two unequal or unlike terms. Creative analogies, therefore, can bring powerful and unexpected insights to apparently asymmetrical relationships, inventing harmonizing correspondences that literally did not exist before being made.[22] Not just any analogy but the most dramatically meaningful one singled out from a swarm of possible linkages is at the core of human creation. Insight with a gasp derives from such intensely concentrated psychobiological experiences of unity in multiplicity.

As we are well into the digital age, what might venerable analogy still say to those posthistorians who relish the absence of equivalences, the irony of eternally incompatible modes of otherness?[23] Again, a Primo Levi short story puts it best. In "They Were Made to Be Together," two schematically conceived lovers disport themselves in flatland. The wittily named Plato and Surpha exist as slender lines against a backdrop of brown rectangles for houses, blue zigzags for water, green segments for trees, points for locations. But miraculously, during a brief interlude of love-making "Plato felt his outline deliciously assume a new outline, so much so that one of its sides reproduced in the negative, with great precision, the girl's corresponding side: they were made for one another."[24] The narrator could have been speaking of analogy when he mused that, in that magical moment of fusion, the lovers intuited an infinitely richer, more complex, and solid world freeing them temporarily from the insubstantial and level horizon.

Levi's tale recalls the fascination many late eighteenth-century painters had for the dialogic juxtaposition of outline drawing or cast shadow with volumetric sculpture. This famous strategy—commemorated in Pliny's account of the Corinthian maid and the invention of painting—owes, I think, in no small measure to its analogical potential. David, Flaxman, Piranesi, and Wright of Derby played with the perennial problem of bridging the mimetic gap separating ideal form from real embodiment, ontological void from transcendent substance, thin present from thick antiquity. I propose that such pictorial and poetic evocations of the fullness that comes with momentary merging or, at least, the establishment of the conditions for a close relationship appear to be the same as the "binding problem" perplexing researchers into perceptual categorization. Cognitive psychologists simply phrase it gracelessly in terms of how different stimulus inputs to different parts of the brain are bound together so as to produce a single, unified experience.

Levi's compassionate metamorphosis of characters as diagrams into solids in the round is the reverse of allegory. Founded on the inadequacy of human judgment, the latter genre feeds on despair arising from the inability to establish an objectively verifiable source of referentiality. The interpreter is an obsessed surgeon, stripping away the literal surface of the work to uncover a higher meaning concealed beneath lying appearances. These merely constitute an *integumentum,* a rind for the critic to peel back.[25] Analogy, on the contrary, makes visible things desire to be together. Simultaneity is its stock in trade, achieved by inlaying a collage of equivalences rather than violently inserting foreign material into an equally impermeable matrix.[26] A sort of pictorial haiku, this mosaic technique invites comparisons, since recognizing differences forms a prelude to discovering likenesses.[27] From the suturing graphics of Callot, Rembrandt, Goya, Blake, and Bewick to the intarsia of Netscape (fig. 100), discovering connections involves just such a balancing of internal tensions with evident contradictions. More recently, Nam June Paik has created witty portrait-monuments of famous artists from a collage of antique television sets. *John Cage*'s TV statue is aptly strung together with piano wire; *Charlotte Moorman* seductively dangles a violin from fingertips composed of electronic gear; *Van Gogh*'s vintage monitors are covered with its namesake's characteristic brushstrokes and color palette.[28]

In these comical and good-natured personifications, analogy recycles modernism's beautiful technological detritus, allowing the viewer to go back and forth between the past and present. Demonstrating the tenuousness of formal harmony both points up and summons us to rectify the instabilities, disarray, and dislocations operating in the world outside the aesthetic composition. Analogy as compressive, transformative—placing a premium on invention and insight—can even be seen as part of a global ecological mission since it does not add

100

Home Page, Netscape 2.0. An Internet
World Wide Web page browser.
(Photo: courtesy Donald
Williamson.)

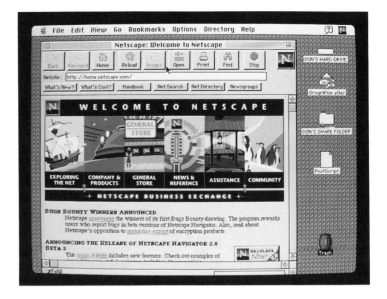

to disposable commodities, but reuses and reconfigures them. Considering patterns or, better, societies and their divergent artifacts as potentially congruent might allow us to enter the twenty-first century less
incoherently, more open to new combinations.

Lastly, I want to step back to go forward. For some time, it has
seemed to me that academic culture wars derive from the essentialist
impasse of yearning for an original, holistic experience while claiming
that none is possible. Even this denial is not original, since Socrates,
Plato, and Aristotle claimed that there was no substitute for direct,
authentic encounters with noumena,[29] all the while acknowledging
that the "real thing" could not be taxidermically preserved once it
entered, diluted, into the communications network of the lifeworld.
Imitations thus had the useful function of *approximating* the unattain-
able higher forms. In important ways, as I have tried to demonstrate
throughout these essays, the verisimilar, approximating illusions of
classical epistemology are not the immersive, simulating delusions they
have become in Debord's critique of scopic regimes.[30] In pondering the
mechanism of analogical thought, a diverse group of philosophers—
chief among them Plato, Aquinas, Mill, and Wittgenstein—admitted
the coexistence of incommensurable realms. They did not, however,
fragment them into cybernetic bits or multiply them *ad infinitum* with

no hope of correlation. Even Leibniz's monads were extended the promise of harmonization. So, while experiences mean different things to different people in different contexts, pure arbitrariness and complete unrelatedness is a shortsighted version of a bigger picture.

I have no intention of minimizing the problem of establishing appropriate distinctions while searching for links among historical and contemporary *membra disjecta.* The ongoing task of asking whether to call different classes of objects by the same term or indicate them by the same image will not disappear. Ambiguity and disproportion are inevitable between living things and their representations, no matter how close the match. The transfer from a familiar to an unfamiliar referent lands us in an equivocal region.[31] The difficulty is finding enough similarity to warrant giving a common name to disparate items while acknowledging their significant variations. *Analogia,* then, should not be confused with establishing identity or isomorphism. When combined together, the prefix *ana* and the noun *logos* etymologically mean "according to due ration," "according to the same kind of way."[32] As a *method,* it establishes a proportional relationship either among single items or among a group of embodied properties existing under diverse conditions and adapted to multiple purposes. Vision makes an imaginative leap, embarking on a dialectical process of seeing affinities not easy to convey in words.

Devised originally to handle concepts not at home in any category, analogy returns us to recent studies of consciousness. According to Lakoff, the brain develops "image-schema"[33] to perform intuiting, sorting, and associating functions required in those ambiguous cases where the phenomenal world is not already classified. What is exciting for the continuing relevance of analogy is that after many stimulus inputs, particular neuronal groups will be selected in patterns. *Similar* signals will not only activate the previously selected neuronal groups in one map, but they will *cross over* to another map or even to a whole group of maps because their operations are linked together by reentry channels. (Note that a "map" is a sheet of neurons in which the points on the sheet are systematically related to the points on a sheet of receptor cells.)

Whether contemplating how electronic technologies abruptly bring the tribes of mankind face to face in all their otherness or how they redirect information flows outward into virtual communities, learning how to connect in new ways while disconnecting from the old, remembered ways will increasingly preoccupy us. Some of the most significant ideas about panhuman characteristics are emerging not in the bitterly conflicted disciplines of the humanities, once committed to an overarching view of cultural life, or in the endlessly subdivided social sciences of which anthropology is a prime example,[34] but in the biological sciences. And, paradoxically, given the current textualization of art history, the image forms the centerpiece of this new transcategorical thinking about the nature of apprehension.

Since the brain is "body-minded," it is responsible for shaping an image of our entire being. A feeling, in the poetic simile of Antonio Damasio, is a momentary view onto a portion of this corporeal landscape.[35] Analogies are possible because over time, our insight into the somatic topography becomes juxtaposed with things lying outside the individual body. This affective and epistemic organization offers the possibility of integrating mind and surroundings, self with non-self, because human beings appear to merge signals from different sensory sources similarly and signal across brain areas in a concerted interaction.

If Damasio is accurate in claiming that there is "no single region of the human brain equipped to process simultaneously representations from all the sensory modalities active when we experience sound, movement, shape, color in perfect temporal and spatial registration,"[36] then a biological operation akin to the rhetorical function of analogy must be responsible for the synaesthetic convergences of discrete information distributed all over the brain occurring when we think coherently. Uncannily reminiscent of Leibnizian apperception, the memory of a face, person, voice, or touch is present to the mind only in separate, monadic views. Sensation does not capture the entire aspect but analogously constructs enough of an object to warrant the designation of likeness. Rethinking venerable analogy in conjunction with the emergent study of consciousness, then, throws into dramatic relief the enduring issue of what knowing about "others," distant peoples, remote times, and our most intimate selves, properly consists of.

1. Although Nicholas Negroponte, in *Being Digital* (New York: Alfred A. Knopf, 1995), is enthusiastic about the digital age, he, as well as other more critical writers on the future of information technology such as Jeremy Rifkin and Clifford Stoll, make no attempt to link our high-tech reality with historical examples of visuality from which we might usefully learn.

2. Doomsayers for the book include Neil Postman, *Technopoly: The Surrender of Culture to Technology* (New York: Knopf, 1992); and Sven Birkerts, *The Gutenberg Elegies: The Fate of Reading in the Electronic Age* (Winchester, Mass.: Faber & Faber, 1994).

3. See William J. Mitchell, *The Reconfigured Eye: Visual Truth in the Post-Photographic Era* (Cambridge, Mass., and London: MIT Press, 1994); and his *City of Bits: Space, Place, and the Infobahn* (Cambridge, Mass., and London: MIT Press, 1995).

Notes

4. See my *Artful Science; Enlightenment Entertainment and the Eclipse of Visual Education* (Cambridge, Mass., and London: MIT Press, 1994), xxiv.

5. For its modern instantiation see, especially, Adorno. Rolf Wiggershaus, *The Frankfurt School: Its History, Theories and Political Significance* (Cambridge: Polity Press, 1994), 597–608.

6. Murray Krieger, *Theory of Criticism: A Tradition and Its System* (Baltimore and London: Johns Hopkins University Press, 1976), 220.

7. Linda Brodkey, "The Value of Theory in the Academic Marketplace: The Reception of *Structuralist Poetics*," in *Rhetoric in the Human Sciences,* ed. Herbert W. Simons (London, Newbury Park, and New Delhi: Sage Publications, 1989), 168.

8. Noam Chomsky, *Syntactic Structures* (Cambridge, Mass.: MIT Press, 1957).

9. Dean Keith Simonton, *Greatness: Who Makes History and Why* (New York and London: The Guilford Press, 1994), 55–56.

10. Marcel Danesi, *Giambattista Vico and the Cognitive Science Enterprise* (New York: Peter Lang, 1994), 36, 46–49.

11. See, especially, Mark Johnson, *The Body in the Mind: The Bodily Basis of Meaning, Imagination, and Reason* (Chicago and London: University of Chicago Press, 1987), xxxvi–xxxviii; and George Lakoff, *Women, Fire, and Dangerous Things: What Categories Reveal about the Mind* (Chicago and London: University of Chicago Press, 1987), 8.

12. Interestingly, philosophers are now lamenting this same fragmenting process that accompanied the death of the Cartesian foundational subject. See Michel Meyer, *Of Problematology: Philosophy, Science, and Language,* trans. David Jamison with Alan Hart (Chicago and London: University of Chicago Press, 1995), 8.

13. For the importance of Geertz's conception of culture as "an historically transmitted pattern of meanings embodied in symbols," see Robert Darnton, *The Kiss of Lamourette: Reflections in Cultural History* (New York and London: W. W. Norton, 1990), 336.

14. See, for example, Paul M. Churchland, *The Engine of Reason, the Seat of the Soul: A Philosophical Journey into the Brain* (Cambridge, Mass., and London: MIT Press, 1995), 264–170; and William G. Lycan, *Consciousness* (Cambridge, Mass., and London: MIT Press, 1995), 1–8.

15. Martha C. Nussbaum, "Poetry and the Passions: Two Stoic Views," in *Passions and Perceptions: Studies in Hellenistic Philosophy of Mind,* Proceedings of the Fifth Symposium Hellenisticum, ed. Jacques Brunschwig and Martha C. Nussbaum (Cambridge: Cambridge University Press, 1993), 148–149.

16. Jacques Derrida, *Memoirs of the Blind: The Self-Portrait and Other Ruins,* trans. Pascale-Anne Brault and Michael Naas (Chicago and London: University of Chicago Press, 1993), 4.

17. Homi Bhabha, *The Location of Culture* (New York and London: Routledge, 1994), 48–51.

18. Anne Hollander, *Suits and Sex* (New York: Alfred A. Knopf, 1995), 19.

19. Cited by Alain Finkielkraut, *The Defeat of the Mind,* trans. Judith Friedlander (New York: Columbia University Press, 1995), 35.

20. The term is from Anthony Giddens, *The Consequences of Modernity* (Stanford: Stanford University Press, 1990), 21.

21. Liz McMillen, "The Meaning of Animals," *Chronicle of Higher Education* (April 21, 1995), A12.

22. Daniel C. Dennett, *Darwin's Dangerous Idea: Evolution and the Meaning of Life* (New York: Simon & Schuster, 1995), 512–513.

23. Churchland, *Engine of Reason,* 11–19, 298. For the importance of the emotions and feelings in neural representations, see Antonio R. Damasio, *Descartes' Error: Emotion, Reason, and the Human Brain* (New York: G. P. Putnam's Sons, 1994), 223–244; and Owen Flanagan, *Consciousness Reconsidered* (Cambridge, Mass., and London: MIT Press, 1992), 102.

24. See, for example, Francisco J. Varela, Evan Thompson, and Eleanor Rosch, *The Embodied Mind: Cognitive Science and Human Experience* (Cambridge, Mass., and London: MIT Press, 1993), xvi–xvii.

25. Bennett Reimer, "What Knowledge Is of Most Worth in the Arts?" in *The Arts, Education, and Aesthetic Knowing: Ninety-First Yearbook of the National Society for the Study of Education,* ed. Bennett Reimer and Ralph A. Smith (Chicago and London: University of Chicago Press, 1992), 20–50.

26. One such blueprint is Robert N. Beck, *Center for Imaging Science: A Plan for the Future* (Chicago: University of Chicago, 1995).

27. Victor Margolin, "Design History or Design Studies: Subject Matter and Methods," *Design Issues,* 11 (Spring 1995), 9–11.

28. Gianni Vattimo, *The End of Modernity: Nihilism and Hermeneutics in Post-Modern Culture,* trans. Jon R. Snyder (Cambridge: Polity Press, 1988), 47.

29. Jean Baudrillard, *Simulacra and Simulation,* trans. Sheila Faria Glaser (Ann Arbor: University of Michigan Press, 1994), 55–56.

30. See my *Voyage into Substance: Art, Science, Nature, and the Illustrated Travel Account, 1760–1840* (Cambridge, Mass., and London: MIT Press, 1984), chapter 2: "The Natural Masterpiece."

31. John Markoff, "And Now Computerized Sensibility," *New York Times* (May 15, 1995), C4. For the eclipse of keyboard-centric views of word processors by that of computers as small, smart objects or even spaces you enter, see David Weinberger "In Your Interface," *Wired* (September 1995), pp. 134–135.

32. My last two books analyzed in different ways the durability with which vision is coupled with negative metaphors. This *préhistoire* is given inadequate and short shrift in Martin Jay's *Downcast Eyes: The Denigration of Vision in Twentieth-Century French Thought* (Berkeley, Los Angeles, and London: University of California Press, 1993); see especially chapter 2, "Dialectic of Enlightenment," 85ff., which is cursory and derivative in its assessment.

33. John Dewey, *Experience and Nature,* 2d ed. (La Salle, Ill.: Open Court, 1961), 288.

34. See, for example, Neil Postman, *Conscientious Objections: Stirring Up Trouble about Language, Technology, and Education* (New York: Alfred A. Knopf, 1988), xiv.

35. Barbara Hoffman, "Digital Technology, Cyberspace, and the Arts," *CAA News* (May/June 1995), 6–7.

36. Donna Haraway, "A Manifesto for Cyborgs: Science, Technology and Socialist Feminism in the 1980's," *Socialist Review* 15 (March–April 1985), 65–107.

37. Hal Foster, *Compulsive Beauty* (Cambridge, Mass., and London: MIT Press, 1993), 158–159, 163–164.

38. See, for example, George H. Birch, *Education without Impact: How Our Universities Fail the Young* (New York: Lane Press, 1994); Robert and Jan Solomon, *Up the University: Recreating Higher Education in America* (New York: Wesley Publishing Company, 1994); and Eli M. Noam, "Electronics and the Dim Future of the University," *Science,* 270 (October 13, 1995), 247–249.

39. Donald E. Stokes, "The Impaired Dialog between Science and Government and What Might Be Done about It," paper delivered at the Nineteenth Annual AAAS Colloquium on Science and Technology Policy (Washington, D.C., April 7, 1994). Also see his forthcoming *Pasteur's Quadrant: Basic Science and Technological Innovation* (Washington, D.C.: The Brookings Institution, 1996).

40. Ethan M. Katsch, *Law in a Digital World* (New York and Oxford: Oxford University Press, 1995), has suggested that law must join other disciplines in entering a graphic world opened up by the computer. See pp. 152–153.

41. Dewey, *Experience and Nature,* 86.

42. Elizabeth W. Bruss, *Beautiful Theories: The Spectacle of Discourse in Contemporary Criticism* (Baltimore and London: Johns Hopkins University Press, 1982), 79. Also see Daniel Herwitz, *Making Theory/Constructing Art: On the Authority of the Avant-Garde* (Chicago and London: University of Chicago Press, 1993), 195, for Arthur Danto's pervasive notion that theory is the defining ingredient of art. Peter Brooks, "Aesthetics and Ideology: What Happened to Poetics?" *Critical Inquiry,*

20 (Spring 1994), 515, asserts that ideological criticism has degenerated into self-importance and posturing.

43. Rosalind E. Krauss, *The Optical Unconscious* (Cambridge, Mass., and London: MIT Press, 1993), 2.

44. For the confusion of power with persuasion in the new sophistic propounded by Stanley Fish, see Martha C. Nussbaum, *Love's Knowledge: Essays on Philosophy and Literature* (New York and Oxford: Oxford University Press, 1990), 222.

45. For the distinctions between the old pragmatism and the "new pragmatism" of Richard Rorty, with its emphasis on script, vocabulary, and constructed narration, see the excellent discussion by John E. Smith, *America's Philosophical Vision* (Chicago and London: University of Chicago Press, 1992); and John Pattrick Diggins, *The Promise of Pragmatism: Modernism and the Crisis of Knowledge and Authority* (Chicago and London: University of Chicago Press, 1994), 492. For the Emersonian connection, see Cornel West, *The American Evasion of Philosophy: A Genealogy of Pragmatism* (Madison: University of Wisconsin Press, 1989), 73–74.

46. Thomas F. Reese contrasts the more hierarchical pedagogical models of German emigrés, such as Panofsky, with Dewey's call for a study that integrates art into our lives. See his "Mapping Interdisciplinarity," *Art Bulletin* (forthcoming).

47. See, for example, John LaPuma and David Shiedermayer, *Ethics Consultation: A Practical Guide* (New York: Jones & Bartlett Publishers, 1994).

1   THE VISUALIZATION OF KNOWLEDGE FROM THE ENLIGHTENMENT TO POSTMODERNISM

1. See M. Mitchell Waldrop, "Learning to Drink from a Fire Hose," *Science,* 248 (1990), 674.

2. For this all too prevalent view, see Judith R. Brown and Steve Cunningham, "Visualization in Higher Education," *Academic Computing* (March 1990), 24.

3. I have examined this "grammatological" aspect of eighteenth-century aesthetics in my *Symbol and Myth: Humbert de Superville's Essay on Absolute Signs in Art* (Cranbury, N.J.: Associated University Presses, 1979). See especially chapter 4, "Kant, Schema, Sign." More recently, I have discussed the resurrection of this word-image polemic in light of poststructuralism's "theoretical" appropriation of art history. See my "The Eighteenth Century: Toward an Interdisciplinary Model," *Art Bulletin,* 70 (March 1988), 6–24. More pointedly, perhaps, the hegemonic aspect of literary control over pictorial hermeneutics has become more insistent as our culture is becoming undeniably ever more visual. The academic economics of this takeover has yet to be deconstructed.

4. For an excellent analysis of the distinction made in midcentury France between *artisans* and *artistes,* that is, between "decorator" or "minor art" practitioners of an *art rocaille* and the "intellectual" painters, sculptors, and architects of the *grand goût* (shored up by pro-antique critics) who scorned them, see Marianne Roland-Michel, *La Joüe et l'art rocaille* (Paris: Arthena, 1984). Italy, Germany, and England (although to a lesser extent) experienced this reversal when they sent their young artists to study in a now "classical" Rome under the tutelage of Winckelmann, that lover of ancient allegory and of a "poetic" art that went beyond the senses. Da-

vid Irwin, "On the Imitation of the Painting and Sculpture of the Greeks (1755)," in Irwin, ed., *Winckelmann: Writings on Art* (London: Phaidon, 1972), 61–85.

5. Yve-Alain Bois, "Malevitch, le carré, le degré zéro," *Macula,* 1 (1976), 28–49.

6. Wendy Steiner, *The Colors of Rhetoric: Problems in the Relation between Modern Literature and Painting* (Chicago and London: University of Chicago Press, 1982), 179–181.

7. Benjamin H. D. Buchloh, "Allegorical Procedures: Appropriation and Montage in Contemporary Art," *Artforum,* 21 (September 1982), 43–56. On collage as the twentieth-century all-purpose device, see Glenn Watkins, *Pyramids at the Louvre: Music, Culture, and Collage from Stravinsky* to *The Postmodernists* (Cambridge, Mass., and London: Harvard University Press, 1994), 1–4.

8. Anthony Vidler, *The Writing of the Walls: Architectural Theory in the Late Enlightenment* (New York: Princeton Architectural Press, 1987), 43. Vidler connects late eighteenth-century architectural "physiognomics" to the modern tradition.

9. While postmodern experience is that of visualization, paradoxically postmodernist criticism privileges the linguistic signifier, as in Althusser's notion of ideology as *langue* or Baudrillard's notion of the fetish as *code.* See Benjamin H. D. Buchloh, "Ready Made, Objet Trouvé, Idée Reçue," in *Dissent* (Boston: Institute of Contemporary Art, 1986), 107–122.

10. James Foley and Andries Van Dam, *Fundamentals of Interactive Computer Graphics* (Reading, Mass.: Addison-Wesley, 1982).

11. Michel Bret, "Procedural Art with Computer Graphics Technology," *Leonardo,* 21, no. 1 (1988), 3–10.

12. Benoît Mandelbrot, *The Fractal Geometry of Nature* (San Francisco: Freeman, 1982).

13. Otto Mayr et al., *Holographie. Medium für Kunst und Technik,* exhibition catalogue (Munich: Deutsches Museum, 1984).

14. An optimistic sign is the Getty Center for Education in the Arts' DBAE Program. See Elliot W. Eisner, *The Role of Discipline-Based Art Education in America's Schools* (Los Angeles: Getty Center for Education in the Arts, 1987).

15. The deep connection between a logocentrism and what might be termed a "numerocentrism" must also be stressed. Recall the Phoenician origin of numeral letters, their subsequent spread to Greece, Rome, Syria, and Arabia, and their ouster of a primitive mode of expressing numbers *orally and through gestures.* See Georges Ifrah, *From One to Zero: A Universal History of Numbers,* trans. Lowell Bair (New York: Viking, 1980), especially 241–310.

16. To my mind the finest analysis of the metaphor of writing and the book for structuring *all* experience is that of Hans Blumenberg, *Die Lesbarkeit der Welt* (Munich: Suhrkamp Verlag, 1986).

17. See, for example, Stephen M. Kosslyn, "Aspects of a Cognitive Neuroscience of Mental Imagery," *Science,* 240 (June 17, 1988), 1621–1626. Also see, in the same issue, Michael I. Posner, Steven E. Petersen, Peter T. Fox, and Marcus E. Raichle, "Localization of Cognitive Operations in the Human Brain," 1627–1631.

18. Eric L. Schwartz, "Images of the Mind," in *Tod Siler: Metaphorms: Forms of Metaphor,* exhibition catalogue (New York: New York Academy of Sciences, 1988), 1–2. In addition to making possible new art forms, neuroscience has begun to change the traditional philosophy of mind. See Patricia Smith Churchland, *Neurophilosophy: Toward a Unified Science of the Mind-Brain* (Cambridge, Mass.: MIT Press, 1986).

19. I am grateful to Robert N. Beck, director of the University of Chicago's Center for Imaging Science, for demonstrating and explaining the operations of this new technology. The people involved in this work include, in addition to Beck, Chin-Tu Chen, David N. Levin, and Charles Pelizzari.

20. Kenneth Snelson. "An Artist's Atom" (unpublished paper), 51. Also see my essay, "The New Immaterialism: Kenneth Snelson Imagines the Atom," in *Kenneth Snelson: The Nature of Structure,* exhibition catalogue (New York: New York Academy of Sciences, 1989), 51–57.

21. J. S. Bell, *Speakable and Unspeakable in Quantum Mechanics: Collected Papers on Quantum Philosophy* (Cambridge: Cambridge University Press, 1987). See especially the title chapter, 169–172; "Bertelmann's Socks and the Nature of Reality," 139–158; and "Six Possible Worlds of Quantum Mechanics," 181–195.

22. Thomas A. DeFanti, "Cultural Roadblocks to Visualization," *Computers in Science* (January–February 1988), 5–6.

23. Robert S. Wolff, "The Visualization Challenge in the Physical Sciences," *Computers in Science* (January–February 1988), 16–25.

24. William H. Kruskal, "Visions of Maps and Graphs," in *Proceedings of International Symposium on Computer-Assisted Cartography: Auto-Carto II* (1975) (Washington, D.C.: Bureau of the Census, 1977), 27–36; and Kruskal, "Criteria for Judging Statistical Graphics," in *Utilitas Mathematica,* 24 (May 1982), 283–310.

25. Hermann Chernoff, "Graphical Representations as a Discipline," in *Graphical Representation of Multivariate Data* (New York: Academic Press, 1978), 1–11. I am grateful to William H. Kruskal for having drawn my attention to Chernoff's work and, indeed, to the larger problem of representation in statistical analysis.

26. See E. F. Loftus, *Eyewitness Testimony* (Cambridge, Mass.: Harvard University Press, 1980).

27. Cited in Frederick Burwick, "The Hermeneutics of Lichtenberg's Interpretation of Hogarth," *Lessing Yearbook,* 19 (1987), 168. For the proliferation of "visuals" in the courtroom, note the existence of the Atlanta-based firm Medical Legal Illustrations, Inc., founded in 1988, and the Chicago-based firm Legal Graphics Inc., founded in 1989.

28. See Shoshana Zuboff, *In the Age of the Smart Machine* (Cambridge, Mass.: Harvard University Press, 1988).

29. George Berkeley, *A Treatise Concerning the Principles of Human Knowledge* [1710], in his *A New Theory of Vision* (New York: E. P. Dutton & Co., 1919), 121, sect. XVIII.

30. Vilém Flusser, "The Photograph as Post-Industrial Object: An Essay on the Ontological Status of Objects," *Leonardo,* 19, no. 4 (1986), 329–332.

31. The literature on Piranesi is vast. See especially Ian Jonathan Scott, *Piranesi* (London and New York: Academy Editions and St. Martin's Press, 1975); John Wilton-Ely, *The Mind and Art of Giovanni Battista Piranesi* (London: Thames & Hudson, 1978); Norbert Miller, *Archäologie des Traums* (Munich and Vienna: Hanser Verlag, 1978); *Piranesi e la cultura antiquaria: Gli antecedenti e il contesto: Atti di Convegno* (Rome: Multigrafica Editrice, 1983; 1st ed., 1979); Marguerite Yourcenar, *The Dark Brain of Piranesi and Other Essays,* trans. Richard Howard (New York: Farrar, Straus, Giroux, 1984), 88–128; Andrew Robison, *Piranesi: Early Architectural Fantasies: A Catalogue Raisonné of the Etchings* (Chicago and London: University of Chicago Press, 1985).

32. David Bindman, *Blake as an Artist* (Oxford: Phaidon, 1977), 38–39.

33. Giambattista Piranesi, *Le Antichità Romane di . . . Architetto veneziano. Tomo secondo. Contenente gli avanzi di Monumenti Sepocrali di Roma e dell'agro Romano* (Rome: Presso l'Autore, 1756), frontispiece.

34. Charles Singer, *The Evolution of Anatomy: A Short History of Anatomical and Physiological Discovery to Harvey* (New York: Alfred A. Knopf, 1925), 111–135.

35. Zofia Ameisenowa, *The Problem of the Écorché and the Three Anatomical Models in the Jagiellonian Library,* trans. Andrzej Potocki (Wroclaw: Zaklad Narodowy im. Ossolinskich, 1963), 44–46.

36. While Piranesi's graphic innovations have been studied in relation to scenography (see, for example, *Piranèse et les français, 1740–1790,* exhibition catalogue [Rome: Edizioni dell'Elefante, 1976]), their connection to medical books remains unexplored. One would like to know, for example, what impact Giovanni Maria Lancisi's 1714 edition of the lost plates of Eustachius (1550–1574), or Albinus's *Explicatio tabularum anatomicorum Bartholomei Eustachii* (Leiden, 1744), made on him. On their history and importance, see Howard B. Adelmann, *Marcello Malpighi and the Evolution of Embryology,* vol. 1 (Ithaca: Cornell University Press, 1966), 634–636. More specifically, what did Piranesi learn from that masterpiece of eighteenth-century anatomy, Albinus's *Tabulae sceleti et musculorum corporis humani* (Leiden, 1737), about the analysis of structure and its presentation within an evocative pictorial context? For innovations in eighteenth-century medical books, see André Hahn, *Paule Du Maître,* and Janine Samion-Contet, *Histoire de la médecine et du livre médicale à la lumière des collections de la Bibliothèque de la Faculté de Médecine de Paris* (Paris: Olivier Perrin Editeur, 1962), 265ff. John Wilton-Ely in *The Mind and Art of Piranesi* (London and New York: Thames and Hudson, 1978), 45–80, used anatomical metaphors to describe Piranesi's archaeological work.

37. Mary A. B. Brazier, *A History of Neurophysiology in the Seventeenth and Eighteenth Centuries: From Concept to Experiment* (New York: Raven Press, 1984), 138–143.

38. For G. E. Lessing's attempt to establish laws separating spiritual, temporal poetry from corporeal, spatial painting, see his: *Laocoön: An Essay on the Limits of Painting and Poetry* (1766), trans. Edward Allen McCormick (Baltimore and London: Johns Hopkins University Press, 1984).

39. For Fontana's silent sanctuary of colored anatomical waxes, created by his chief worker in wax, Clemente Susini (1754–1814), for Florence's Museo Fisica e Storia Naturale (inaugurated in 1776) and, subsequently, for Vienna's Josephi-

nium, see Mario Bucci, *Anatomia come arte* (Florence: Edizione d'Arte Il Fiorino, 1969), 189–191.

40. See, for example, Ferrante Imperatore, *Historia Naturale di . . . Napolitano nella quale ordinatamente si tratta della diversa conditione di minere, pietre pretiose, & altre curiosità. Con varie Historie di pianti, & animali, fin hora non date in luce* (1599; Venice: Presso Combi, & La Noù, 1672) foldout plate. Also see Paula Findlen, "Containment: Objects, Places, Museums," *Thresholds,* 11 (1995), 7.

41. On the foundation of anatomical museums and natural history collections between 1528 and 1850, see F. J. Cole, *A History of Comparative Anatomy from Aristotle to the Eighteenth Century* (London: Macmillan, 1944), 443–463. On the educative value of eighteenth-century museums, see Paul Holdengräber, "A Visible History of Art," *Studies in Eighteenth-Century Culture,* 17 (1987), 107–117.

42. R. P. Claude du Molinet, *Le Cabinet de la bibliothèque de Sainte Geneviève, divisé en deux parties* (Paris: Chez Antoine Dezallier, 1692), plate 5.

43. For the growing body of scholarship on early collecting, see Paula Findlen, "The Museum: Its Classical Etymology and Renaissance Genealogy," *Journal of the History of Collections,* 1 (1989), 59–78.

44. Jean-Jacques Scheuchzer, *Physique sacrée, ou histoire naturelle de la Bible, vol. 1* (Amsterdam: Chez Pierre Schenk et Pierre Mortier, 1732), plate LVII.

45. Bryan G. Norton, *Why Preserve Natural Variety?* (Princeton: Princeton University Press, 1987), 151–156.

46. See my *Voyage into Substance,* 305–320.

47. See my "Characters in Stones, Marks on Paper: Enlightenment Discourse on Natural and Artificual *Taches*," *Art Journal,* 44 (Fall 1984), 233–240.

48. For an excellent discussion of the commerce and procedures of printmaking, see Victor I. Carlson and John W. Ittmann, *Regency to Empire: French Print-Making 1715–1814,* exhibition catalogue (Minneapolis: Minneapolis Institute of Arts, 1985).

49. William Schupbach, *The Paradox of Rembrandt's 'Anatomy of Dr. Tulp'* (London: Wellcome Institute for the History of Medicine, 1982), 32–34.

50. "Supercollider," *Chicago Tribune* (June 13, 1988), 11.

51. M. Ruse, "Is Biology Different from Physics?" in R. G. Colodny, ed., *Logic, Laws and Life: Some Philosophical Complications* (Pittsburgh: University of Pittsburgh Press, 1977), 91–109. Also see R. J. Faber, *Clockwork Garden: On the Mechanistic Reduction of Living Things* (Amherst: University of Massachusetts Press, 1986), xi.

52. See my "'Peculiar Marks': Lavater and the Countenance of Blemished Thought," *Art Journal,* 46 (Fall 1987), 185–192.

53. For some contemporary clinical implications of the physiognomic concept of formal perfection, see Barbara M. Stafford, John La Puma, M.D., and David L. Schiedermayer, M.D., "One Face of Beauty, One Picture of Health: The Hidden Aesthetic of Medical Practice," *Journal of Medicine and Philosophy,* 11 (1989), 213–230.

54. Max Kozloff, "Johns and Duchamp," *Art International,* 8 (March 20, 1964), 138–146.

55. G. W. Leibniz's "elegant artifice" was proposed, first, in the *De arte combinatoria* (1666), and again, later, in *Towards a Universal Characteristic* (1677). See *Leibniz Selections,* ed. Philip P. Wiener (New York: Charles Scribner's Sons, 1951), 17–25.

56. G. C. Lichtenberg, *Über Physiognomik wider die Physiognomen. Zur Beförderung der Menschenliebe und Menschenkenntniss,* ed. K. Riha (Steibbach: Anabas Verlag, 1970).

57. Plato, *Republic* 6. 509D–511E; and *Sophist* 235D–236C.

58. For the most thorough analysis of these *chiaroscuro* epistemological metaphors, as they evolved in Platonism and Neoplatonism, see Wesley Trimpi, *Muses of One Mind: The Literary Analysis of Experience and Its Continuity* (Princeton: Princeton University Press, 1983), esp. 113–120, 212–216.

59. For the arguments against this claim, see Robert G. Turnbull, "The Role of the 'Special Sensibles' in the Perception Theories of Plato and Aristotle," in Peter K. Machamer and Robert G. Turnbull, eds., *Studies in Perception: Interrelations in the History of Philosophy and Science* (Columbus: Ohio State University Press, 1978), 4–23.

60. For over two decades the British educator William Baldwin has argued that school curricula should group geography with English and mathematics as foundation subjects for precollege education. His argument rests on the thesis that there are four basic types of human intelligence with their respective educational counterparts: literacy, articulacy, numeracy, and graphicacy. See Mark Monmonier and George A. Schnell, *Map Appreciation* (Englewood Cliffs: Prentice Hall, 1988), 4. The irony remains, however, that during this past decade we have witnessed the extinction of geography programs at the precollege and college levels. One has to wonder whether, among the several reasons for this demise, there was not the old logocentrism embodied in the belief that visual media do not sufficiently stimulate the *intellectual* aspects of our mental processes. For early evidence of this conflict between text and image on maps, see Arthur Robinson, *The Look of Maps: An Examination of Cartographic Design* (Madison, Milwaukee, and London: University of Wisconsin Press, 1966), 55–57. Significantly, there are no illustrations in this book!

2   DISPLAY AND THE RHETORIC OF CORRUPTION

1. See my *Artful Science: Enlightenment Entertainment and the Eclipse of Visual Education* (Cambridge, Mass., and London: MIT Press, 1994), chapter 1, "The Mind's Release."

2. James Coates, "Multimedia's the Word," *Chicago Tribune* (June 4, 1993), section 9, pp. 1–2.

3. Victor Margolin, "Design History or Design Studies: Subject Matter and Methods," *Design Studies,* 13 (April 1992), 115.

4. Friedrich Kittler, "Gramophone, Film, Typewriter," *October,* 41 (Fall 1986), 101–164.

5. See my *Body Criticism: Imaging the Unseen in Enlightenment Art and Medicine* (Cambridge, Mass., and London: MIT Press, 1991), esp. 24–45; and chapter 1 in this volume.

6. For a prominent spokesman, with a strong history of ideas approach, see the collected writings of G. S. Rousseau, *Enlightenment Crossings: Pre- and Post-Modern Discourses: Anthropological* (vol. 1); *Enlightenment Borders: Pre- and Post-Modern Discourses: Medical, Scientific* (vol. 2); *Perilous Enlightenment: Pre- and Post-Modern Discourses: Sexual, Historical* (vol. 3) (Manchester: Manchester University Press, 1991).

7. Paul Roberts, "Electronics Ethics," *Aldus Magazine,* 4 (June 1993), 15–18.

8. For the suggestion that forgery is a special case of all artistic work, see James Elkins, "From Original to Copy and Back Again," *British Journal of Aesthetics,* 33 (April 1993), 114.

9. Steve Lohr, "Across the Computer Divide, the Nerds face the Dummies," *New York Times* (June 6, 1993), 1, 4.

10. See my "Art of Conjuring, Or How the Romantic Virtuoso Learned from the Enlightened Charlatan," *Art Journal,* 52 (Summer 1993), 22–30.

11. For our continuing reverence for, and objectification of, supposedly authentic and culturally pure experiences, see, Scott Rankin's color/stereo video art production *The Pure* (1993).

12. François-Saneré Chérubim d'Orléans, *La dioptrique oculaire, ou la théorique, la positive, et la méchanique, de l'oculaire dioptrique en toutes ses espèces* (Paris: Chez Thomas Jolly & Simon Benard, 1671), dedication.

13. Christine Buci-Glucksmann, *La folie du voir. De l'esthétique baroque* (Paris: Editions Galilée, 1986), 33–34.

14. Bruno Latour, *Science in Action: How to Follow Scientists and Engineers through Society* (Milton Keynes: Open University Press, 1987), 21–29, 133–135.

15. On the denigration of vision in twentieth-century French theory, see Martin Jay, "Ideology and Ocularcentrism: Is There Anything behind the Mirror's Tain?" in *Force Fields: Between Intellectual History and Cultural Critique* (New York and London: Routledge, 1993), 134–136.

16. On the mistaken analogy betwen language and the visual arts, developed in Saussurian-inspired structuralist and poststructuralist theory, see David Summers, "Conditions and Conventions: On the Disanalogy of Art and Language," in Salim Kemal and Ivan Gaskell, eds., *The Language of Art History* (Cambridge: Cambridge University Press, 1992), 181–212.

17. David Summers, "Why Did Kant Call Taste a 'Common Sense?'" in Paul Mattick, Jr., ed., *Eighteenth-Century Aesthetics and the Reconstruction of Art* (Cambridge: Cambridge University Press, 1993), 147–148.

18. For the tenacity of the linguistic analogy in the philosophy of perception, see Margaret Atherton, *Berkeley's Revolution in Vision* (Ithaca and London: Cornell University Press, 1990), 195–198. On the fascination for hieroglyphics as a universal, and esoteric, language during the later eighteenth century, see my *Symbol and*

Myth: Humbert de Superville's Essay on Absolute Signs in Art (Cranbury, N.J.: Associated University Presses, 1976), 78–94.

19. See my "Voyeur or Observer? Enlightenment Thoughts on the Dilemma of Display," *Configurations* 1 (Fall 1992), 95–128.

20. On the deep connections between the Enlightenment and romanticism, see Laurence S. Lockridge, *The Ethics of Romanticism* (Cambridge: Cambridge University Press, 1989), 73.

21. On the overstepping of legitimate boundaries, see Bruno Latour, *The Pasteurization of France,* trans. Alan Sheridan and John Law (Cambridge, Mass., and London: Harvard University Press, 1988), 187.

22. See my "Instructive Games: Apparatus and the Experimental Aesthetics of Imposture," in Walter Pape and Frederick Burwick, eds., *Reflecting Senses: Perception and Appearance in Literature, Culture, and the Arts* (Berlin and New York: W. de Gruyter, 1995).

23. See, for example, David Vincent, *Literacy and Popular Culture. England, 1730–1914* (Cambridge: Cambridge University Press, 1989), 6.

24. J. Paul Hunter, *Before Novels: The Cultural Contexts of Eighteenth-Century Fiction* (New York and London: W. W. Norton, 1990), 82–83; and Roger Chartier, "The Practical Impact of Writing," in *A History of Private Life,* vol. 3, *Passions of the Renaissance,* ed. Roger Chartier, trans. Arthur Goldhammer (Cambridge, Mass., and London: Belknap Press of Harvard University Press, 1989), 119–121, 130–132.

25. For the religious and political background leading to the eventual suppression of the Jesuit order, see Christopher M. S. Johns, *Papal Art and Cultural Politics: Rome in the Age of Clement XI* (Cambridge: Cambridge University Press, 1993), 2–12.

26. *Iconographia emblematica Triplicis ad Deum Tri-Unum mysticae viae, purgationae, Illuminativae unitivae: splendoribus sanctorum* (Augsburg: Ignatius Verhelst, 1779).

27. See, for example, Claire Richter Sherman, "Beyond the Photo Archive: Imaging the History of Psychology," *Visual Resources,* 9 (1992), 39.

28. For this dominant theme in Goya, see Janis Tomlinson, *Goya's Tapestry Cartoons* (New Haven and London: Yale University Press, 1991), 154–156.

29. Lorraine Daston, "Marvelous Facts and Miraculous Evidence in Early Modern Europe," *Critical Inquiry,* 18 (Autumn 1991), 93–124.

30. David Hume, *Of Miracles* (La Salle, Ill.: Open Court, 1987), 161.

31. Lorraine Daston, *Classical Probability in the Enlightenment* (Princeton: Princeton University Press, 1988), 320–321.

32. E. S. Shaffer, *"Kubla Khan" and the Fall of Jerusalem: The Mythological School in Biblical Criticism and Secular Literature* (Cambridge: Cambridge University Press, 1975), 63–64, 86–91.

33. Naomi Schor, *Reading in Detail: Aesthetics and the Feminine* (New York and London: Methuen, 1987), 84. On the dominance of "detailism" in all facets of contem-

porary cultural criticism, see Alan Liu, "Local Transcendence: Cultural Criticism, Postmodernism, and the Romanticism of Detail," *Representations,* 32 (Fall 1990), 75–113.

34. For the importance of this trope within the eighteenth-century emblem tradition, see Franz Anton, Graf von Sporck, *Der sogennante Sinn-Lehr und geistvolle . . . Todtentanz* (Vienna: Gedruckt bey Johann Thomas Edlen von Trattnern, 1767).

35. See my "The Postmodern Aesthetics of Medical Ethics," in Tobin Siebers, ed., *Bio-Technological Utopias* (Ann Arbor: University of Michigan Press, 1994).

36. E. Leonard Rubin, "Toll Booths on the Information Highway—A Legal Perspective," *Chicago,* 17 (Spring 1995), 1–3.

37. See, for example, Hal Foster, ed., *The Anti-Aesthetic: Essays on Postmodern Culture* (Port Townsend, Wash.: Bay Press, 1983), xv.

38. Jeffrey Barnouw, "The Beginnings of 'Aesthetics' and the Leibnizian Conception of Sensation," in Mattick, *Eighteenth-Century Aesthetics,* 95.

3 THE EIGHTEENTH CENTURY AT THE END OF MODERNITY

1. This essay, commissioned for the twenty-fifth anniversary of the American Society for Eighteenth-Century Studies, forms a sequel to my state-of-the-field essay, "The Eighteenth Century: Towards an Interdisciplinary Model," *Art Bulletin,* 79 (March 1988), 6–24.

2. For Walter Benjamin's understanding of modernity as a shock to the neurological system, see Susan Buck-Morss, "Aesthetics and Anaesthetics: Walter Benjamin's Artwork Essay Reconsidered," *October,* 62 (Fall 1992), 16–17.

3. Leonard Barkan, *The Gods Made Flesh: Metamorphosis and the Pursuit of Paganism* (New Haven and London: Yale University Press, 1986), 56.

4. On the computer as a revolutionary medium, see Frank Biocca, "Communication without Virtual Reality: Creating a Space for Research," *Journal of Communications,* 42 (Autumn 1992), 5–22.

5. Ronald Lee Fleming, "Saving Shopping Centers: An Owlish View, or, Give a Hoot for Enhancement," *The Forum: Bulletin of the Committee on Preservation* [Society of Architectural Historians], 21 (April 1993).

6. Wesley Trimpi, "Review of *The Cambridge History of Literary Criticism,* Vol. I: *Classical Criticism,*" *Ancient Philosophy,* 12 (1992), 510.

7. G. S. Rousseau, paper in the panel "Are the Disciplines Dead? Cross-Disciplinary Approaches to Eighteenth-Century Studies," Annual Meeting of the American Society for Eighteenth-Century Studies, Providence, Rhode Island, April 24, 1993. Also see his seminal essays on the state of modern scholarship collected in *Enlightenment Borders: Pre- and Post-Modern Discourses: Medical, Scientific* and *Perilous Enlightenment: Pre- and Post-Modern Discourses: Sexual, Historical* (Manchester: Manchester University Press, 1991).

8. James A. Winn, "The Intellectual Economy of Interdisciplinary Scholarship" (forthcoming).

9. Hélène Cixous, "Clarice Lispector," in *"Coming to Writing" and Other Essays,* ed. Deborah Jenson (Cambridge, Mass., and London: Harvard University Press, 1991), 62.

10. For the relation between material progress and moral decline, see Malcolm Jack, *Corruption and Progress* (New York: AMS Press, 1989), ix.

11. Reflexive anthropology has led in the celebration of the impossibility of systematically knowing the elusive "Other." See Marshall Sahlins, "Goodbye to Tristes Tropiques: Ethnography in the Context of Modern World History," the 1992 Ryerson Lecture, *The University of Chicago Record,* 27, no. 3 (1993), 2–7.

12. Marjorie Perloff, *Radical Artifice: Writing Poetry in the Age of Media* (Chicago and London: University of Chicago Press, 1991), 11.

13. William Keach, *Shelley's Style* (New York and London: Methuen, 1984), 25.

14. Friedrich Kittler, "Gramophone, Film, Typewriter," *October,* 41 (1987), 102.

15. Hal Foster, ed., *The Anti-Aesthetic: Essays on Postmodern Culture* (Port Townsend, Wash.: Bay Press, 1983), xv–xvi.

16. Gilles Deleuze and Félix Guattari, *Anti-Oedipus: Capitalism and Schizophrenia,* trans. Robert Hurley, Mark Seem, and Helen R. Lane (Minneapolis: University of Minnesota Press, 1983), xx.

17. Fredric Jameson, *Late Marxism: Adorno, or, the Persistence of the Dialectic* (New York: Verso, 1991), 232.

18. Michel Foucault, *Discipline and Punish: The Birth of the Prison* (New York: Pantheon Books, 1977), 221.

19. Ronald Schleuer, Robert Con Davis, and Nancy Mergler, *Culture and Cognition: The Boundaries of Literary and Scientific Inquiry* (Ithaca and London: Cornell University Press, 1992), 201.

20. Fredric Jameson, in *The Political Unconscious: Narrative as a Socially Symbolic Art* (Ithaca and London: Cornell University Press, 1981), 35, noted that Althusser's sweeping negativity is based on Lacan's notion of the Real.

21. See Edward Said, *Orientalism* (New York: Vintage Books, 1978), 7–14, for the wide-ranging importance of Gramsci's notion of hegemony as a form of cultural leadership where certain forms predominate over others.

22. See, for example, Terry Eagleton, *The Ideology of the Aesthetic* (London: Basil Blackwell, 1990), 13, on the politicization of the aesthetic.

23. For the aesthetic as a kind of knowing that relies on nuanced assessments of sensory experience and feeling, see Jeffrey Barnouw, "The Beginnings of 'Aesthetics' and the Leibnizian Conception of Sensation," in Paul Mattick, Jr., ed., *Eighteenth-Century Aesthetics and the Reconstruction of Art* (Cambridge: Cambridge University Press, 1993), 52–95.

24. Ernest Gellner, *The Devil in Modern Philosophy,* ed. I. C. Jarvie and Joseph Agassi (London and Boston: Routledge & Kegan Paul, 1974), 4–7.

25. For the connection between the new criticism and interdisciplinarity, see the exchange between Oscar Kenshur, "Demystifying the Demystifiers: Metaphysical Snares of Ideological Criticism," *Critical Inquiry,* 14 (Winter 1988), 335–353; and Robert Markley, "What Isn't History: The Snares of Demystifying Ideological Criticism," *Critical Inquiry,* 15 (Spring 1989), 647–657.

26. Werner Schneiders, "Die Mission der Philosophie," in Werner Schneiders, ed., *Aufklärung als Mission. La Mission des Lumières. Akzeptanzprobleme und Kommunikationsdefizite. Accueil réciproque et difficultés de communication* (Marburg: Hitzeroth, 1993), 11–21.

27. Ernest Lee Tuveson, *The Avatars of Thrice Great Hermes: An Approach to Romanticism* (Lewisburg, Pa.: Bucknell University Press, 1982), 106.

28. Isaiah Berlin, *The Crooked Timber of Humanity: Chapters in the History of Ideas* (New York: Alfred A. Knopf, 1991), 5.

29. Mark C. Taylor, *Disfiguring: Art, Architecture, Religion* (Chicago and London: University of Chicago Press, 1992), 101–102.

30. Judith N. Shklar, *Ordinary Vices* (Cambridge, Mass., and London: Harvard University Press, 1984), 48. I am grateful to Tobin Siebers for having drawn my attention to this book.

31. Gerald N. Izenberg, *Impossible Individuality: Romanticism, Revolution, and the Origins of Modern Selfhood, 1787–1802* (Princeton: Princeton University Press, 1992), 264, 310.

32. Tobin Siebers, *The Romantic Fantastic* (Ithaca and London: Cornell University Press, 1984), 35.

33. For the historical connection between vandalism and a logic of denunciation, see Dominique Poulot, "Revolutionary 'Vandalism' and the Birth of the Museum: The Effects of a Representation of Modern Cultural Terror," in Susan Pearce, ed., *Art in Museums* (London and Atlantic Highlands, N.J.: Athlone Press, 1995), 192–213.

34. Amy M. Spindler, "African Prince of Pieces Stitches Cultures Together," *New York Times* (May 3, 1993), B1, B4.

35. Anthony Vidler, *The Architectural Uncanny: Essays in the Modern Unhomely* (Cambridge, Mass., and London: MIT Press, 1992), x.

36. James M. Rosen is currently the William S. Morris Eminent Scholar in Art at Augusta College, Augusta, Georgia.

37. Philippe Lacoue-Labarthe and Jean-Luc Nancy, *The Literary Absolute: The Theory of Literature in German Romanticism,* trans. Philip Barnard and Cheryl Lester (Albany: State University of New York Press, 1988), 11.

38. John M. Hoberman, "Creating the 'New Man': German and Soviet Sports Photographs between the Wars," in *This Sporting Life, 1878–1991,* exhibition catalogue, ed. Ellen Dugan (Atlanta: The High Museum, 1992), n.p.

39. Although they proved permeable in actual discussion, such binary constructions provided the titles and topics for panels at the symposium "Politicized Edu-

cation and Its Discontents," University of Chicago Humanities Institute, May 27–May 28, 1993.

40. Jürgen Habermas, "Modernity—An Incomplete Project," in Foster, *The Anti-Aesthetic*, 9–12.

41. Lorraine Daston, "Marvelous Facts and Miraculous Evidence in Early Modern Europe," *Critical Inquiry,* 18 (Autumn 1991), 93–124.

42. Paul Barolsky, "Cellini, Vasari, and the Marvels of Malady," *Sixteenth-Century Journal,* 24, no. 1 (1993), 41–42.

43. Jean Baudrillard, "The Ecstasy of Communication," in Foster, *The Anti-Aesthetic,* 130.

44. Veronica Hollinger, "Cybernetic Deconstructions: Cyberpunk and Postmodernism," *Mosaic,* 23 (Spring 1990), 29–44.

45. See, for example, the *Arachnet Electronic Journal of Virtual Culture,* existing only in electronic form. The Society for Literature and Science, which has many eighteenth-century scholars as members, is also at the forefront of exploring the interface between interdisciplinarity and technology.

46. See my "Present Image, Past Text, Post Body: Educating the Late Modern Citizen," *Semiotica,* 91, nos. 3/4 (1992), 195–198.

47. David Summers, "Conditions and Conventions: On the Disanalogy of Art and Language," in Salim Kemal and Ivan Gaskell, eds., *The Language of Art History* (Cambridge: Cambridge University Press, 1992), 181–212.

48. This artisanal and design potential inhered in the practical side of the Enlightenment. See Antoine Picon, *French Architects and Engineers in the Age of Enlightenment,* trans. Martin Than (Cambridge: Cambridge University Press, 1988), 119.

49. Victor Margolin, *Design: Discourse: History/Theory/Criticism* (Chicago and London: University of Chicago Press, 1989), 4–5.

50. Cheryl Buckley, "Made in Patriarchy: Toward a Feminist Analysis of Women and Design," in Margolin, *Design Discourse,* 251–262.

51. Clive Dilnot, "The State of Design History. Part II: Problems and Possibilities," in Margolin, *Design Discourse,* 236.

4   THE NEW IMAGIST

1. Vic Sussman, "Policing Cyberspace," *US News & World Report* (January 23, 1995), 55–60.

2. Andy Meisler, "TV Getting a Closer Look as a Contributor to Real Violence," *New York Times* (December 14, 1984), A1, A13.

3. Guy Debord, *Society of the Spectacle* (Detroit: Black & Red, 1977), Aphorism 10.

4. Goldie Blumenstyck, "Networks to the Rescue?" *Chronicle of Higher Education* (December 14, 1994), A21.

5. Chad J. Kainz, *Multimedia Basics* (Chicago: Multimedia & Visualization Center, 1994), 3.

6. Even the Getty Center's five national conferences (dating back to 1987), reflecting deeply on the future of arts education in light of technology, have not addressed this specific problem. See "The Arts: Central to Education and School Reform," *The Getty Center for Education in the Arts,* 14 (Winter 1994–1995), 10–12.

7. Richard P. Cunningham, "Journalism: Toward an Accountable Profession," in *The Public Duties of the Professions, A Hastings Center Report,* Special Supplement (February 1987), 15.

8. David L. Wilson, "A Key for Entering Virtual Worlds," *Chronicle of Higher Education* (November 16, 1994), A19, A21.

9. David Porter, "Assembling a Poet and Her Poems: Convergent Limit-Works of Joseph Cornell and Emily Dickinson," *Word & Image,* 10 (July–September 1994), 208.

10. Annie-France Laurens and Krzysztof Pomain, eds., *L'Anticomanie. La collection d'antiquités aux 18e et 19e siècles* (Paris: Editions de L'Ecole des Hautes Etudes en Sciences Sociales, 1988), 209–218.

11. Note that three federal agencies have joined in an effort to integrate science and humanities studies at the undergraduate level. NSF, NEH, and FIPSE are making awards as part of an initiative entitled "Leadership Opportunity and Science and Humanities Education."

12. Dave Hickey, *The Invisible Dragon: Four Essays on Beauty* (Los Angeles: Art Issues Press, 1993), 10, similarly argues for the efficacy of images through their sheer beauty.

5 MAKING IMAGES REAL

1. Joseph Alper, "Biomedicine in the Age of Imaging," *Science,* 261 (July 30, 1993), 560.

2. Selected papers from this symposium will be published in two issues of the annual *Advances in Visual Semiotics: The Semiotic Web* (Bloomington: University of Indiana, 1996).

3. Robert N. Beck, "Issues of Imaging Science for Future Consideration," *Proceedings of the National Academy of Sciences of the United States of America,* 90, no. 21 (November 1, 1993), 9803–9807.

4. Robert P. Crease, "Biomedicine in the Age of Imaging," *Science,* 261 (July 30, 1993), 560–561.

5. The Getty Art History Information Program (AHIP) with the ACLS organized a groundbreaking national conference in the fall of 1992 on the new information technologies. One of their exciting recommendations was that humanities scholars be enlisted to interpret the impact of information technology on society and to promote that technology in research and teaching. I am making a different, but complementary, point.

6. On anthropology's continuing role as an orienting discipline, see Ernest Gellner, "What Do We Need Now? Social Anthropology and Its New Global Context," *TLS* (July 16, 1993), 3–4.

1. Nicholas Jardine, "A Trial of Galileos," essay review, *Isis,* 85 (June 1994),
279–283.

2. See, for example, Jonathan Barnes, "Like Us, Only Better," *Classics, TLS* (April
23, 1994), 3–4.

3. George Stocking, "On the Limits of 'Presentism' and 'Historicism' in the Histo-
riography of the Behavioral Sciences," editorial in *Journal of the History of the Behavioral Sciences,* 1 (1965), 215.

4. Nancy S. Struever, *Theory as Practice: Ethical Inquiry in the Renaissance* (Chicago:
University of Chicago Press, 1992), xi.

5. Burton Bollag, "The 'Great Equalizer,'" *Chronicle of Higher Education* (June 29,
1994), A17–A19.

6. Johann Zahn, *Specula physico-mathematico-historica notabilium ac mirabilium scien-
dorum in qua mundi mirabilis oeconomia,* 3 vols. (Nuremberg: Sumptibus Joannis
Christophori Lochner, 1696).

7. The baroque materialization of divinity appears to be returning in contemporary "religion and environment" studies. See, for example, Sallie McFague, *The
Body of God: An Ecological Theology* (New York: Fortress Press, 1993).

8. See my *Voyage into Substance: Art, Science, Nature, and the Illustrated Travel Account,
1760–1840* (Cambridge, Mass., and London: MIT Press, 1984), chapter 3: "The
Fugitive Effect."

9. Robert N. Beck, "The Future of Imaging Science," *Advance in Visual Semiotics,
The Semiotic Web* (Bloomington: University of Indiana Press, 1996).

10. He has written a series of books on this theme. See, for example, Neil Postman, *Conscientious Objections: Stirring up Trouble about Language, Technology, and Education* (New York: Alfred A. Knopf, 1988), xiii.

11. Gregory Ulmer, *Teletheory: Grammatology in the Age of Video* (New York and London: Routledge, 1989), 45.

12. For the distinction between "natural" and "artificial" grotesque compositions
(and the latter's connection to electronic imagery), see my *Body Criticism: Imaging
the Unseen in Enlightenment Art and Medicine* (Cambridge, Mass., and London: MIT
Press, 1991), 266–280, 329–340.

13. On hypertext as the teacher of the future, see Richard A. Lanham, *The Electronic Word: Democracy, Technology, and the Arts* (Chicago and London: University of
Chicago Press, 1994), 219.

14. Mitchell M. Waldrop, *Complexity: The Emerging Science at the Edge of Order and
Chaos* (New York: Simon & Schuster, 1992), 13.

15. See my "Conjuring: How the Romantic Virtuoso Learned from the Enlightened Charlatan," *Art Journal,* 52 (Summer 1993), 22–30; "Instructive Games:
Apparatus and the Experimental Aesthetics of Imposture," in Walter Pape and

Frederick Burwick, eds., *Reflecting Senses: Perception and Appearance in Literature, Culture, and the Arts* (Berlin and New York: W. de Gruyter, 1995).

16. Howard Gardner, *Art Education and Human Development*, Occasional Paper 3 (Los Angeles: The J. Paul Getty Trust, 1990), 49.

17. Mihaly Csikszentmihalyi, "Design and Order in Everyday Life," *Design Issues,* 8 (Fall 1991), 27.

18. John Brinkerhoff Jackson, *A Sense of Place, a Sense of Time* (New Haven and London: Yale University Press, 1993); see the chapter, "Working at Home."

19. Simon Schaffer, "The Consuming Flame: Electrical Showmen and Tory Mysticism in the World of Goods," in John Brewer and Roy Porter, eds., *Consumption and the World of Goods* (London and New York: Routledge, 1993), 489–526.

20. This is the thesis of Jonathan Crary's *Techniques of the Observer: On Vision and Modernity in the Nineteenth Century* (Cambridge, Mass., and London: MIT Press, 1991); and in "Unbinding Vision," *October,* 68 (Spring 1994), 21–44.

21. Microscopy, historically, was a case in point. See my *Body Criticism,* chapter 5, "Magnifying."

22. Richard Coyne, "Heidegger and Virtual Reality: The Implications of Heidegger's Thinking for Computer Representations," *Leonardo,* 27, no. 1 (1994), 66–68.

23. Anders Michelsen, "Jeff Wall," *Art Factum,* 46 (December 1992), 33.

24. William Gibson, *Count Zero* (New York: Ace Books, 1987), 119.

25. For example, that assembled by Bonnier de la Mosson (died in 1747). See John Whitehead, *The French Interior in the Eighteenth Century* (New York: Dutton Studio Books, 1992), 28–29.

26. For what little is known about him, see my *Artful Science: Enlightenment Entertainment and the Eclipse of Visual Education* (Cambridge, Mass., and London: MIT Press, 1994), 182–186.

27. Charles Rabiqueau, *Le microscope moderne, pour débrouiller la nature par le filtre d'un nouvel alémbic chymique où l'on voit un nouveau méchanisme physique universel* (Paris: Chez l'Auteur et Demonville, 1781), 1.

28. William A. Covino, *The Art of Wondering: A Revisionist Return to the History of Rhetoric* (Portsmouth, N.H.: Boynton/Cook Publishers, 1988), 9.

29. Mark Franko, *The Dancing Body in Renaissance Choreography (c. 1416–1589)* (Birmingham, Ala.: Summa Publications, 1986), 22–23.

30. Philippe Desan, *Naissance de la méthode (Machiavel, La Ramée, Bodin, Montaigne, Descartes)* (Paris: Librairie A.-G. Nizet, 1987), 10.

31. Christine Buci-Glucksmann, *La folie du voir. De l'esthétique baroque* (Paris: Editions Galilée, 1986), 29.

32. Diskin Clay, *Lucretius and Epicurus* (Ithaca and London: Cornell University Press, 1983), 86.

33. Mihaly Csikszentmihalyi, *Flow: The Psychology of Optimal Experience* (New York: Harper & Row, 1990), 16–22.

34. Anne Barclay Morgan, "Art and Technology: Tomorrow's Palette," *Art in America* (April 1994), 36–42.

35. Richard Buchanan, editorial, *Design Issues, 9* (Fall 1992), 3–4; and "Rhetoric, Humanism, and Design," in *Discovering Design* (Chicago and London: University of Chicago Press, 1995).

36. Keith Thomas, introduction to Jan Bremmer and Herman Roodenburg, eds., *A Cultural History of Gesture* (Ithaca: Cornell University Press, 1991), 5.

37. Evlyn Gould, *Virtual Theater from Diderot to Mallarmé* (Baltimore and London: Johns Hopkins University Press, 1989), 1.

38. On the effort, stretching from the Enlightenment to romanticism, to put illusion in a mentalized space, see Frederick Burwick, *Illusion and Drama: Critical Theory of the Enlightenment and Romantic Era* (University Park: Pennsylvania State University Press, 1991), 17.

39. See Mario Biagioli, *Galileo Courtier: The Practice of Science in the Age of Absolutism* (Chicago and London: University of Chicago Press, 1993), for the aristocratic etiquette of Tuscan science.

40. Steven Shapin, *A Social History of Truth: Civility and Science in Seventeenth-Century England* (Chicago and London: University of Chicago Press, 1994), 97.

41. For the situation of the writer, see Peter France, *Politeness and Its Discontents: Problems in French Classical Culture* (Cambridge: Cambridge University Press, 1992), 106.

42. On Lavoisier's intellectualization of chemistry, see Jan Golinski, *Science as Public Culture: Chemistry and Enlightenment in Britain, 1760–1820* (Cambridge: Cambridge University Press, 1992), 137.

43. Louis-Sébastien Mercier, *Le nouveau Paris,* 6 vols. (Brunswick and Paris: Chez Frédéric Heweg & Chez Fuchs, 1800), 6:15.

44. Ibid., 2:123, 165–170.

45. Ibid., 3:93–125; 5:193.

46. [Noël Retz], *Mémoire pour servir à l'histoire de la jonglerie, dans lequel on démontre les phénomènes du mesmérisme* (London and Paris: Chez Méquignon, 1784), 2–3.

47. Alan Gauld, *A History of Hypnotism* (Cambridge: Cambridge University Press, 1992), 5.

48. Jean-Baptiste Bonnefoy, *Analyse raisonné des rapports des commissaires chargés par le roy de l'examen du magnetisme animal* (Lyons and Paris: Chez Prault, Imprimeur du Roi, 1784), 65–66.

49. Heinz Schott, "Neurogamies. De la relation entre mesmérisme, hypnose et psychanalyse," in *L'Âme au corps. Arts et sciences, 1793–1993,* exhibition catalogue, ed. Jean Clair (Paris: Réunion des Musées Nationaux, 1993), 142–153.

50. Jan Goldstein, *Console and Classify: The French Psychiatric Profession in the Nineteenth Century* (Cambridge: Cambridge University Press, 1987), 87.

51. Eusèbe Salverte, *Des rapports de la médecine avec la politique* (Paris: Chez Moreau, 1806), 152–156.

52. Ray Quintanilla, "Future of Magic Could be Illusion," *Chicago Tribune* (July 15, 1994), section 2, pp. 1, 6.

53. Rabiqueau, *Le microscope moderne,* 160–162.

54. Charles Rabiqueau, *Le spectacle du feu élémentaire ou cours d'électricité expérimentale* (Paris: Chez Jombert, Krapen, Duchesne, 1753), 240. Also see Laura Bossi, "L'Âme électrique," in *L'Âme au corps,* 162–163.

55. Charles Rabiqueau, *Prospectus du cabinet du Mr. . . .* (Paris: Chez l'Auteur, Chez Cailleau, Imprimeur-Libraire, 1772).

56. Vartan Gregorian, "Technology, Scholarship, and the Humanities: The Implications of Electronic Information," *Leonardo,* 27, no. 2 (1994), 129.

57. John D. Callaway, *The Thing of It Is: With Reflections on Chicago and the Problem Society* (Ottawa, Ill.: Jameson Books, 1994), 278.

7   THE NATURAL HISTORY OF DESIGN: HUMBERT DE SUPERVILLE AND POSTMODERN THEORY

1. Richard Buchanan, "The Design of Design: Reflections and Conference Summary," *Design at the Crossroads: A Conference Report,* CIRA Working Papers, no. 3 (June 1991), 10.

2. Natalie Angier, "Why Birds and Bees, Too, Like Good Looks," *New York Times* (February 8, 1994), B8. Also see Irenäus Eibl-Eibesfeldt and Christa Sütterlin, *Im Banne der Angst. Zur Natur und Kunstgeschichte menschlicher Abwehrsymbolik* (Munich and Zurich: Piper, 1992).

3. Humphrey Wine, "The End of History? Painting in France c. 1770–1880," in *Tradition and Revolution in French Art 1700–1800: Paintings and Drawings from Lille,* exhibition catalogue (London: National Gallery of Art, 1993), 20.

4. See, for example, Paul Ekman, "Facial Expression and Emotion," *American Psychologist,* 48 (April 1993), 384–392.

5. Martin Weyl, *Passion for Reason and Reason of Passion: Seventeenth-Century Art and Theory in France, 1648–1683* (New York, Bern, Frankfurt-am-Main: Peter Lang Verlag, 1989), 117–121.

6. Richard J. Campbell and Victor Carlson, *Visions of Antiquity: Neoclassical Figural Drawing,* exhibition catalogue (Los Angeles and Minneapolis: Los Angeles County Museum and the Minneapolis Museum of Arts, 1993), 15.

7. See chapter 3 in this volume. Also see Dominique Poulot, "Patrimoine et esthétique du territoire," *Espaces et Sociétés,* special issue (December 1992), 15–16.

8. Régis Michel, *Le Beau idéal ou l'art du concept,* exhibition catalogue (Paris: Editions de la Réunion des Musées Nationaux, 1989), 8.

9. Marco Diani, "Immateriality Takes Command," in Diani, ed., *The Immaterial Society: Design, Culture, and Technology in the Postmodern World* (Englewood Cliffs, N.J.: Prentice Hall, 1992), 1–12.

10. Cited in Ellis Shookman, "Pseudo-Science, Social Fad, Literary Wonder: Johann Caspar Lavater and the Art of Physiognomy," in Shookman, ed., *The Faces of Physiognomy: Interdisciplinary Approaches to Johann Caspar Lavater* (Columbia, S.C.: Camden House, 1993), 17.

11. On Lavater's thousand-letter alphabet, see Christoph Siegrist, "'Letters of the Divine Alphabet'—Lavater's Concept of Physiognomy," in Shookman, *Faces of Physiognomy,* 32.

12. The classic study of their rediscovery remains that of Giovanni Previtali, *La Fortuna dei primitivi dal Vasari ai neoclassici* (Turin: Einaudi, 1964).

13. Henri Loyrette, "Seroux d'Agincourt et les origines de l'histoire de l'art médieval," *Revue de l'Art,* 48 (1980), 40–56.

14. Andrew Ladis, "Charity Triumphant: The Role of the Virtues and Vices in Giotto's Arena Chapel," paper delivered at Folger Library Consortium Workshop, "How Images Mean," Washington, D.C., March 4–5, 1994.

15. See my "Arena of Virtue and Temple of Immortality: An Early Nineteenth-Century Museum Project," *Journal of the Society of Architectural Historians,* 35 (March 1976), 21–34.

16. See Sylvia Lavin, *Quatremère de Quincy and the Invention of a Modern Language of Architecture* (Cambridge, Mass., and London: MIT Press, 1992); Dominique Poulot, "The Birth of Heritage: 'le moment Guizot,'" *Oxford Art Journal,* 11, no. 2 (1988), 46; and Dominique Poulot, "La naissance du musée," in Regis Michel and Philippe Bordes, eds., *Aux armes et aux arts!* (Paris: Adam, 1988), 201–231.

17. Victor Margolin, "The Politics of the Artificial," lecture, California College of Arts and Crafts, San Francisco, April 21, 1992.

18. For the complex politics of the Koninklijke Nederlandse Akademie van Wetenschappen (especially the Instituut van Wetenschappen, Letteren, en Schoone Kunsten) of which Humbert was a member, see *Van Wapenhandel tot Wetenschapsbedrijf. De Koninklijke Nederlandse Akademie van Wetenschappen in het Trippenhuis te Amsterdam,* exhibition catalogue (Amsterdam: Snoeck-Ducaju & Zoon, 1993), 38–47.

19. On the postmodern return to narrative as a metacode, on the basis of which transcultural messages about a shaped reality can be transmitted, see Hayden White, *The Content of Form: Narrative Discourse and Historical Representation* (Baltimore and London: Johns Hopkins University Press, 1987), 1–3.

20. On the intense interest in the problem of interpretation, see Joel C. Weinsheimer, *Eighteenth-Century Hermeneutics: Philosophy of Interpretation in England from Locke to Burke* (New Haven and London: Yale University Press, 1993), x–xi.

21. Daniel Simeoni, "Language Processes and the Metalinguistic Puzzle," in Diani, *The Immaterial Society,* 139.

22. Homi Bhabha, "Conclusion: Race, Time and the Revision of Modernity," *The Location of Culture* (London: Routledge, 1993), 239.

23. John Dewey, "The Development of American Pragmatism," *Philosophy and Civilization* (New York: Minton, Balch & Company, 1931), 14.

8   AN IMAGE OF ONE'S OWN

1. "Interview: Barbara Maria Stafford," *Sculpture,* 13 (May–June 1994), 12–15.

2. Charles Taylor, *Multiculturalism and the "Politics of Recognition"* (Princeton: Princeton University Press, 1992), 33.

3. Quite to the contrary. See, for example, chapters 3 and 5 in this volume.

4. Gunnar Swanson, "Graphic Design Education as a Liberal Art: Design and Knowledge in the University and the 'Real World,'" *Design Issues,* 10 (Spring 1994), 54.

5. For the historical association of images with illiteracy, see my *Body Criticism: Imaging the Unseen in Enlightenment Art and Medicine* (Cambridge, Mass.: MIT Press, 1991); *Artful Science: Enlightenment Entertainment and the Eclipse of Visual Education* (Cambridge, Mass.: MIT Press, 1994); and chapter 1 in this volume.

6. See, for example, Neil Postman, *Technopoly: The Surrender of Culture to Technology* (New York: Alfred A. Knopf, 1992).

7. Herbert George, "The Place of a Studio Art Program within the Humanities Core," typescript (May 1994).

8. Victor Margolin, "The Age of Communication: A Challenge to Designers," *Design Issues,* 10 (Spring 1994), 67; and "Expanding the Boundaries of Design: The Product Environment and the New User," in Marco Diani, ed., *The Immaterial Society: Design, Culture and Technology in the Postmodern World* (Englewood Cliffs, N.J.: Prentice-Hall, 1992), 71–82.

9. Theologians have seen the importance of the "vision of the good" for moral life; why not for other aspects of living as well? See Stanley Hauerwas, *Vision and Virtue: Essays in Christian Ethical Reflection* (Notre Dame: Fides Publishers, 1974), esp. 30–47.

10. W. J. T. Mitchell, *Picture Theory: Essays on Verbal and Visual Representation* (Chicago: University of Chicago Press, 1994).

11. Michiko Kakutani, "Biography as a Blood Sport," *New York Times* (May 20, 1994), B6.

12. Hauerwas, *Vision and Virtue,* 41.

13. Semir Zeki, *A Vision of the Brain* (Cambridge, Mass.: Blackwell Scientific, 1993).

14. Coleen Cordes, "Technology as Religion?" *Chronicle of Higher Education* (April 27, 1994), A10, A15.

15. Terry Eagleton, *The Ideology of the Aesthetic* (London: Basil Blackwell, 1990).

16. Denise K. Magner, "Job-Market Blues," *Chronicle of Higher Education* (April 27, 1994), A17, A20.

1. Frank Biocca, "Communication within Virtual Reality: Creating a Space for Research," *Journal of Communication,* 42 (Autumn 1992), 9.

2. Michael A. Shapiro and Daniel G. McDonald, "I'm Not a Real Doctor, but I Play One in Virtual Reality: Implications of Virtual Reality for Judgments about Reality," *Journal of Communications*, 42 (Autumn 1992), 94.

3. Peter Paaw, *Anatomy with Commentary on Hippocrates* (Lyons: Iodocum a Colster, 1616), 62.

4. William Cowper, *An Anatomical Treatise on the Muscles of the Human Body,* 2d(?) ed. (London: R. Knaplock, 1724), pl. 12.

5. Ronald Dworkin, "The Right to Death," *New York Review of Books* 38 (January 31, 1991), 14, 16.

6. I was prompted to think about the equivocal nature of our contemporary usage in a conversation with Simon Schaffer about his work on values and Victorian science.

7. On the connection between ethics, aesthetics, and statistics, see my *Body Criticism: Imaging the Unseen in Enlightenment Art and Medicine* (Cambridge, Mass.: MIT Press, 1991), chapter 1, "Dissecting."

8. Johann Caspar Lavater, *Essays on Physiognomy. Designed to promote the Knowledge and the Love of Mankind . . .* (1792), vol. 3 part II, pl. facing p. 271.

9. Barbara M. Stafford, John La Puma, and David L. Schiedermayer, "One Face of Beauty, One Picture of Health: The Hidden Aesthetic of Medical Practice," *Journal of Medicine and Philosophy,* 14 (1989), 213–230.

10. It was a frequent simile in Martha B. Denckla's talk, "Brain Behavior Insights through Imaging," in the conference on "Brain Imaging and Learning Disabilities."

11. Ronald Kotulak, "Epidemic of Violence and Stress Is Devastating Kids' Brains," *Unlocking the Mind,* part 4, *Chicago Tribune,* (April 14, 1993), 1, 18.

12. Ronald Kotulak, "Reshaping Brain for Better Future," *Chicago Tribune* (April 15, 1993), 1, 18–19.

13. Gerd Gigereiszer, Zeno Swiftink, Theodore Porter, Lorraine Daston, John Beatty, and Lorenz Krüger, *The Empire of Chance: How Probability Theory Changed Science and Everyday Life* (Cambridge: Cambridge University Press, 1989), 298–291.

14. David M. Eddy, "Medicine, Money, and Mathematics," *American College of Surgeons Bulletin,* 77 (June 1992), 43.

15. Harvie Ferguson, *The Science of Pleasure: Cosmos and Psyche in the Bourgeois World View* (London and New York: Routledge, 1990), 249.

16. James Elkins, "From Original to Copy and Back Again," *British Journal of Aesthetics,* 23 (April 1993), 114.

17. François-Saneré Chérubim d'Orléans, *La dioptrique oculaire* (Paris: n.p., 1671), 298.

18. Joan L. Kirsch and Russell A. Kirsch, "Storing Art Images in Intelligent Computers," *Leonardo,* 23, no. 1 (1990), 99.

19. Robert Marrone, *Body of Knowledge: An Introduction to Body/Mind Psychology* (New York: State University of New York Press, 1990), 4.

20. Hubert Markl, "Genetics and Ethics," in *Alexander von Humboldt Stiftung Mitteilungen,* 54 (1990), 1.

21. Stafford, *Body Criticism,* chapter 3, "Conceiving."

22. Leon R. Kass, "Looking Good: Nature and Nobility," in his *Toward a More Natural Biology and Human Affairs* (New York: The Free Press, 1985), 318.

23. N. Katherine Hayles, *Chaos Bound: Orderly Disorder in Contemporary Literature and Science* (Ithaca: Cornell University Press, 1990), 274.

24. Markl, "Genetics and Ethics," 6.

25. Petrus Camper, *Dissertation physique: traits du visage* (Utrecht: B. Wild & J. Altheer, 1791), pl. 5.

26. Maureen McNeil, Ian Varcoe, and Steven Yearley, eds., *The New Reproductive Technologies* (New York: St. Martin's Press, 1990), 87–89.

27. Norman D. Cook, *The Brain Code: Mechanisms of Information Transfer and the Roles of the Corpus Callosum* (New York: Methuen, 1986), 10–20.

28. On this point, see also Howard Gardner, *Art, Mind, and Brain: A Cognitive Approach to Creativity* (New York: Basic Books, 1982), 235–240; and *Frames of Mind: The Theory of Multiple Intelligences* (New York: Basic Books, 1983), 4–6.

29. Jerre Levy and Susan Levin, "Left and Right Brain Perceptional Functions: Implications for Learning," in conference on "Brain Imaging and Learning Disabilities."

30. Cook, *The Brain Code,* 211.

31. Yehuda Elkana, "The Epistemology of the Opposition to Science," in William R. Shea and Beat Sitter, eds., *Scientists and Their Responsibilities* (Canton, Mass.: Watson Publishing International, 1989), 171–188.

32. Jack Goody, *The Logic of Writing and the Organization of Society* (Cambridge: Cambridge University Press, 1986), 136, 140–144.

33. See the catalogue of the recent exhibition at the British Museum, ed. Mark Jones, *Fake? The Art of Deception* (Berkeley: University of California Press, 1991).

34. See Kass, *Toward a More Natural Science,* 331, on the innate tendency toward dissembling as manifested in the animal world.

10 PICTURING AMBIGUITY

1. See my *Body Criticism: Imaging the Unseen in Enlightenment Art and Medicine* (Cambridge, Mass., and London: MIT Press, 1991), chapter 5, "Magnifying." Also see chapter 11 in this volume, which complements this essay.

2. See Barbara M. Stafford, John La Puma, and David L. Schiedermayer, "One Face of Beauty, One Picture of Health: The Hidden Aesthetic of Medical Practice," *The Journal of Medicine and Philosophy,* 14 (1989), 213–230.

3. Victor Turner, "Betwixt and Between: The Liminal Period in *Rites du passage,*" in *The Forest of Symbols: Aspects of Nolembu Ritual* (Ithaca and London: Cornell University Press, 1967), 96–99.

4. Lynne B. Dixon, *Diderot, Philosopher of Energy: The Development of His Concept of Physical Energy, 1745–1769* (Oxford: The Voltaire Foundation, 1988), 50.

5. William Hooper, *Rational Recreations, in Which the Principles of Numbers and Natural Philosophy are Clearly and Copiously Elucidated, by a Series of Easy, Entertaining, and Interesting Experiments. Among Which are All Those Commonly Performed with the Cards,* 4th ed., 4 vols. (London: Printed for B. Law and Son, G. G. and J. Robinson, 1794), 1: Advertisement.

6. Ibid., 2:13–14, 43–48.

7. Mark Roskill and David Carrier, *Truth and Falsehood in Visual Images* (Amherst: University of Massachusetts Press, 1983), 80–86.

8. Hooper, *Rational Recreations,* 1:iv–v.

9. Hooper, *Rational Recreations,* 1:vi–vii.

10. See chapter 1 in this volume.

11. George Turnbull, *Observations upon Liberal Education, In All Its Branches: Containing the Substance of What Hath Been Said upon That Important Subject by the Best Writers Ancient or Modern. With Many New Remarks Interspersed: Designed for the Assistance of Young Gentlemen, Who Having Made some Progress in the Useful Sciences are Desirous of Making Further Improvements* . . . (London: Printed for A. Miller, 1742), 127.

12. Ibid., 126.

13. Louis Joblot, *Descriptions et usages de plusieurs nouveaux microscopes, tant simples que composez; avec des nouvelles observations faites sur une multitude innombrable d'insectes, & d'autres animaux de diverses expèces, qui naissent dans des liqueurs preparées, & dans celles qui ne le sont point* (Paris: Chez Jacques Collombat, Imprimeur Ordinaire du Roy & de l'Académie Royale de Peinture & Sculpture, 1718), Avertissement.

14. Pierre Cazeneuve, "La Génération spontanée d'après les livres d'Henri Baker et de Joblot," *Revue Scientifique,* 31 (4th ser. 1, 1894), 161–166.

15. Joblot, *Descriptions,* 44–45.

16. Ibid., Avertissement.

17. Henry Baker, *The Microscope Made Easy: or the Nature, Uses, and Magnifying Powers of the Best Kinds of Microscopes Describes, Calculated, and Explained: For the Instruction of Such, Particularly, as Desire to Search into the Wonders of the Minute Creation, tho' They Are Not Acquainted With Optics,* 2d ed., 2 vols. (London: Printed for R. Dodsley, 1744), 1:ii–iv.

18. Ibid., 1:72, 90–91.

19. Ibid., 2:138–139.

20. David Brett, "The Interpretation of Ornament," *Journal of Design History,* 1, no. 2 (1988), 106.

21. Baron Frédéric-Guillaume de Gleichen (called Russworm), *Dissertation sur la génération, les animalcules spermatiques, et ceux d'infusions, avec des observations sur le sperme, et sur différentes infusions* (Paris: De l'Imprimerie de Digeon, An VII), 197–198.

22. Ibid., 160–161.

23. Ibid., 66–69.

24. [John Turberville Needham], *An Account of some New Microscopical Discoveries Founded on An Examination of the Calamary, and Its Wonderful Milt-Vessels (Each of Which tho' They Exceed Not a Horse-Hair in Diameter . . .)* (London: Printed for F. Needham, 1745), 2–4.

25. John Hill, *Essays in Natural History and Philosophy Containing A Series of Discoveries, by the Assistance of Microscopes* (London: Printed for J. Whiston and P. White, P. Vaillant, and L. Davis, 1752), 60–61.

26. Ibid., 3–4, 6.

27. John Ellis, *The Natural History of Many Curious and Uncommon Zoophytes, Collected from Various Parts of the Globe . . . Systematically Arranged and Described by the Late Daniel Solander* (London: Printed for Benjmain White and Son, 1786), vi–vii.

28. Cited in Turner, "Betwixt and Between," 105.

29. Jean Ellis, *Essai sur l'histoire des corallines et d'autres productions marines du même genre, qu'on trouve communement sur les côtes de la Grande-Bretagne et d'Irlande, auquel on a joint une description d'un grand polype de mer,* trans. from the English (The Hague: Chez Pierre de Hondt, 1756), 1, 18–22, 27.

30. Ellis, *Natural History,* 9, 19, 145–151.

31. Ibid., 15.

32. On the diagnostic and prognostic signs of skin disease, see Anne-Charles de Lorry, *Tractatus de Morbis Cutaneis* (Paris: Apud P. Guillelmen Cavelier, 1777), 73–113.

33. Ellis, *Natural History,* 16, 39, 40, 47, 53, 54–55.

34. Robert Willan, *On Cutaneous Diseases. I: Containing Ord. I. Papulae; Ord. II. Squamae; Ord. III. Exanthemata; Ord IV. Bullae* (Philadelphia: Published by Kimber and Conrad, 1809), 13, 27, 47, 144–146, 163.

35. See the continuation of Willan's unfinished project to standardize nomenclature in Thomas Bateman, *A Practical Synopsis of Cutaneous Diseases, According to the Arrangement of Dr. Willan, Exhibiting a Concise View of the Diagnostic Symptoms and the Method of Treatment,* 2d ed. (London: Longman, Hurst, Rees, Orme, and Brown, 1813), viii.

36. Abbé Jacques-François Dicquemare, "Dissertation sur les limites des règnes de la nature," in *Observations sur la physique, sur l'histoire naturelle et les arts: avec des planches en taille-douce, dédiées à Mgr. Le Comte d'Artois,* ed. Abbé Rozier, 10 vols. (Paris: Chez Ruault, 1773–1777), 8:371–372.

37. Ibid., 8:376.

38. Félix Vicq d'Azyr, "*Table* pour servir à l'histoire naturelle & anatomique des corps organiques ou vivans, présentée dans la séance publique de l'Académie Royale des Sciences, le 12 novembre 1774," in *Observations sur la physique,* 4:479.

39. Joseph-Adrien Lelarge de Lignac, *Lettres à un amériquain sur l'histoire naturelle de Mr. de Buffon; et sur les observations microscopiques de Mr. Needham, quatrième partie* (Hamburg: n.p., 1751), 62–69, 74–82, 182.

40. René-Antoine Ferchault de Réaumur, *Mémoires pour servir à l'histoire des insectes,* 7 vols. (Paris: De l'Imprimerie Royale, 1734–1755).

41. Charles de Geer, *Mémoires pour servir à l'histoire naturelle des insectes,* 9 vols. (Stockholm: De l'Imprimerie de L.L. Grefing, 1752–1770).

42. Pierre Lyonnet, *Traité anatomique de la chenille, qui ronge le bois de saule, augmenté d'une explication abrégée des planches et d'une description de l'instrument et des outils dont l'auteur s'est servi pour anatomiser à la loupe & au microscope, & pour déterminer la force de ses verres, suivant les règles de l'optique, & méchaniquement* (The Hague: Chez Pierre Gosse Jr., & Daniel Pinet; and Amsterdam: Chez Marc-Michel Rey, 1762), xviii.

43. Ibid., xix.

44. Ibid., v–vii.

45. See my *Symbol and Myth: Humbert de Superville's Essay on Absolute Signs in Art* (Cranbury, N.J.: Associated University Presses, 1979), 43–58.

46. Hendrik Punt, *Bernard Siegfried Albinus (1697–1770). On "Human Nature." Anatomical and Physiological Ideas in Eighteenth-Century Leiden* (Amsterdam: B.M. Israël B.V., 1983), 14–17.

47. J. Schuller tot Persum-Meijer, *Petrus Camper (1722–1789). Onderzoeker van Nature,* exhibition catalogue (Groningen: Universiteits Museum, 1989), 65–68.

48. Lyonnet, *Traité anatomique,* 24–25.

11 DIFFICULT CONTENT, OR THE PLEASURES OF VIEWING PAIN

1. See Francis Haskell, "Titian and the Perils of International Exhibitions," *New York Review,* 37 (August 16, 1990), 8–12, for a critique of museum practice.

2. See, for example, Louis Joblot, *Descriptions et usages de plusieurs nouveaux microscopes, tant simples que composez; avec des nouvelles observations faites sur une multitude innombrable d'insectes, & d'autres animaux de diverses espèces, qui naissent dans des liqueurs préparée, & dans celles qui ne le sont point* (Paris: Jaques Collombat, 1718), pl. 13 and pp. 44–45.

3. Henry Baker, *The Microscope Made Easy; or, the Nature, Uses, and Magnifying Powers of the Best Kinds of Microscopes Described, Calculated and Explained: For the Instruction of Such, Particularly, as Desire to Search into the Wonders of the Minute Creation, tho' They Are Not Acquainted with Optics* . . . , 3d ed., 2 vols. (London: R. Dodsley, 1744), 1:21–25.

4. On eighteenth-century domestic scientific amusements, see M. A. Crawforth, "Evidence from Trade Cards for the Scientific Instrument Industry," *Annals of Science*, 42 (1985), 472–473.

5. George Turnbull, *A Curious Collection of Ancient Paintings, Accurately Engraved from Excellent Drawings, Lately Done after the Originals, by One of the Best Hands in Rome: With an Account Where and When They Were Found and Where They Now Are; and Several Critical, Historical, and Mythological Observations on Them* (London: A. Millar, 1741), 8–9, 39.

6. Crawforth, "Evidence from Trade Cards," 478.

7. Baker, *The Microscope Made Easy*, v–vi.

8. See, for example, Joblot, *Descriptions et usages*, Avertissement, on the "pleasure of seeing the different motions of the blood" in frogs, tadpoles, lampreys, and eels.

9. Baker, *The Microscope Made Easy*, 1:133.

10. Ibid., 1:134–148.

11. Christian Metz, *The Imaginary Signifier: Psychoanalysis and the Cinema* (Bloomington: Indiana University Press, 1977), 94–96. My thanks to Tamara Faulkner for having drawn my attention to the discussion of voyeurism in film studies.

12. John Hill, *An History of Animals: Containing Descriptions of the Birds, Beasts, Fishes, and Insects, of the Several Parts of the World; and Including Accounts of the Several Classes of Animalcules, Visible only by the Assistance of Microscopes* (London: Thomas Osborne, 1752), preface.

13. On scopophilia, see Laura Mulvey, "Visual Pleasure and Narrative Cinema," in Mast and Cohen, *Film Theory and Criticism*, 806–807.

14. John Hill, *Essays in Natural History and Philosophy: Containing a Series of Discoveries, by the Assistance of Microscopes* (London: J. Whiston and P. White, P. Vaillant, and L. Davis, 1752), 1, 3–5.

15. Ibid., 45–55.

16. Ibid., 56.

17. Ibid., 56–57.

18. Ibid., 57–58.

19. Ibid., 75–77.

20. On the spreading out over a surface, for male scrutiny, of female pathology, see Mary Anne Doanne, "The Clinical Eye: Medical Discourses in the 'Woman's Film' of the 1940's," in Susan Rubin Suleiman, ed., *The Female Body in Western Culture* (Cambridge, Mass.: Harvard University Press, 1986), 152–154.

21. Hill, *Essays in Natural History,* 75–80.

22. Gertrude Koch, "The Body's Shadow Realm," *October,* 50 (Fall 1989), 11–12, 15–21.

23. Metz, *The Imaginary Signifier,* 96.

24. "Réaumur," in *Biographie universelle, ancienne et moderne,* 27 (1824), 198–203.

25. René-Antoine Ferchault de Réaumur, *Mémoires pour servir à l'histoire des insectes,* 7 vols. (Paris: L'imprimerie Royale, 1734–1755), 1:13–15. This edition includes the problematic seventh volume "completed" from Réaumur's unpublished notes.

26. Virginia P. Dawson, *Nature's Enigma: The Problem of the Polyp in the Letters of Bonnet, Trembley, and Réaumur* (Philadelphia: American Philosophical Society, 1987), 12.

27. [Charles Bonnet], *Essai de psychologie; ou considérations sur les opérations de l'âme, sur l'habitude et sur l'éducation, auxquelles on a ajouté des principes philosophiques sur la cause première et sur son effet* (London: n.p., 1755), 88–89, 218–220.

28. Réaumur, *Mémoires,* 5:68–72, 77–79, 85–86. Also see pl. 9, p. 86.

29. Ibid., 3:65–66, 343–345.

30. On the "philosophical traveler," whom I see as being similar to the microscopic observer, see Miranda Hughes, "Tall Tales or True Stories? Baudin, Péron, and the Tasmanians, 1802," in Roy MacLeod and Philip F. Rehbock, eds., *Nature in Its Greatest Extent: Western Science in the Pacific* (Honolulu: University of Hawaii Press, 1988), 80–81.

31. Réaumur, *Mémoires,* 1:10.

32. Ibid., 1:11.

33. Ibid., 1:12.

34. Wolf Lepenies, *Das Ende der Naturgeschichte: Wandel kultureller Selbstverständlichkeiten in den Wissenschaften des 18. und 19. Jahrhunderts* (Munich and Vienna: Carl Hanser Verlag, 1976), 30.

35. [Noël-Antoine La Pluche], *Le spectacle de la nature; ou entretiens sur particularités de l'histoire naturelle, qui ont paru les plus propres à rendre jeunes-gens curieux, & à former leur esprit,* 2d ed., 8 vols. in 9 (Paris, 1749–1756), 1:viii.

36. Ibid., 1:ix.

37. Ibid., 1:x–xiii.

38. Ibid., 1:xxi–xxiii.

39. Charles Bonnet, *Contemplation de la nature,* 2d ed., 2 vols. (Amsterdam: Marc-Michel Rey, 1769), 1:ii.

40. Baker, *The Microscope Made Easy,* 1:xv.

41. Ibid., 1:xiii.

42. "Cabinet d'histoire naturelle," *Encyclopédie, ou dictionnaire raisonné des sciences, des arts, et des métiers par une société de gens de lettres mis en ordre et publié par M. Diderot, et quant à la partie mathématique, par M. D'Alembert, 17 vols.* (Paris: Briasson, David l'aîné, Le Breton, Durand, 1751–1780), 2:489.

43. George Turnbull, *A Treatise on Ancient Painting, Containing Observations on the Rise and Progress, and Decline of That Art amongst the Greeks and Romans; the High Opinion Which the Great Men of Antiquity Had of It; Its Connexion with Poetry and Philosophy; and the Use that May Be Made of It in Education* (London: privately printed, 1740), 46. Turnbull's severe and chaste aesthetics—grounded on the analogy of a rational art to language—formed an important precedent for Winckelmann's *History of Art* (1764).

44. Turnbull, *A Curious Collection*, 7.

45. "Cabinet d'histoire naturelle," 489.

46. Ibid., 490.

47. Ibid., 491.

48. "Le Large de Lignac," *Biographie universelle, ancienne et moderne,* 24 (1819), 477–478.

49. [Joseph-Adrien Le Large de Lignac], *Lettres à un amériquain sur l'histoire naturelle de M. de Buffon; et sur les observations microscopiques de Mr. Needham, quatrième partie* (Hamburg: n.p., 1751), 42–44.

50. Ibid., 75.

51. "Cabinet d'histoire naturelle," 491.

52. Turnbull, *Treatise on Ancient Painting,* ix.

53. Ibid., vii, 40.

54. Ibid., 46.

55. Ibid., 125–126, 145–147.

56. See, for example, Andy Grundberg, "Ask It No Questions; The Camera Can Lie," *New York Times* (August 12, 1990), sect. 2, pp. 1, 29.

57. Bob Greene, "Artists Lose When It's Them vs. Us," *Chicago Tribune* (November 7, 1990), sect. 5, p.c.

CONCLUSION: ANALOGY IN AN AGE OF DIFFERENCE

A version of this essay was presented as a paper at the conference "Regimes of Description," Stanford University, January 11–14, 1996.

1. Nadine Gordimer, "Adam's Rib," *New York Review* (October 19, 1995), 28.

2. Philippe Hamon, *Expositions: Literature and Architecture in Nineteenth-Century France,* trans. Katia Sainson-Frank and Lisa Maguire (Berkeley, Los Angeles, Oxford: University of California Press, 1992), 117.

3. Primo Levi, *The Mirror Maker: Stories and Essays,* trans. Raymond Rosenthal (New York: Schocken Books, 1989), 47–51.

4. Cited in Stephen Bann, *The Clothing of Clio: A Study of the Representation of History in Nineteenth-Century Britain and France* (Cambridge: Cambridge University Press, 1984), 3.

5. Note especially the influence of Adorno's negative dialectics project. See Rolf Wiggershaus, *The Frankfurt School: Its History, Theories and Political Significance,* trans. Michael Robertson (Cambridge: Polity Press, 1994), 597–608.

6. Bob Shacochis, "The Enemies of the Imagination," *Harper's* (November 1995), 14.

7. Dave Hickey, "Shining Hours/Forgiving Rhyme," *Art Issues,* 40 (November/December 1995), 11.

8. Antonio R. Damasio, *Descartes' Error: Emotion, Reason, and the Human Brain* (New York: G. P. Putnam's Sons, 1994), 97.

9. Thomas Fuchs, "Gewogen und zu leicht befunden. Herz und Gewissen," in *Das menschliche Herz. Der herzliche Mensch,* exh. cat. (Dresden: Deutschen Hygiene-Museum, 1995–1996), 31–48.

10. Gerald M. Edelman, *Bright Air, Brilliant Fire: On the Matter of the Mind* (New York: Basic Books, 1991), 112.

11. Gary Cziko, *Without Miracles: Universal Selection Theory and the Second Darwinian Revolution* (Cambridge, Mass., and London: MIT Press, 1995), 8–9.

12. The importance of this issue has been summarized by John R. Searle, "The Mystery of Consciousness: Part I and II," *New York Review* (November 2, 1995; November 16, 1995), 61–66; 54–61.

13. Paul and Patricia Churchland and Daniel C. Dennett are proponents of this view. See the latter's *Consciousness Explained* (Boston: Back Bay/Little, Brown, 1994).

14. George Lakoff, *Women, Fire, and Dangerous Things: What Categories Reveal about the Mind* (Chicago and London: University of Chicago Press, 1987), xiv.

15. Herbert Vorgrimler, "Die Erbsünde—kirchliche und päpstliche Erklärung für alle Übel," in *Krank Warum? Vorstellungen der Volker, Heiler, Mediziner,* ed. Frank Beat Keller (Ostfeldern: Cantz Verlag, 1995), 54.

16. Owen Flanagan, *Consciousness Reconsidered* (Cambridge, Mass., and London: MIT Press, 1992), 2; Lakoff, *Women, Fire, and Dangerous Things,* 338; Roger Penrose, *Shadows of the Mind: A Search for the Missing Science of Consciousness* (Oxford: Oxford University Press, 1994), 8–11; and Francisco J. Varella, Evan Thompson, and Eleanor Rosch, eds., *The Embodied Mind: Cognitive Science and Human Experience* (Cambridge, Mass., and London: MIT Press, 1993), xv.

17. Paul Holdengräber, "Between the Profane and the Redemptive: The Collector as Possessor in Walter Benjamin's *Passagen-Werk,*" *Internationale Zeitschrift für Philosophie* 1 (1993), 113–135.

18. Craig Owens, *Beyond Recognition: Representation, Power, and Culture,* ed. Scott Bryson, Barbara Kruger, Lynne Tillman, and Jane Weinstock (Berkeley, Los Angeles, Oxford: University of California Press, 1992), 262.

19. A. W. Heinrich Langhein, *Das Prinzip der Analogie als juristische Methode, Ein Beitrag zur Geschichte der methodologischen Grundlagenforschung vom ausgehenden 18. bix zum 20. Jahrhundert* (Berlin: Duncker & Humblot, 1992), 16–19.

20. Ibid., 26–29.

21. Douglas Hofstadter and the Fluid Analogies Research Group, *Fluid Concepts and Creative Analogies: Computer Models of the Fundamental Mechanisms of Thought* (New York: Basic Books, 1995), 179–180, 295.

22. Bippin Indurkhya, *Metaphor and Cognition: An Interactionist Approach* (Norwell, Mass.: Kluwer, 1992).

23. Deborah L. Jones, "An Anatomy of Allegory: A Study of the Genre, Its Rhetorical Traditions and Its American Renaissance" (Ph.D. diss., University of Sussex, 1988), 7.

24. Levi, *The Mirror Maker,* 16.

25. David Summers, "'Form,' Nineteenth-Century Metaphysics, and the Problem of Art Historical Description," *Critical Inquiry,* 15 (Winter 1989), 378–379.

26. Glenn Watkins, *Pyramids at the Louvre: Music, Culture, and Collage from Stravinsky to the Postmodernists* (Cambridge, Mass., and London: Harvard University Press, 1994), 423–425.

27. Carl Zigrosser, *Multum in Parvo: An Essay in Poetic Imagination* (New York: George Braziller, 1965), 15.

28. Patricia Mellencamp, "The Old and the New: Nam June Paik," *Art Journal,* 54 (Winter 1955), 41–47.

29. David Burrell, *Analogy and Philosophical Language* (New Haven and London: Yale University Press, 1973), 1.

30. On Debord, see Martin Jay, *Downcast Eyes: The Denigration of Vision in Twentieth-Century French Thought* (Berkeley and Los Angeles: University of California Press, 1993), 377–379.

31. Ralph McIverny, *Studies in Analogy* (The Hague: Martinus Nijhoff, 1968), 82.

32. Norbert W. Mtega, *Analogy and Theological Language in the Summa Contra Gentiles: A Textual Survey of the Concept of Analogy and Its Theological Application by St. Thomas Aquinas* (Frankfurt am Main: Peter Lang, 1984), 17.

33. Lakoff, *Women, Fire, and Dangerous Things,* 455.

34. Clifford Geertz, "Culture War," *New York Review* (November 30, 1995), 4–6.

35. Antonio R. Damasio, *Descartes' Error: Emotion, Reason, and the Human Brain* (New York: G. P. Putnam's Sons, 1994), 91–93, 223–244.

36. Ibid., 95.

Page numbers in italics indicate material in illustration captions.